The Multimedia Library
Second Edition

Materials Selection and Use

LIBRARY AND INFORMATION SCIENCE

CONSULTING EDITORS: *Harold Borko and G. Edward Evans*
GRADUATE SCHOOL OF LIBRARY SCIENCE
UNIVERSITY OF CALIFORNIA, LOS ANGELES

Thomas H. Mott, Jr., Susan Artandi, and Leny Struminger
Introduction to PL/I Programming for Library and Information Science

Karen Sparck Jones and Martin Kay
Linguistics and Information Science

Manfred Kochen (Ed.)
Information for Action: From Knowledge to Wisdom

Harold Borko and Charles L. Bernier
Abstracting Concepts and Methods

G. Edward Evans
Management Techniques for Librarians

James Cabeceiras
The Multimedia Library: Materials Selection and Use

F. W. Lancaster
Toward Paperless Information Systems

H. S. Heaps
Information Retrieval: Computational and Theoretical Aspects

Harold Borko and Charles L. Bernier
Indexing Concepts and Methods

Gerald Jahoda and Judith Schiek Braunagel
The Librarian and Reference Queries: A Systematic Approach

Charles H. Busha and Stephen P. Harter
Research Methods in Librarianship: Techniques and Interpretation

Diana M. Thomas, Ann T. Hinckley, and Elizabeth R. Eisenbach
The Effective Reference Librarian

James Cabeceiras
The Multimedia Library, Second Edition: Materials Selection and Use

IN PREPARATION
G. Edward Evans
Management Techniques for Librarians, Second Edition

The Multimedia Library
Second Edition

Materials Selection and Use

James Cabeceiras
Division of Library Science
Department of Instructional Technology
San Jose State University
San Jose, California

1982

ACADEMIC PRESS
A Subsidiary of Harcourt Brace Jovanovich, Publishers
New York   London
Paris San Diego San Francisco São Paulo Sydney Tokyo Toronto

ACADEMIC PRESS, INC.
111 Fifth Avenue, New York, New York 10003

United Kingdom Edition published by
ACADEMIC PRESS, INC. (LONDON) LTD.
24/28 Oval Road, London NW1 7DX

Library of Congress Cataloging in Publication Data

Cabeceiras, James.
  The multimedia library.

  (Library and information science)
  Includes bibliographies and index.
  1. Selection of nonbook materials. 2. Book selection.
3. Audio-visual library service. I. Title. II. Series.
Z689.C12 1982   025.2'1   82-6734
ISBN 0-12-153952-0   AACR2

PRINTED IN THE UNITED STATES OF AMERICA

82 83 84 85   9 8 7 6 5 4 3 2 1

To Chris

While there was light,
So brilliantly did it shine,
That I will forever bask,
In the radiant afterglow.

Contents

3
Selection Aids

4
Systems Approach to Selecting Materials

5
Selecting the Proper Medium

6
Motion Picture Films

7
Filmstrips and Slides

8
Audio Recordings

9
Television

10
Programmed Instruction

11
Maps

12
Models, Realia, and Games and Simulations

13
Microforms

14
Local Preparation of Information Materials

15
Fair Use of Copyright

16
Intellectual Freedom

Preface

Libraries are becoming increasingly involved with various information media forms. Much more has been written about the traditional print media forms, such as books and periodicals, than about the various types of nontraditional media forms that are an essential part of the services that libraries are currently expected to provide their patrons.

In the second edition of *The Multimedia Library,* greater emphasis has been placed on the nonprint media forms, those that have been used for some time in libraries, as well as the new media forms that are growing in popularity as valid library information materials. This investigation of the selection and use of the various types of nonprint media analyzes unique capabilities and advantages of each media form, as well as how each form may be used most effectively and efficiently, and, when applicable, the selection of ancillary equipment (hardware) to accompany a particular medium (software).

This volume has been organized to provide the reader with a foundation in the philosophy, trends, tools, and procedures involved in selection of materials for the multimedia library. It then offers information on particular media forms. Content in both of these areas has been modified to include developments and trends that were not prevalent when the first edition went to press. Organization of material within chapters follows, whenever possible, a prescribed format: the chapters begin with an overview followed by a description of characteristics and a discussion of selection and utilization procedures; the chapters conclude with a selected bibliography and a suggested list of appropriate selection aids.

Given the broad information media selection base provided in the initial chapters of the book, the reader should have the prerequisite knowledge to learn how to select and more intelligently use the various multimedia information forms discussed in subsequent chapters. Also explored are the regulating constraints involved in making information available to the public as well as the leadership role the librarian must assume in order to function successfully in the multimedia library.

Chapter 1 analyzes present and future trends in the field of library science in order to orient the reader toward a multimedia philosophy to which he or she can conscientiously subscribe. An overview of materials selection as it relates to the formulation of policy, standards for the selection of materials and equipment, categories of media, and procedures for the utilization of library materials is presented in Chapter 2. Chapter 3 reviews the function of selection aids and suggests and discusses evaluation criteria. The systems approach to materials selection, so essential to the organized growth of the library, is examined in Chapter 4. Guidelines for applying a knowledge of the properties of the various information media to the selection of the proper medium for a particular task are provided in Chapter 5. Chapters 6–13 explore in some depth the various media found in libraries, with an emphasis on identification and application as well as on the development of criteria for evaluation and selection. Because some libraries often become involved in making their own special materials to better serve patrons' needs, local production of materials is covered in Chapter 14.

Two new subjects are covered in the second edition of *The Multimedia Library*. Chapter 15 examines recently instituted copyright regulations, as well as their implications for both the owner and the user of copyright information. This information is especially important for the multimedia librarian who presently has the technology available to produce and reproduce information in a wide range of media forms. Chapter 16 is devoted to a discussion of intellectual freedom, with the intention of giving the reader a perspective on how selecting, justifying, and advocating the use of information materials in the library is indeed a serious task and must be performed with professional expertise.

1

Trends, Present and Future

Overview

It is essential that the librarian be critically aware of how and where the library fits into the societal matrix and of the kinds of services it provides to justify its existence. Equally important, the librarian must be cognizant of how his or her knowledge, skill, and attitude contribute to the achievement of the library's goals. Libraries have a highly respected history as primary sources for acquiring and dispensing the information needed by the society they serve. To nurture and maintain this reputation, the library must be adaptable to change. As information continues to be generated in ever-increasing amounts, so too must the library grow to accommodate the demands of the omnipresent information explosion.

The library not only acquires information in printed formats, but increasingly builds collections of nonprint information as well. Society is just now embarking on the electronic era, which means that the library, as a dynamic institution, will continue to expand its use of this technology to serve the needs of its patrons. The librarian must develop a perspective as to the role he or she will play in this evolutionary process. Although not intending to overemphasize the dichotomy of the individual roles librarians must play, there is presently a strong tendency among librarians to perceive their orientation as being predominantly either print or nonprint. Regardless of how one perceives his or her orientation, be it print or nonprint, there is a need for both types of knowledgeable professionals, and both can make a valued contribution.

Whatever one's particular inclination, it is critical to know that a multitude of information forms exist, each with its own unique characteristics and objectives for satisfying a particular need. With a basic knowledge of the many information formats circulated by the library, what each format does, and how it is used, the individual librarian can better ascertain his or her role in the overall schema of services and perform that role as capably as possible. Print is here to stay, but it will not be solely in a paper format; it will also be available in a host of electronic forms as well. Likewise, nonprint information media will not become passé, but will also be adapted to incorporate the advantages inherent in the newer electronic technologies.

Implication of Trends

"Change Is the Only Constant"

It is essential that the professional librarian be able to identify with the institution—the library—to which he or she dedicates a career. He or she must know that the profession of a librarian is not now, never was, nor ever will be static; it is an extremely important entity within an ever-changing society and must be responsive to the needs of society. The librarian must realize that the library itself is in a constant state of metamorphosis. Often, change and innovation in the library occur almost imperceptibly, and as a result, trends too often are assimilated but not appreciated. Frequently the librarian is aware only of the present time frame, the here and now. Such a myopic perspective tends to obscure the fact that the library of even the recent past is not the library of today; and that the library of the future will be quite different from today's. It is clearly valuable for the librarian to take the time and effort to analyze the phenomenon of change in the library and the demands it places on the library profession.

Perhaps one of the best ways to analyze current and future library trends is to view them on a continuum that includes not only the present and the future, but the past as well. If we took the time to identify library changes since World War II, it would become apparent that changes have occurred in both degree and kind. Unfortunately, many library patrons, and a few librarians as well, have an extremely limited perspective as to the purpose the library serves and are apt to criticize libraries as being antiquated book museums that have changed very little. Such criticisms are unwarranted, and worse, the people making them are neither aware of nor ready for future changes. As librarians, we need to examine carefully our own philosophy and decide whether we want to be in the vanguard, making changes, or to adopt the less active role of adapting to change. Either way, the process is irreversible; change is inevitable.

Ancient Carthage had a library of scrolls; the medieval monks had libraries of hand-written manuscripts. In the fifteenth century, Johann Gutenberg invented movable type, and thus ushered in the era of mechanical printing. A relatively short time later in 1658, John Amos Comenius published his *Orbus Pictus*, considered to be the first illustrated textbook. As time progressed, more efficient methods of printing, the advent of photography, and the use of color resulted in more, better, and less expensive books.

Since World War II, libraries have been providing information in many different media. Libraries now circulate books (both hardcover and paperback), microform, art prints, periodicals, disc records, audiotapes, games and simulations, motion picture films, slides, filmstrips, models, realia (real things), animals, and minerals. With the exception of four or five of the items listed, none were even available in libraries prior to 1945. Currently, we are beginning to witness the introduction of videotapes and computer terminals into the repertory of services provided. It should be clear from this extremely brief chronology that librarians need not feel they have to defend their institutions against charges that they are static and archaic. Rather, the emphasis must now be placed on how to accommodate for change.

What is needed is an examination of the basic social and technological factors that are affecting our lives and in turn affecting the services provided by libraries. There has been a constant shift in American demographic patterns from rural to urban to suburban living. Currently, however, some futurists are predicting a reverse change from suburban back to large metropolitan or megalopolitan living. The importance of education, which vitally affects a society's need for and attitude toward libraries, is continually expanding. Earlier retirements are generating a group of individuals who are no longer in the labor pool, but are still mentally and physically active and desire more education. A new awareness of the symbiotic relationship between man and his environment is changing attitudes toward the exploitation of nature for personal profit. The future may find man concerned not with the puritan work ethic, but with a communal effort toward group preservation. Financial status may cease to be the determinant of social rank, leading to a reduction of gaps between the current socioeconomic levels of American society. The family unit is undergoing change as well; the nuclear family is replacing the extended family, and at the same time, people are living longer, entering the labor market later, and leaving it earlier. The country is presently experiencing an erosion of the control traditionally ascribed to family and religion. Social, moral, and religious mores are undergoing accelerated and sometimes traumatic changes. These are only some of the more visible societal changes taking place, but they are not the only arbiter of change.

Along with social change is technological change. American society is rapidly evolving from the industrial, machine age to the electronic era. There is a continuing logarithmic increase in the use of automation in just about every human activity. It is astounding to ponder that in less than three quarters of the twentieth century, man was able to proceed from the first heavier-than-air flight to walking on the moon. Not as dramatic, but perhaps more important, is the progress in medicine and health care. Many of the killer epidemics that plagued man in the past are today virtually nonexistent, an achievement not without price. The world, for the first time, is faced with the critical problem of global overpopulation, which generates a whole new set of survival problems. We are now witnessing the emergence of genetic control and manipulation and of biochemical regulation of the brain and intellect.

We are immersed in the epoch of electronic communication, which is changing the concept of the library's role in society. Television as a form of mass communication has resulted in a decline in person-to-person communication, which will be further reduced by electronic information display devices used for one-to-one, man–machine communication. This access to electronic communication implies a myriad of both advantages and problems. Accumulated information available to man is presently doubling every 12 years, and it is projected that by 2000, it will be doubling in 1 year's time.

This vast storehouse of information can be handled electronically, but someone will have to be responsible for its management. The librarian is the obvious choice for this task, and the responsibility and power inherent in that responsibility are awesome. In a management capacity, the librarian will have considerable influence on what kind of information is selected, stored, retrieved, and discarded. Information control requirements will necessitate that the librarian be a highly trained information technologist. As the person controlling this vast amount of information, the librarian will be required to perform a much greater service than is currently being offered by libraries. The librarian must assist society by maintaining and supplying whatever information is needed. But who is to decide what is needed? Such decisions require a librarian who is a skilled, responsive humanist, able to assess individual needs and respond with information that serves mankind. The problem of verbal illiteracy will be replaced by a demand for a higher and more efficient communication literacy. The librarian technologist will insure that information is available for all of society; the librarian humanist will prescribe it to the benefit of the individual.

Types of Materials Circulated

Since it has been established that libraries are in a state of continual change within a changing society, it is appropriate to examine more closely the changes taking place in the materials circulated. It is in the area of material selection and utilization that the library justifies its existence, for if the materials selected are not the best that can be provided and are not in demand or needed by patrons, the library becomes a warehouse of unneeded, unwanted information. Added to this is the concern that acquisitions prove to be economically valid.

Libraries are no longer considered simply as conservators of information; the emphasis now is on the dissemination of information. If the library were only a conservator, then all information would best be acquired on some type of microform and stored in a safe place. But what is the use of information if it cannot be disseminated in its most appropriate media form? Such information needs to be used effectively and efficiently. For this reason, the librarian needs to be aware of the various forms, how they are disseminated, and how they best serve a particular information need. An examination of the types of materials currently being circulated by libraries provides vivid evidence that change is taking place. Furthermore, some of the newer media forms being acquired are a positive indication that what is happening is not for the sole purpose of keeping the library modern; for if this indeed were the case, then libraries would only build collections of these newer media forms. The truth of the matter is that some of the newer forms provide a valuable service, and holdings in many of these areas are growing as fast as, if not faster than, holdings in the book area.

Currently, it is the school library that is in the vanguard of using the vast array of the more modern media forms, but other libraries, from public to academic, are also shifting to some of the newer media forms as demand for them becomes apparent. An examination of some of the newer media will give an idea of the unique characteristics that make them important sources of information.

Paperbacks, although not necessarily a new media form, are increasing in the quantity in which they are being acquired. Somewhat less expensive than hardbound books, they are perceived as a good means of acquiring books of transient value. Not only will the books be in demand for a relatively short time span, but multiple copies can be inexpensively purchased if the demand is great. Also, with the proliferation of books being published, more titles can be purchased in paperback form. The lower price of paperbacks, however, does not give the librarian license to buy haphazardly. If the material is not being used, its acquisition cannot be justified regardless of cost.

Microforms are becoming more prevalent in libraries, but here the librarian must consider a machine system that makes the information available in a readable form. Microforms were first acquired by libraries with the rationale that they resulted in tremendous savings in space. Now it is being realized that there are other benefits. The savings in binding costs of periodicals is considerable; and perhaps even more important, the microform is an inexpensive medium in which to acquire copies of printed matter in their original form. Also available in microform are books and periodicals that are out of print and would otherwise be quite expensive (if indeed they were even available for purchase); microform helps to make out-of-print materials available and affordable.

New techniques in industrial photo-offset printing now make it economically feasible to circulate art prints. The high reproduction quality of art prints are enjoyed and appreciated by the patron.

Improvements in the fidelity of audio recordings, on both disc record and magnetic tape, have resulted in an increased demand for this format. An American home, especially one with teenage children, that has neither a record player nor a tape recorder is rare. The librarian needs to be aware of the demand for information in an audio format and of exactly what kind of audio information needs to be made available.

Packaged games and simulations have opened a whole new vista in information processing. They are becoming extremely popular as group learning and group experiencing activities. Games and simulations require active participation; for not only are the users acquiring information, but they are relating to it emotionally as well.

The enormous growth of (and reliance on) visual literacy is resulting in a population that has a preference for the picture over the printed word. The librarian must be skilled in evaluating visual media and ascertaining their communication effectiveness. Knowledge of how and under what circumstances the material will be used will determine whether it should be in print, slide, filmstrip, or motion picture form.

Models, maps in many forms, and realia are also being acquired as a means of providing information in the best possible form. Again, the librarian must bear in mind that the main criterion for selecting the best format is to determine which format will be most used by the patron.

Television in the form of videotapes and videodiscs is beginning to appear in libraries. Much of the information in video formats is currently being used in the library, but with the tremendous number of videotape recorders being purchased for home use, libraries can expect requests for more information in this format and that it be available for use outside the library. Videodisc players are also being marketed; and it can be expected that they too will be purchased in considerable numbers, which in turn will demand that libraries acquire and circulate information in the new videodisc formats.

The microcomputer, which is now available at a price that the library can afford, is opening a new era of information service. Librarians involved with the use of microcomputers need to be trained to use them to their fullest potential. This will require librarians to develop skills in selecting computer programs, and perhaps have a basic knowledge of computer languages in order to select, store, and retrieve information.

These various media, their introduction, growth, and use by the library, are prima facie evidence that the library is in a state of metamorphosis. It is essential to remember that today's library patron is continually exposed to a wide variety of communication media forms and selects those he or she personally considers best for any particular information need; the librarian, therefore, must select and have available those media that best serve those needs.

Trends in Library Service

Contingent on the types of materials provided by the library are the services it provides. Here is another indication that the library is not a static institution. Because many of the newer materials require some type of device to gain access to their information (e.g., listening to a disc record requires a record player), the library provides a service by having the necessary equipment available either for loan or for use in the library. This means that the library is now a facility that provides the properly designed space for using the new media. No longer are there just tables for reading; we now see a trend toward the learning center concept in the physical organization of the library, wherein the patron can use a whole array of media in an ideally designed environment. Private spaces for individual or group use are becoming prevalent.

A library provides a vast array of community information services in a wide assortment of media forms. Mobile and branch libraries are now accepted forms of service. Among other services provided by the library are book talks and interviews with authors to stimulate patrons interest in certain books, story hours for children to help explore the world of literature, discussions and debates on popular issues to support free and critical inquiry, community bulletin boards to inform the public of items of general interest, reference services to aid in the dissemination of information, public service displays to advertise information about the community, film festivals to promote patron appreciation of film as an art form, and art shows to foster cultural growth.

Cable television is making an appearance as a library service. Many of the services listed in the preceding paragraphs can be transmitted via cable television directly into the homes and businesses of the library service area. The ever-growing electronic refinements in television, with the use of such exotic devices as laser beams and holography, will generate a still greater expansion of library services. Eventually the library will be able to transmit, via television, information requested by individual subscribers. It is anticipated that such service will be common before the end of this century (i.e., within the next two decades).

In summary, the library is capable of providing just about any type of information service in any media format currently available in a technological society. This is not to imply that the library is the community's temple of omniscience. Rather, in concert with educational institutions, mass communication institutions, and centers of entertainment, a community has access to virtually all the information in the treasury of mankind. It is the librarian, by the judicious accession and distribution of information, who provides the information services needed by the community and best obtained from a library. Such a task can only be accomplished by a highly skilled professional librarian.

Impact of Electronic Technology

Possibly the greatest change that will occur in libraries is presently on the horizon of information science. It is conceivable that in the near future (i.e., within 20 years), libraries will be interconnected with a vast electronic information network. Electronic devices in local libraries will have direct and immediate access to information stored in regional, national, and international centers. This information will be retrievable and transmittable directly to the patron's home or place of employment. Furthermore, this information will be reproduced on a cathode ray tube (CRT) or in some form of hard copy (e.g., paper, videodisc, or microform).

The patron's access to the entire world's storehouse of information will be attained via the local library. Libraries will be responsible for analyzing requests for information and having the expertise to interpret them by using a man–machine interface system as a means of retrieving the exact information needed. This task cannot be performed by the unskilled patron, because it requires knowledge in the operation and efficient use of information systems.

Retrieving electronically stored information will be only part of the library profession's task. It will also include determining what data are to be entered into the information bank, to what media format the data are to be committed, and what (if any) information is to be rejected or discarded. The system will include a feedback loop with a two-way flow of information between the smallest library and the largest information bank. Obviously such a system will involve a highly sophisticated electronic network managed by capably trained professionals. Incidentally, these systems are not merely in scientists' minds—they are presently leaving the laboratory, and early prototypes are being field-tested.

It is difficult to comprehend the impact electronic technology is having and will continue to have on the library. The library could become the manager of all of mankind's recorded information worthy of being preserved, with the ability to make this information directly accessible on demand to any patron anywhere. The librarian will need to be acquainted with the procedures involved in materials selection, to develop efficient systems approaches to implementing the procedures, to be aware of how information can be distributed vis-à-vis copyright laws, and to defend and preserve the principles of intellectual freedom.

Although there will be many stages or plateaus of development prior to the realization of the ultimate electronic information bank, to say that such a phenomenon is unrealistic is to deny what is currently happening. The library has always been changing (although at times these changes have seemed imperceptible), but the changes that are occurring presently—the use of sophisticated forms of television, the installation of computer terminals—are of a much greater scope. The time when a library can accept or reject the idea of incorporating newer types of media into its repertory of services has long passed; rather, the situation now is that the library must plan on how soon and to what degree it can provide all the information services demanded by society.

Adaptable Philosophy for the Present and Future

Every librarian, whether new to the profession or enjoying many years of service, should take time to develop a philosophy and to evaluate it periodically in order to determine if it is still providing guidelines for the fulfillment of professional goals. Actually, there is no one best philosophy for the librarian; for in the final analysis, "best" is measured by its usefulness in attaining goals. Perhaps at this point it would be beneficial to stop reading this textbook and prepare a written statement of your personal philosophy as a librarian. Can you work with your philosophy? Can you derive daily work goals and objectives from it? Is it a true statement? Can you defend it? Does it make a genuine contribution to the profession? Finally, is your philosophy compatible with the particular institution that employs you or from which you are seeking employment?

Too often, librarians (and other professionals as well) perform their professional obligations without concern for a philosophy or perhaps reflect a philosophy formulated by someone else that may provide little or no guidance for achieving personal professional goals. The librarian must be aware of how society is functioning, investigate the needs of the particular community in which he or she functions, know the goals of his or her particular library, and do a critical, introspective analysis of him or herself as a person and as a librarian.

This entire chapter has been devoted to present and future trends in the library. It has irrefutably stated that the library is a dynamic, evolving institution involved with change within a changing society. Granted, the rate of change varies among libraries; the librarian must nevertheless ask, "How well do I cope with change?" Some people are always eager to adopt every innovation that arrives on the scene; others prefer adhering to the "tried and true." To aid in answering this question, the librarian should analyze his or her philosophy and that of the institution for which he or she works using a continuum with innovation at one end and tradition at the other. By placing both his or her own philosophy and that of the institution on this continuum, the librarian can assess if the philosophies are where he or she feels they should be. Bear in mind that this is not a "goodness" measurement; it is only an objective examination. All media, regardless of whether they have been around for centuries or are new, exotic, and futuristic, must meet the criterion of being the best means of serving the patron's needs. The printed book is not about to, and perhaps never will, disappear from the library; it is much too valuable, for it contains a treasury of information and enjoyment unobtainable in any other form. However, there is an ever-growing demand for information in other media that cannot be overlooked.

In formulating or reviewing a philosophy, there are various continua that can be objectively used, such as the following:

innovator	traditionalist
technologist	humanist
direct society	serve society
provide all that is available	provide best that is available
specialist	generalist
nonprint oriented	print oriented

The librarian must ask where he or she would place him or herself with regard to being a technologist or a humanist? Does he or she feel the library should direct society or serve it? Of course, directing and serving society are both honorable endeavors, but the librarian must decide where he or she truthfully fits on this continuum. In selecting materials, should the librarian provide the patron with everything available for a particular need, or should only the best materials be provided? Finally, does the librarian perceive him or herself, on the basis of training, ability, and attitude, as a highly skilled narrow specialist or as a competent, broad generalist?

A philosophy must measure up to or even exceed the librarian's professional goals. The library is a mainstay of society and must be in the control of people who can guide its destiny. There is an ever-growing reliance on the library as the institution for preserving all information and making it available on demand. The growth of the library parallels society's ability to generate new information. The Library of Congress has over 336 miles of shelves and is still growing. The librarian is responsible for analyzing the needs of society as regards information and having a philosophy that allows for the design and implementation of a complete information system. It is both a difficult and a delicate task. It can only be delegated to the type of leadership that knows precisely where it is going—and how it is going to get there.

Considerations

The amount of information being produced annually is growing exponentially, and concomitant to this growth is the diversity of patrons' interests and the increased intensity of their demands. As a result, libraries have increased both their dimensions and their areas of specialization, with the net effect of broadening their information bases. The library must resort to some method of systems analysis in determining what types and forms of information media are to be acquired. The library is becoming a more complex operation, and the librarian functioning in this type of milieu can no longer perform within a superior–

subordinate structure with a system of specifically prescribed directives. Rather, he or she must adopt the professional attitude of obtaining individual self-fulfillment by providing input as to how the institution is to achieve its goals. This means that the individual must now contribute to the design of the library's objectives, policies, and procedures. By following such a course, a process of shared commitment and responsibility is created, resulting in a greater sense of professional fulfillment for the librarian, while improving the services provided by the library. This process of altering the role of the librarian from one of performing in a tightly structured hierarchy to one of contributing input to how the library should function means that the whole institution can change from a reacting to an action-initiating modus operandi. In pursuing the role of professional leader, the librarian must be aware that institutions have a strong tendency to maintain the status quo. However, the avant-garde librarian has the support of continuing technological developments and increased patron demand that predicate, if not mandate, that changes must take place. The librarian must determine if he or she will influence, shape, and control these developments and demands, or simply react to them as they occur.

In order to function effectively and still guide the destiny of the library, the professional librarian will have to know how to cope intelligently and objectively with the key change factors that continue to occur (e.g., exponential growth coupled to the needs of a postindustrial or electronic society), the technological advances that are taking place, and the effect of these on the library specifically and society in general. The librarian will need to know how to initiate change as well as how to predict its ultimate effects. Finally, the librarian will need to know how to analyze what information is being generated, select what is needed and wanted, store it, and then ultimately make it accessible on demand in the format best suited for a particularly diagnosed request. This is no easy task, and obviously it will not be the responsibility of one person or group of people, but rather it should and will be in the charge of a team of librarians who use a systems approach and are continually learning how to adapt to the modern, forward-looking, and ever-evolving library.

Selected Bibliography

Atkinson, Frank. *Librarianship: An Introduction to the Profession*. Hamden, Connecticut: Shoe String Press, 1974.
Benge, Ronald C. *Libraries and Cultural Change*. Hamden, Connecticut: Shoe String Press, 1970.

Buckland, Michael K. *Book Availability and the Library User.* New York: Pergamon Press, 1975.

Carey, R. J. P. *Library Guiding: A Program for Exploiting Resources.* Hamden, Connecticut: Shoe String Press, 1974.

Communications Tomorrow. Washington, D.C.: World Future Society, 1976–.

Estabrook, Leigh, ed. *Libraries in a Post-Industrial Society.* Phoenix: Oryx Press, 1977.

Garrison, Guy G. *Total Community Library Service. Washington, D.C., 1972.* Chicago: American Library Association, 1973.

Hammer, Donald P., ed. *The Information Age: Its Development, Its Impact.* Metuchen, New Jersey: Scarecrow Press, 1976.

Kochen, Manfred. *Information for Action: From Knowledge to Wisdom.* New York: Academic Press, 1975.

Lancaster, Frederick W. *Toward Paperless Information Systems.* Library and Information Science Series. New York: Academic Press, 1978.

Martin, Lowell A. "User Studies and Library Planning." *Library Trends* 24(January 1976) 483–496.

Orr, James M. *Libraries As Communications Systems.* Westport, Connecticut: Greenwood Press, 1977.

Poole, Herbert. *Academic Libraries by the Year 2000.* New York: R. R. Bowker, 1977.

Robotham, John S., and La Fleur, Lydia. *Library Programs: How to Select, Plan and Produce Them.* Metuchen, New Jersey: Scarecrow Press, 1976.

2

Materials Selection

Overview

When selecting and promoting the use of library materials, it is best to think of the library as a facility that dispenses information in a vast array of media forms. There is no single media form that can be considered as the best; rather, there are many media forms, and each has attributes and capabilities that may be best suited for a particular patron, need, or situation. The task of the librarian is to select those media forms that communicate a specific body of information most effectively. It is essential for the librarian to have an acquaintance with and a working knowledge of the various media forms available.

Formulation of Policy

Before embarking on a program of materials selection, it is necessary to establish a clearly stated, precise policy for materials selection. This policy should spell out the guidelines by which materials are to be considered for acquisition. Ideally, the formulation of a materials selection policy should involve all who are concerned with the operation and utilization of the library. This would include those who provide or allocate funds (in the case of publicly funded libraries, it would be a member of the legislative body), whoever is in charge of administering the library, librarians with expertise in materials selection, and representatives from the community which the library serves. It is quite conceivable that some members of the policymaking group would serve only in an advisory or ex officio capacity, but their input is nevertheless vital to the success of the task.

In developing a materials selection policy, it is recommended that a systems analysis approach be followed. Basically, this requires that all the system components that either affect or are affected by materials selection and utilization are analyzed in an effort to determine the library's requirements and the components' contribution to the program. Regardless of the type of library, these components would include at least the following:

1. purpose of the library
2. community served and its needs
3. scope and depth of the collection
4. type of information needed to be acquired
5. budget
6. space
7. established guidelines
8. policy governing use of materials
9. hardware requirements
10. characteristics of various media
11. media preferences
12. trends in information packaging

Purpose of the Library It must always be borne in mind that regardless of the information or media form selected, its function is to serve the purpose of the library. Unfortunately for purposes of selection, the library almost invariably has a multitude of purposes that need to be clearly understood and stringently followed in considering the acquisition of media. The prescribed purpose could be to support the informational needs of a particular school curriculum, to cater to leisure time or recreational needs, to be a depository of reference or archival information, to provide information for vocational and avocational development, or to keep abreast of the latest information being generated that is of value or could possibly be requested. These purposes must be defined and delineated prior to any selection of media.

Community Served and Its Needs It is important to ascertain the scope of the community to be served as regards age, occupation, ethnic composition, ability, interests, and projected informational needs. Obviously the informational needs of a school community could differ considerably from those of a retirement community. Concomitant with information needs are media preferences. Whereas a school community may have a preference for filmstrips and motion picture films because of large-group utilization of information, a retirement community may have a propensity toward books, video recordings, and other materials that are consumed on a more individual basis.

Scope and Depth of the Collection   The librarian needs to know how broadly and to what depth the collection should be developed. The very nature of the library will provide some direction. If it is an academic library serving a particular curriculum, obviously both the scope and depth of acquisitions will have to be made to comply with that need. Scope essentially refers to how broadly an area or topic of information should be considered for acquisition, whereas depth refers to how much detail is necessary. Simply stated, scope can be equated with extensiveness, and depth with intensiveness. A well-defined policy regarding scope and depth of collection will not only guide what is selected, but can also alleviate any problems of censorship. If controversial material is acquired, then any objection to it can usually be resolved by indicating (and proving) that the material acquisition was made within the boundaries of library policy.

Type of Information Needed to be Acquired   Too often, information is acquired in print form without a real consideration of the type of information being selected. It is vital to know which format is best for a particular information type. If a patron wants to enjoy a particular musical selection, he or she would obviously choose a recording over a printed score; but which would be better if the patron wants to learn the musical score, the printed work or the recording? Understanding how a pole vaulter performs can best be achieved by a film, but should the film be in sound or silent? It is necessary to know the characteristics of various types of information in order to determine which formats are best suited for effective communication of that information.

Budget   There is always a concern as to how many dollars are to be allocated for various information materials. The policy of the library needs to provide direction as to how much of the budget should be used for which type of material. Budget allocations need to be reviewed at least annually to determine if they are still in compliance with current needs and trends. The importance of budget cannot be understated; it is all pervasive in the selection process. Without it, nothing can be purchased; if it is limited, it can present constraints as to which media form can be acquired. Ideally, it might be nice to have a popular novel available in both book and motion picture formats, but perhaps all your library can afford is a paperback version. Do not consider budget as something ugly that impedes the development of the library collection; rather, consider it as a challenge that requires judicious selection procedures. Be well aware of the fact that if budget were not a problem and were truly unlimited, selection would be no problem; the library would just buy everything that was available and would not need the skills of a professional librarian to determine precisely the information needed and its best format. More likely than not, budgets are prepared with allocations for specific media forms, which advantageously assures a balance of various media forms in the collection. However, it is also advantageous when a librarian is truly not biased toward any particular medium and feels free to select the medium best suited to a particular information need.

Space Needless to say, library materials take up space. What must be determined is the space needs of various types of media in terms of both storage and utilization. Storage may require special shelving and a controlled environment (e.g., microforms should be stored in closed drawers or cabinets that are relatively dustfree, dark, and low in relative humidity). Some media can be used outside the library, whereas others can only be used inside the library. The librarian must be aware of the space available and how it must or can be best utilized.

Established Guidelines Available to the librarian are a vast array of guidelines that can be used in selecting various media formats. On a national level, both the American Library Association (ALA) and the Association for Educational Communications and Technology (AECT) have published guidelines for kinds and amounts of material that should be in various types of libraries. There are also guidelines published by many state library and audiovisual associations that may be more applicable for a particular area. Listed in most guidelines are minimal media requirements in both kind and amount for particular types of libraries. The data available in these guidelines are invaluable in determining how a particular library collection measures up to a set of accepted, recommended norms. Established guidelines provide essential information for the development of a selection policy.

Policy Governing Use of Materials The librarian must establish conditions under which materials are to be used. This includes who is allowed to use the collection, any direct cost or charges to the patron, whether a particular media form can only be used in the library or whether it can be charged out, how long a period of time it can be charged to a particular patron, any restrictions as to the kind of patron who can use a particular medium, charges for damaging or losing materials, enforcement of overdue penalties, and rules for using equipment and/or facilities.

Hardware Requirements In addition to knowing what kind of equipment and facilities are needed for using the various information media, the librarian must know the required ratios of material to related equipment. It would be ridiculous to have a library of 500 films and have only one motion picture projector. To assist the librarian in this task, there are established guidelines that contain tables that give minimum as well as ideal ratios of material to equipment requirements. Attention must also be given to any maintenance that will be necessary for materials and equipment, because this too can affect what material can be selected in terms of media type, quality, and quantity.

Characteristics of Various Media Media characteristics can govern access to and use of a particular medium as well as conditions of use. Motion picture films, for example, tend to be used by instructional departments (i.e., teachers), civic groups, and organizations and are usually presented to large groups. A book, on the other hand, is used by an individual; and, if used by a group at the same time, multiple copies must be made available. Motion pictures require the use of equipment and proper audio and visual conditions, whereas a book is *nonmediated* (i.e., does not require equipment) and can be read just about anywhere. It would be a good exercise for the librarian to chart out the characteristics of the various media as to physical characteristics, equipment needed and its characteristics, and conditions of use in his or her particular library.

Media Preferences It is commendable to analytically determine which medium is best for a particular information type, but the medium will not be beneficial if it is not used by the patron. Filmstrips tend to be enjoyed by children, but tend to have less appeal for adults if not accompanied by an audio recording. Some people are addicted to books, whereas others can easily adapt to the same information when it is on microform. The librarian should develop and nurture a "feel" for the media preferences of the library's patrons. However, this does not preclude the librarian from introducing and encouraging the patron to use other media forms that are better suited to the nature of the information the patron is seeking.

Trends in Information Packaging Since the librarian cannot alter trends in how information is made available, library acquisition policy should not be restrictive to the point that if something worthwhile were to appear on the market, the librarian could not acquire it. Rather, the policy should encourage the librarian to be forward looking. Microcomputers, for example, are becoming more prevalent in libraries; but if policy restricts the use of a new or different information format, then an opportunity to provide a valuable service may well be lost. In this age of rapid and phenomenal technological advances, it is advisable that the librarian be critically aware of the ways information is being dispensed. Some children's books are made of materials that are virtually indestructable. Motion pictures are now available in both 8-mm and 16-mm formats in open reel or self-threading cartridges and in several video formats. The computer, with its huge storage capabilities, is now available to libraries. The librarian must be ready to incorporate these new trends into the library schema and to make projections as to how soon a media form may become obsolete. It would be foolish to commit the library to a particular media form that becomes obsolete while the information it contains is still of value.

By using the preceding components in formulating selection policy, the librarian will essentially be following the tenets of systems analysis. All the aspects of media selection and utilization will be critically scrutinized. Acquisition of materials will be performed within specifically prescribed parameters that will guide the librarian in making professional, intelligent, valuable, and useful selections of information media.

Selection Standards

In developing the library collection, the librarian must determine whether the kinds of materials being acquired are adequate in number for his or her particular library. To address this concern, there are available a host of recognized standards to which the librarian can refer. These standards are published by professional library associations that periodically research the problems of selection standards and generate what they believe to be appropriate levels of service for particular types of libraries. The unique advantage in having professional associations develop standards is that the standards are prepared by and, therefore, are a consensus of the beliefs of the librarian's professional peers as to the legitimate needs for the modern library.

Library standards serve several functions. They provide the guidelines by which to measure the size of a collection against a recognized published standard. If a librarian wants to start a new collection of a particular type of medium, then the standards give an indication of absolute minimum number necessary. If the minimum cannot be attained to initiate the collection, then it is not feasible to even consider embarking on it. If a particular type of information requires mediation, the standards will indicate how many pieces of equipment are necessary, that is the ratio of hardware to software. The standards assist the librarian in preparing budget justifications, especially in cases in which the individual responsible for making budget decisions has little idea as to what is a fair and adequate allocation. Not only do the standards give numbers for material and complementing equipment, they also provide standards for personnel, kinds and degree of services the library can provide, and procedures for organizing the collection.

There are several things to look for when examining library selection standards. The librarian should find out the source of the standards and verify that the source is knowledgeable and experienced in dealing with the needs of the particular type of library for which the librarian works. It is also important to know which association or group is responsible for the endorsement because this information can be extremely valuable in justifying selection procedures. The librarian should determine whether the standards are qualitative or quantitative. *Qualitative* standards tend to be philosophical, citing the purpose of the library and why it should pursue a distinctive type of action in building a collection. *Quantitative* standards, on the other hand, are purely statistical and cite specific amounts of material for a particular size of library. The librarian can then choose the set of standards that are most applicable for the library's geographical area; these standards are usually available at the national, state, and regional level. The librarian must also ascertain the type of library (e.g., public, school, academic, or special library) to which the standards apply and the precise purpose for which the standards were developed (i.e., for facility, collection, equipment, or services). The date when the standards were made is also extremely important because since standards are often made by professional organizations, the members of which volunteer their services, the task is usually not undertaken on an annual basis, and any set of standards that is more than 5 years old could very well be obsolete and inappropriate to the librarian's purpose. Finally, the librarian must consider whether the standards are realistic for his/her particular library. There could very well be unique circumstances related to the library that would tend to invalidate the position taken in the published standards. In essence, the librarian must be able to justify using a particular set of standards and to demonstrate that these will prove useful in building the library collection.

Materials and Equipment Selection

When involved with materials and equipment selection, the librarian needs to be familiar with the characteristics of the various information media. The first consideration is which media form(s) is(are) best suited to a particular body of information, bearing in mind the patron's receptivity to the form(s). A filmstrip may be best for a particular body of information, but if the patron is adverse to filmstrips, maybe an illustrated text is preferable. If a media form requires some type of audiovisual equipment to gain access to the information, such equipment needs to be compatible with both the patron's ability to operate it and the conditions and environment in which it will be used.

In order to select information forms more intelligently, it is best to categorize them into classes and to specify how access to the information is gained. The ordering of the media that follows ranges from simple to complex, and should not be considered as a taxonomy or hierarchy, but rather, as a means for easy identification of the form and its characteristics. The term *mediated* refers to the equipment (*hardware*) necessary to gain access to the information (*software*).

1. *Objects*   These items can be considered realia (i.e., the "real" thing), and include anything in its natural state whether it be animal, vegetable, or mineral; living or preserved; original or synthesized. Still another category is objects that represent the "real" thing, such as models and replicas.

2. *Visual, still, nonmediated media*   This is the category with which most people are familiar. It includes the printed word (verbal symbols), graphics and drawings (nonverbal symbols), art prints, and illustrations and photographs (still pictures). The user of this information has direct access to it; it does not require the use of equipment in order to be read or viewed.

3. *Visual, still, mediated media*   This includes slides, filmstrips, and information appearing on the CRT of a computer. Viewing this information requires the use of some type of electrical–optical equipment to project it onto a screen.

4. *Visual, motion, mediated media*   This category is the silent motion picture film in either color or black and white. The most prevalent format is the Super 8-mm film packaged in either open reel or cartridge (film loop). Much less prevalent is the 16-mm silent motion picture film.

5. *Audio, nonmediated, media*   Often overlooked in the library is the use of resource people who can come into the library and give talks.

Musical instruments also fall into this category although few libraries are involved with them.

6. *Audio, mediated media*   This includes both audio disc and audio tape recordings that are available in a variety of playing speeds and formats.

7. *Audio, still, visual, mediated media*   Sound filmstrips and sound slides fall into this category. The visuals (filmstrips or slides) are discrete entities and must be viewed on some type of optical projection equipment, whereas the audio (disc or tape) require some kind of electronic playback. The audio tracks are duplicated on two sides or tracks with one side or track having an audible tone for manually advancing the visuals. The other side or track has an inaudible tone that automatically advances the visual when used on special sound–slide or sound–filmstrip projectors.

8. *Visual, motion, audio, mediated media*   This category includes the sound motion picture film in either black and white or color and is predominantly available in a 16-mm format, although some producers offer the option of obtaining certain titles that are available in Super 8-mm. Television is also in this category (i.e., video tape and video disc recordings).

9. *Consumable media*   This category is used to identify those items that are, in a sense, consumed in the process of being used. Included are items that are constructed or compounded by the patron and cannot be returned to their original state, coloring books, and textbooks or workbooks in which it is intended that the user will write.

10. *Manipulative media*   Games, simulations, teaching machines, and computer terminals fit into this category. These are essentially devices that the patrons, either singly or in small groups, have to manipulate in order to obtain information or achieve a desired objective.

Bear in mind that although these categories are described as entities, which indeed they are, they can be used in combination with other categories—or it may even be advisable to have information available in several media formats. It is the librarian's responsibility to know the characteristics, advantages, and disadvantages of various media, and to know which are economically feasible and best suited for his or her particular library. Any medium selected should be in the best format available, not necessarily the format preferred by the librarian. The librarian should have an open mind when selecting a media format; too often he or she will only select those forms that are most familiar or comfortable, and, as a result, the library becomes somewhat congested with information conforming to a particular format. Remember, it is the information that determines the format, not the reverse.

Major Categories of Media

Libraries are involved in a wide range of media, and the librarian needs to be aware of the various media categories. No longer can it suffice for materials to be classified simply as print or nonprint, or mediated or nonmediated. Classifying material as print or nonprint is ambiguous and not very helpful; print information can be found in many media (e.g., paper, microform, computer, videodisc). Mediated, as opposed to nonmediated, indicates only whether or not it is necessary to have some device or piece of equipment to gain access to information. For instance, a book does not require any device, whereas a film requires a piece of projection equipment. But, with the proliferation of information available today, it could well be that some information items are available in both mediated and nonmediated forms. A book can be available in a bound copy, or it can be available on microfilm. It is still a book; however in the latter form, it requires the use of a microfilm reader in order to be read. Considering whether an item is mediated assists the librarian in a search. There would obviously be no need to search for a videotape if the library does not have access to videotape playback equipment.

The task of categorizing media appears to be quite simple, and indeed it is for the librarian who has a working knowledge of the various kinds of media and can categorically define how they are used. If the librarian is requested to construct a bibliography in microform media only, an awareness of the various microform formats would be critical in making intelligent selections. In fact, much of this book is devoted to an examination of the various media currently found in libraries.

The task of learning the various media categories is quite simple, and indeed most people are familiar with most of them as an integral part of their everyday lives. The benefit of such learning is realized when the librarian becomes involved in selection and needs to know what medium is best for a particular need or situation. The categories are not finite or closed, and it is possible that some information forms could be assigned to more than one category; but again, knowing the various categories, the librarian will know what a particular medium does and how it can be used. The following categories are based primarily on the physical characteristics of the items.

Art Prints An *art print* is either an original work of art (a painting) or a facsimile. It can be either framed or unframed. An original work of art can have any width or length and peculiar or odd-sized paintings can possibly pose a storage problem. A reproduction, on the other hand, can be available in the same size as the original or can be enlarged or reduced to a more manageable size (e.g., 51 × 61 cm [20 × 24 inches]). The value of art prints is basically twofold: They can be used for studying the styles and techniques of various artists, or they can be loaned out simply for esthetic appreciation. Patrons accustomed to having art prints available in their own homes quite often become regular users of this type of library service. Some libraries integrate art prints into the picture file collection (see the section entitled pictures), but if the art print collection is substantial in size, it should be regarded as a specific category.

Books   Most books in libraries are bound with hard covers; however, paperback books are becoming more prevalent. Reference books, and more specifically, encyclopedias, are generally available in hard cover. Selection aids are also available in book form, both hard cover and paperback. Books are also classified as fiction or nonfiction. A more specific classification is that of a *textbook*, the definition of which (depending on the situation) can be quite nebulous. Some librarians consider any book, even a novel, a textbook if it is required reading for a particular course of instruction. Under a more specific definition, a textbook would be a book that investigates a particular area of study and organizes information in a concise format by which the reader can receive instruction and learn and verify information by virtue of its accuracy and authenticity. Dissertations or research papers would be considered quasi textbooks because although they are not primarily intended to instruct, they do inform and provide scholarly information.

Community Resources   Community resources include things available in or from the community and fall into two major areas: (*a*) things in the community that cannot be brought to the library but must be seen on actual location and would be classified as *field trip items;* and (*b*) things from the community that can be brought into the library and would be called *local realia*. A subarea or type of this category would be *resource persons,* people available to the library who can make a contribution to a topic for which the librarian is preparing a bibliography.

Computers   Although it is unlikely that individual libraries will be housing their own computers, there is a growing number of computer terminals available to the library patron. The computer terminal is the means by which the user can introduce, obtain, and interact with information stored in a computer. Basically, the computer terminal looks like a combination typewriter and television screen. The keyboard is the channel whereby the user can communicate *to* the computer, and the plasma screen (which looks like a television tube) is the source from which the user gets information *from* the computer. The information appearing on the screen can be either print or graphic, and with some computer terminals, there is a light-sensitive pen that the user can touch against the screen as a means of *responding* to information generated and presented by the computer. The computer terminal is also capable of producing hard copy (i.e., a paper printout of information supplied to it by both the user and the computer). Computer programs are now designed for use by the novice and require no experience whatever. The librarian's prime task is to select, or contribute to the selection of, programs that will be stored in the computer for patron use. Most of these computers are extremely easy to operate and require very little instruction—usually a few typewritten directions will suffice. The computer can also be used to handle administrative and recordkeeping functions.

Filmstrips   These require viewing equipment. A filmstrip is a continuous strip of photographic film containing a series of still pictures intended to be viewed separately. Filmstrips can be either captioned or uncaptioned. They are primarily available in a 35-mm half, single, or double frame format (half frame and single frame are synonomous). Some companies now have filmstrips available in a 16-mm format. On occasion, books are accompanied with *shortstrips*, which are small filmstrips usually only 8–10 frames in length. *Sound filmstrips*, as the name indicates, are filmstrips accompanied with sound by either disc record or audiotape (reel or cassette). A few years ago, a filmstrip was marketed with the sound information right on the filmstrip, but it never gained wide commercial acceptance.

Kits   A universally accepted definition of the term kit is lacking because producers of kits do not use the term the same way. It will have to suffice to say that a *kit* is a collection or package of two or more items on a particular topic. Therefore, if a producer packages two or more items and calls it a kit, it should be so classified. As an example, a producer will package several filmstrips and call it a kit, whereas another producer will call it a series. Usually a kit must be purchased as a complete unit, but a series of filmstrips can be purchased separately. Perhaps a true kit would be a *multimedia kit*, which contains a variety of media (books, recording, filmstrips, guides, dittoes, etc.) or realia (coins, artifacts, minerals, etc.) dealing with a particular topic.

Maps and Charts   A *map* or *chart*, for the purpose of definition, is identified as a single, unbound, discrete item capable of being examined as a complete entity. Maps and charts vary in size, from items that can be held in one hand, to panels mounted on an entire wall. Maps are usually identified as to type of projection (Mercator, polyconic, orthographic, equal area, polar, etc.) and purpose (political, geographic, topographic, demographic, vegetation, economic, etc.). Some maps are made of paper and can be folded when not in use; others have cloth backing, and are intended to be rolled when stored. Still other maps are textured or three dimensional and made of plastic. Charts could be pictorial, diagrams, floor plans, blueprints, layouts, or flowcharts. *Atlases* are actually books of maps and as such could be categorized as books. Also, *globes* although often considered maps, are really *models* of the earth, satellites, solar system, or stars.

Microforms   These require viewing equipment. *Microforms* are any information that has been reduced photographically and requires the use of some type of magnifying device to be made readable. Microforms are available in a host of formats, physical sizes, and degrees of magnification. Most common is *microfilm,* available in reel or cartridge and in 35-mm or 16-mm formats. *Microfiche* refers to microform available on sheets of film (7.5 × 12.6 mm [3 × 5 inch], 11 × 15.2 mm [4 × 6 inch], 12.6 × 17.7 mm [5 × 7 inch], etc.). *Aperture cards* are computer cards containing pieces of microform (usually 35-mm microfilm). A *microopaque* card is an opaque piece of cardboard on which photographically printed information has been micrographically reduced. *Ultrafiche* is a microfiche with a very high micrographic reduction (50× –210×).

Motion Pictures   These require viewing and possibly listening equipment. Although motion pictures are available in many formats, libraries are usually involved with 16-mm, Super 8-mm, and standard or regular 8-mm formats. (Commercial theatres use 35-mm and 70 mm formats.) Films are available with sound tracks or silent, and the sound track can be either magnetic or optical.

Pamphlets   The term *pamphlet* varies in definition among librarians, but it is generally an unbound work of one or more pieces of paper stapled together. Pamphlets usually provide information on topics of interest; they are not intended to be exhaustive in their contents, but to provide the reader with some specific information. Pamphlets vary in size from small foldouts to stapled materials printed in a variety of sizes.

Periodicals   Periodicals are not to be confused with pamphlets. Although in physical appearance they may look like some pamphlets, they are published on a regular, or periodical, basis, identified by title, and classified by volume, issue, and date. It may be said that a periodical has continuity. Incidentally, accumulated periodicals can be bound, and many of them are available in microform.

Pictures Pictures differ from maps and charts in that they are either photographs of objects or works of art that are drawn or painted. Pictures are available as photographs, various kinds of graphics, and illustrations. A librarian can inexpensively build a fine collection of pictures by clipping them out of discarded publications. Often these clipped visuals can be mounted on cardboard to give them a quality worthy of display. The end product of this effort of clipping, mounting, and gathering various kinds of pictures will be a picture file; if continually developed and built on, a picture file can become a compendium of visuals used for study, the development of visual statements or stories, or pure esthetic appreciation. This is best exemplified by the compilation of pictures for use as study prints, accompanied by textual explanatory materials on the subject. This is somewhat different from using art prints (discussed previously—original art or reproductions, framed or unframed) for circulation to patrons for display and appreciation in their own homes.

Programmed Instruction This may require equipment. Programmed instruction includes materials designed to instruct the learner in a prescribed sequence of (*a*) stimulus (giving information), (*b*) response (providing the learner with an opportunity to answer or respond), and (*c*) reinforcement (giving the learner immediate feedback on his or her responses). Programmed instruction can be either of the linear or of the branching type. It is available in linear texts and scramble texts for use in teaching machines, or in a program to be used with a computer. Programmed instruction can be subcategorized as anything from a book to a host of media, both print and nonprint.

Real Things and Models Real things and models cover a multitude of materials and can vary in size from very small to extremely large. Real things, also called realia, include items such as live animals, animal specimens, minerals, plants, manufactured items, and works of art. A model, on the other hand, is a representation of a real thing that has been enlarged or reduced, a cutaway or cross-section simplified or modified for easier viewing or understanding, or even a replica blowup, miniaturization, or diorama. A replica, of course, could be classified as a real thing in some cases.

Recordings: Audiotape These require listening equipment. Audiotapes are available in various speeds identified in inches per second (ips). The common commercial speeds are $1\frac{7}{8}$, $3\frac{3}{4}$, and $7\frac{1}{2}$ ips. Tapes are available in open reel, cassette, or cartridge formats. Recordings can be monaural, stereophonic, or quadraphonic. The major types of information found on recordings are music, storytelling, reading, speeches, recitals, and sound effects.

Recordings: Disc These require listening equipment. Disc recordings are available in various speeds or revolutions per minute (rpm). The speeds are 16⅔, 33⅓, 45, and 78 rpm. The 16⅔-rpm record is called a transcription, and 78-rpm recordings are obsolete and no longer in production. Information found on disc recordings is of basically the same type as that found on audiotape recordings. Recordings can be monaural, stereophonic, or quadraphonic.

Recordings: Videotape These require viewing and listening equipment. Videotape recordings are becoming more available to libraries. Libraries favor the helical scan format to the quadruplex format because helical scan equipment costs a fraction of the quadruplex equipment. Videotapes are available in open reel or cassette and range from ¼ to 2 inches (0.6 to 5.1 cm) in width. Recent developments have been made with videodiscs, and they will soon be available in libraries. Videotape programs can be purchased commercially or produced locally.

Simulations and Games Simulations and games are being packaged to provide the patron with a wide range of learning and recreational activities. They can be as simple as a printed scenario and as complex as boxes with playing boards, counters, dice, spinning discs, etc. Simulations and games are intended to provide active participant behavior.

Slides (Photographic) These require viewing equipment. Slides differ from filmstrips in that they are individually mounted photographs and not placed on one continuous piece of film. In this way, they can be rearranged, augmented, and deleted. The prevalent size is 2 × 2 inches (5.1 × 5.1 cm), which is a measurement of the entire slide including the mount. Greatest use of slides is in the area of local production and the visual arts (art, architecture, sculpture, etc.).

Transparencies (Overhead) These require viewing equipment. Overhead transparencies are used extensively in education. They are usually mounted on 26- × 30-cm (10¼- × 11¾-inch) frames and contain a base transparency and possibly overlay transparencies. The major types of transparencies are clear acetate (on which information is drawn with a pen), thermal (heat process), and diazo (low-speed photographic). Polarized transparencies, through the use of special materials and equipment, give an illusion of motion when projected.

These categories can, if needed, be expanded or reduced, depending on the type of bibliography being prepared. The list can serve as a classification guide in categorizing media. It can also be invaluable when the librarian must decide on exactly what kind of selection aid should be used in searching for a particular type of item.

Materials Utilization

It is the responsibility of the librarian to create and maintain conditions that are conducive to the use of information materials. Concern must be given to cataloging, storage, circulation, equipment needs, maintenance, and place of use. There are many excellent books available on the cataloging of print and nonprint materials to which the librarian can refer. Some libraries will use one system for cataloging print materials and other types of cataloging systems for the various types of nonprint materials. It would be well for the librarian to analyze the various cataloging options available and to determine which is most appropriate for his or her particular library. With regard to equipment storage, the general approach is to segregate and store materials by their particular formats; however, some libraries have attempted to use a semi-integrated approach in which some nonprint items that lend themselves to being stored on bookshelves are shelved with books. The circulation procedures for print materials are fairly well standardized, but these procedures vary for mediated nonprint materials. Consideration must be given to the type of equipment needed, its cost and complexity of operation, the environment in which it is to be used, and the amount of time that must be allowed to enable the patron to use the equipment advantageously.

The matter of equipment is perhaps the greatest factor that divides librarians into two groups: those that prefer print materials and those that prefer nonprint materials. There is a common agreement that information should be available in a variety of media forms, nevertheless, some librarians just do not feel comfortable with the responsibility involved in the maintenance and supervision of patron use of equipment. About the only feasible solution to this dilemma is to establish a library that uses enough equipment to warrant the services of an equipment technician. The librarian is then solely responsible for providing information in any media form necessary and does not have to attend to equipment utilization. Regardless of who is responsible for equipment utilization, equipment selection should be based on ease of operation, physical safety of the user, durability, easy maintenance, and resistance to obsolescence during its life expectancy.

Maintenance programs need to be developed for all materials and equipment in the library. A plan should be devised whereby maintenance procedures can be periodically performed. There are several categories of maintenance to be considered: (*a*) the maintenance that must be performed every time an item is used—this may entail nothing more than a cursory inspection and preparation for its next use, (*b*) the maintenance that is required to repair any damage or wear incurred during use of the item, and (*c*) the maintenance that is performed periodically, regardless of the extent of use of a particular item.

Some thought must be given to where material is to be used. In the case of nonmediated materials, the patron may use them just about anywhere. Information that requires equipment to make it accessible needs space for its use, and if the material is to be taken outside the library, provision must be made to acquire portable equipment that can be loaned. If equipment cannot be loaned, the librarian must determine from the patron exactly what kind of equipment will be used to make the information accessible when it is taken out of the library.

Materials Control

Ancillary to the selection and utilization process is material control. This includes where material can or should be used, charging and reservation procedures, competence of the patron, and supervision. Some material by its very nature should only be used in the library, for example, reference and archive materials as well as materials that because of cost, limited number, or difficulty of use should be used only in the library.

Some materials can be charged out on a first come, first served basis, but other materials such as films and videotapes, because they are often used with large groups, should be booked on a reservation basis to ensure their availability to the requester. Provision should be made to determine the competence of the patron to operate some of the mediated materials. If the material is used only in the library, and if it is economically feasible, a staff member can serve as the equipment operator and as an instructor in proper equipment utilization. Any mediated material and/or equipment taken out of the library should only be used by a person whose competence in using the equipment has been confirmed by the library.

The aspect of material supervision is important if what is acquired by the library is to be used effectively and efficiently. Actually, the best use is the kind in which the material is never handled by the patron. Unfortunately, this is neither efficient nor practical. The material has to get into the hands of the user when it is needed, for as long as is practical. The patron needs to be made aware of the responsibility entailed in using material, and, if necessary, required to pay for its use as a form of a damage insurance fee. If damage is incurred, the patron should be held liable for the cost of repair. Materials can be expected to receive normal wear, but it is for the librarian to ensure that materials receive a fairly respectable time–life use.

Vital to materials selection is the recordkeeping necessary to maintain control of the collection. It is only by keeping copious records that accurate assessments can be made as to how often an item is used, or if it is being used at all. Too often in the selection process, the person who does the selecting is neither involved nor concerned with the kind of use materials receive. This is truly a situation in which a systems analysis approach is critical to the successful operation of the library, for not only does the librarian in charge of selection acquire material, but he or she is also responsible for its successful use. The librarian can discharge this responsibility simply by obtaining utilization feedback. Thus, decisions regarding selection are made not only on what is available in the marketplace, but also on the projected use of material, which is based on utilization records. Incidentally, this is not a ponderous task, especially when the recordkeeping can be relegated to a computer, which can provide utilization data on command.

Weeding

Libraries have always been concerned with selection to the point that they continually refine procedures for acquisition. However, some libraries have been somewhat reluctant to come to grips with devising a systematic method for removing material from the collection. Depending on the type of library, its rate of acquiring materials, and its storage space, there are obviously different approaches to weeding. Also, the purpose, or intent, (and extent) of use of materials determines the scope and depth of any weeding process. What is needed is a comprehensive, integrated approach to weeding that is both justifiable and does not leave the librarian with regrets or negative afterthoughts about removing (or not removing) material from the collection. It is really only in the past 20 years that researchers have been making any concerted effort to examine this problem. Most libraries only consider it a problem when they start to run out of storage space. Perhaps the first step in weeding should occur when the material is originally selected. At that time, a determination should be made, if possible, as to how long the information, material, or equipment will be of value. If such a time period can be ascertained, it becomes simply a matter of recording for future reference as to when a particular item should be withdrawn from the collection.

Still another aspect with regard to weeding is the rate of use. The utilization record would indicate whether an item, because of insufficient use, should be withdrawn from the collection. Conversely, rate of use could also indicate the need for additional copies. The recordkeeping is not difficult once a system has been set up; the main task is to develop a set of valid criteria as to when any item should be considered for withdrawal. The end result of having the weeding process begin when an item is initially considered for selection and end when it is removed from the collection is that the library will be operating at top level of material utilization. It will not waste space and will assure maximum use of the items selected.

Integrated Approach to Materials Selection

By utilizing an integrated approach to material selection, the librarian can proceed to acquire materials in the appropriate media. Basically, the task involves selecting the best information, in the proper format, for a particular type of patron. With regard to the best information, the librarian has a wide collection of selection aids and tools at his or her disposal that can facilitate the task by identifying the information needed for a particular type of library and from whom the information is available, and by providing a description and possibly even an evaluation of the content. Having found this information, the librarian's next step is to determine which formats would be most applicable for the patron's need, or, conversely, determining which formats are available that are suited to the patron.

Finally, the librarian can ascertain the type of patron and patron needs the library will have to serve by developing a profile of patron needs and preferences. This can be achieved by keeping current with the professional literature that cites trends in what materials are being received and acclaimed by patrons as well as with research that substantiates patron preferences. The individual librarian should solicit feedback from patrons. In some cases, such as school and academic libraries, the faculty provide excellent input as to what materials are needed. With the public library, the librarian needs to be aware of how extensively current materials are being used and of any information trends prevalent in the community or society in general.

Often, the task of deciding on a particular format is eliminated because there is no choice; for example, the information is available in book form only. All that remains is to resolve that the information itself is suited to the patron's needs and preferences. If the information is available in several formats then a decision must be made as to which formats are best with regard to cost/effectiveness; that is, which format will give the best return for the amount of money invested. There will be occasions when several formats will be equally beneficial. If this is the case, all formats should be acquired. However, if there are budget or space constraints, it is advisable to investigate the extent to which similar types of information already in the library are utilized in the various formats. In the final analysis, it is the extent of use that confirms whether the information and format was the best selected.

In general, small public libraries and branch libraries are inclined to select print materials that are nonmediated, along with a small collection of audio recordings. Large public libraries, though still oriented toward nonmediated print materials, tend to purchase the more expensive, one-of-a-kind mediated nonprint materials and their complementary equipment and to provide space in the library for using such information. The rationale is that the large central library can distribute to the branch libraries or the branch library can refer patrons to the large central library.

School and community college libraries are committed to an integrated approach by virtue of the type of patron served (i.e., students, who use information in independent, small- and large-group configurations). Unfortunately, many of these libraries will only grant students access to the more expensive information formats via a teacher, when, in fact, the student is the true consumer and should therefore have direct access to all materials.

The integrated approach can be further justified by the fact that information formats are selected with the patron in mind and should be comfortable for him or her to use. Considering that as much as 15% of the adult population in the United States is classified as functionally illiterate (i.e., cannot read a classified ad or competently fill out a job application), the need for an integrated information format approach becomes evident. Material has to be available in a multitude of formats, if for no other reason than to have it in a form in which the patron can assimilate it. It would be wonderful if a patron could go to a library and present identification listing his or her language and communication assimilation profile so that the librarian could provide the information requested in a format suited to the patron's ability. Librarians can no longer deny the fact that an integrated approach to material selection and utilization is essential if the library is to be used by all patrons entitled to its services.

Perhaps the most important aspect of the integrated approach is the tremendous advances being made with electronic technology in the area of information processing. The time is not far off when all library patrons, through the use of their personal computers and television systems, will have access to all types of information in practically all available formats. All librarians, regardless of the type of library they serve, should be cognizant of this trend and use it to their best advantage. Electronic technology does not result in eliminating the need for a librarian; rather, it makes information processing a more sophisticated and efficient process. This requires a highly skilled and professionally trained librarian.

Evaluation Procedures

Although at times evaluation procedures may seem cumbersome and time consuming, they are nevertheless vital in measuring the degree of success to which the library is achieving its intended goals. Evaluation has to be conducted as an ongoing process and must encompass every facet of the library's operation. In regard to material selection, it has to involve the entire gamut of material utilization from intended acquisitions to the ultimate removal of an item from the collection. The entire evaluation process is somewhat cyclical in nature, with the data gathered being used to provide information for decision making in every other phase of the utilization process.

The process of material utilization logically begins with selection. With knowledge of the types of information materials and formats that the library needs to acquire, the librarian, using professional selection aid tools, can determine the availability and locate published reviews and evaluations of these materials and formats. If the reviews and evaluations provide sufficient information to make an acquisition decision, the material can be purchased. If adequate review and evaluative information are lacking, it is recommended that samples of the material under consideration be requested for local preview and evaluation. To conduct local evaluation of material, the librarian needs to prepare proper evaluation forms and procedures, to identify persons who can reliably evaluate the material. The librarian can then use this evaluative data to make an objective buy–no buy decision.

When the material is acquired, processed, and made available for consumption, records should be kept as to how well it serves the needs of the patrons. This may entail nothing more than a record of how many times the information is requested or charged out to a patron, but it would be most beneficial if information could be obtained as to how well it was appreciated by the user. Use data will indicate how often an item is requested, if additional copies should be acquired, and if and when it should be removed from the collection. Knowing how well an item was appreciated by the patron indicates not only the extent to which certain types of information are preferred, but also why they are preferred. Currently, libraries that are starting to utilize computer systems for controlling circulation can easily obtain much of the necessary data. With this information, the librarian can be more precise in selecting material with an awareness that patron preferences may reveal the need for a different type of material. In essence, the evaluation information will give more specificity to the selection process. It is the librarian's responsibility to develop procedures for soliciting feedback from patrons. Ideally, the information should be processed and analyzed by a computer, which would considerably reduce the number of man-hours required to gather information and to make ultimate selection decisions.

Many librarians are reluctant, or feel they do not have the time to conduct a thorough evaluation of material acquisition and utilization, but the benefits that can be accrued from evaluation cannot be overlooked. The library will be providing patrons with materials they need and want, an economical number of materials will receive greater use, library space will be more efficiently used, and a greater degree of cost/effectiveness will be realized. Evaluation procedures are vital to the systems process; for in essence, they inform the system as to how well it is doing. Evaluation not only tells the system what it has done, but also what it should consider doing; stated simply, selection of materials begins and ends with evaluation.

Selected Bibliography

Asheim, Lester, and Fenwick, Sara I., eds. *Differentiating the Media*. Chicago: University of Chicago Press, 1975.

Broadus, Robert N. *Selecting Materials for Libraries*. New York: H. W. Wilson, 1973.

Brown, James W. *Educational Media Yearbook*, fifth edition. New York: R. R. Bowker, 1978.

Brown, James Wilson. *New Media in Public Libraries: A Survey of Current Practices*. Syracuse: Gaylord Bros., 1976.

Hicks, Warren B., and Tillin, Alma M., eds. *Managing Multimedia Libraries*, second edition. New York: R. R. Bowker, 1977.

Katz, William A. *Collection Development: The Selection of Materials for Libraries*. New York: Holt, 1980.

Prostano, Emanuel T., ed. *Audiovisual Media and Libraries: Selected Readings.* Littleton, Colorado: Libraries Unlimited, 1972.

Selection Aids

International Index to Multi-Media Information. New York: R. R. Bowker, 1970.

Perkins, Flossie L. *Book and Non-Book Media: Annotation Guide to Selection Aids for Educational Materials.* Urbana: National Council of Teachers of English, 1972.

Rufsvold, Margaret I. *Guides to Educational Media: Films, Filmstrips, Multimedia Kits, Programmed Instruction, Recordings on Discs and Tapes, Transparencies, Videotapes,* fourth edition. Chicago: American Library Association, 1977.

Sive, Mary Robinson. *Selecting Instructional Media: A Guide to Audiovisual and Other Instructional Lists.* Littleton, Colorado: Libraries Unlimited, 1978.

3

Selection Aids

Overview

Whether employed in a professional or trade vocation, a person must have tools in order to perform properly. The lawyer without law books or the mechanic without wrenches would be rendered inoperative. Likewise, the librarian without reference tools would be unable to perform in a professional capacity. When deciding what materials will be in a library collection, the librarian must have access to a comprehensive set of tools, that is, selection aids.

A knowledge of the selection aids available and the functions they perform is essential for the librarian involved in acquisitions. Actually, the professional librarian is in a rather advantageous position as regards selection of materials, because invariably the information being considered for acquisition is located somewhere in a selection aid. The problem is determining which selection aid has the necessary information, or which reference tool should be used to find the selection aid that will assist the librarian in the decision-making process. Although some prime selection aids can facilitate the search for materials, it is often necessary to have a large host of selection aids in order to do the job completely and to one's professional satisfaction.

Purpose of a Selection Aid

Selection aids provide the necessary information as to what is available for the library collection—where it can be obtained, what it does, how well it does it, and its bibliographic characteristics, physical formats, and possible uses. Using parts or all of the information selection aids provided, the librarian can authoritatively select new materials and justify their inclusion in the library collection. Because of the huge proliferation of information in the world today—a growth that is increasing annually in logarithmic proportions—it is essential that the librarian become an expert in using selection aids. If we consider that it took 1750 years to double the amount of information available at the birth of Christ, 150 years to double it again, only 60 years for the next doubling, and presently, a short 12 years to double existing information, then we quickly realize that it is impossible, and perhaps unnecessary, for a library to acquire and house all the information generated. It is the selection aids that provide the best sources of information as to exactly what to acquire.

General Functions of Selection Aids

Knowing the various functions of selection aids facilitates categorizing them and provides the means whereby one has available the proper selection aid at the proper time. A selection aid, although primarily used for assisting in acquisition, also helps in locating sources of information. When used to their fullest potential, selection aids become primary locators of information, making them indispensable tools of the skilled librarian.

Selection aids perform the following general functions:

1. *Buying guides*   If the librarian intends to acquire material, its cost must be determined. The price of the item is usually listed as the cost per unit. Information such as volume discounts, optional payment plans, replacement of damaged materials policy, and the purchase of individual items in a series must generally be obtained directly from the manufacturer's catalog, which makes manufacturer catalogs a primary selection aid. Because price structures are in a continual state of flux, selection aid tools used for pricing must be kept current.

2. *Reference tools*   Selection aid tools are not primarily intended for reference purposes; they do however, provide an expedient means of locating information. Depending on the type of information being sought, there is a selection aid tool that can facilitate the search. Conversely, some tools intended primarily for referencing purposes can double as selection aid tools.

3. *Checklists*   The professional librarian is always concerned as to how his or her library measures up to some standard of an acceptable

collection in numbers, titles, and types of materials. There are selection aid standards that provide this information in varying degrees. The ALA, regional, and state organizations have published standards for various types of libraries. There are also selection aids that provide lists of titles for particular types of collections (e.g., *El-Hi: Textbooks in Print*).

4. *Evaluative tools* If there is a concern for quality control, selection aid tools that evaluate materials can be of considerable assistance. They eliminate the tedious and time-consuming task of evaluating acquisitions. Unfortunately, less than one third of all the books published annually receive anything in the way of a bona fide review or evaluation. There are several organizations that provide a varying degree of evaluation services. Professional periodicals, such as *Booklist* and *Innovator*, devote sections of their issues to the evaluation of recent releases. There are also indexes (e.g., *Book Review Index*) that give information as to where reviews can be located.

5. *Sources of précis of particular materials* To be able to make an intelligent selection, the librarian needs to have some annotative information regarding the material considered for acquisition. In some cases, it is possible to extrapolate précis information from reviews. The précis needs to provide information succinctly and without distortion. To be worthwhile, it should be brief, but complete. Usually the best précis is obtained from the publishers' catalogs.

6. *Means of keeping abreast of new materials* The librarian interested in maintaining the collection and keeping it up to date with the latest releases should subscribe to selection aids that are published on a monthly, or at least an annual, basis and that indicate new releases. Some professional aids, such as *Forthcoming Books in Print*, provide this service; but it is also advantageous to be on publishers' mailing lists, which provide a steady stream of information on new and forthcoming releases.

7. *Locators of out-of-print materials* Knowing what materials are out of print is another important concern. It is good to note that many paper-print materials that are out of print are available in microform. Perhaps the best selection aid tool for this task is *Books On Demand*. Many libraries, when weeding their collections of old materials (which more likely than not would be out of print), should consider consulting *10,000 Old Books with Current Value* since they may be disposing of books that have some monetary value.

8. *Guides to materials in a particular format* The librarian may have need of information in a particular format, and a selection aid tool that only catalogs certain types of materials is especially useful (e.g., *Books in Print, NICEM Index to Educational Overhead Transparencies*).

9. *Locator of materials that fall within various categories*   Some selection aids cross-index information, which, in essence, categorizes material for convenient location by publisher, author, subject, age, suitability, medium, etc. (e.g., *Educator's Guide to Free Filmstrips*).

10. *Indexes*   An indexing selection aid is valuable for providing location information. Usually, this type of selection aid only refers the user to where additional information can be found or to where certain information is indexed.

Obviously, there is no single selection aid capable of performing all these functions to the extent needed by each librarian. However, by having the right combination of selection aids, the librarian can have fingertip access to an astronomically large listing of sources of information. The proper combination can be achieved by performing an analytical evaluation of the selection aids acquired for your professional use. It is one thing to have the tools and know how to use them, but you must first know how valuable the tool is for your purposes.

Components To Be Examined
When Evaluating a Selection Aid

Before evaluating a selection aid, you must determine what specific function you want it to serve. It is not fair to condemn a particular selection aid because it does not, for example, have complete bibliographical descriptions when, indeed, this is not its intended purpose. The librarian must first ascertain what information the aid claims to provide, and then evaluate how accurately, easily, thoroughly, and completely the information is provided. Incidentally, it is for this reason that the librarian needs more than one selection aid tool; when similar aids make identical claims, the evaluator should ascertain which one does the best job. If you have two similar selection tools, and one is far superior to the other, then the poor one will never be used and would not have been acquired if it had been properly evaluated before it was acquired. In evaluating selection aids, consider the adage: "If you can't use it—you don't need it."

Performing a systematic evaluation of selection aid components is essential. The librarian should never make prior assumptions, rather, examine in detail those components he or she wants included. The following components give an idea of what should be evaluated in a selection aid; the degree to which it satisfies a particular need will determine its particular worth as a tool.

1. *Authorship*   What are the author's credentials? How does he or she select entries—by committee, with information from people in the field, etc.? Is there more than one author?

2. *Publication data*   Is the work new? How is it kept up to date—with supplements or entirely new editions? When was it first published? Are back issues available or necessary? What is the frequency of publication? Are new entries so indicated?

3. *Bibliographic entries*   These can list, author, title, edition, place, publisher, date, paging, volumes, illustrations, plates, portraits, maps, indexing, and cost. Depending on the medium, listings on nonprint materials would provide such information as whether the material was produced in color or black and white, its speed, running time, and format, whether it has captions, its size and dimension, and whether it has sound or is silent.

4. *Scope and coverage*   What is the purpose of the selection aid? How wide is the range of subject matter included? To what type of library, information area, or patron is it applicable? How many different entries are listed? Does it include all materials available in a particular area, or does it only include those of a specific genre?

5. *Purpose*   What service is the selection aid supposed to provide? How well is the purpose achieved? Is the purpose expressly stated, and does it state parameters of coverage? Is the purpose too broad or too narrow? Is the purpose consistent in the information it provides on each entry, and is it complete?

6. *Arrangement*   Is the information conveniently arranged for your purposes? Is the arrangement form dictionary, class, subject, age, or interest group? Are class numbers or Library of Congress (LC) card numbers given? Are index tabs provided? Is any type of convenient color coding used (e.g., colored type or colored pages)?

7. *Physical characteristics*   What is the type (soft or hard cover) and quality of the binding? What is the quality and durability of the paper? Is the layout of information consistent, orderly, and efficient to read? Is the print large enough and easy to read; are devices such as bold type or italicized print used? If updated supplements are used, are they of the same quality as the original volume? Are the overall dimensions (size) of the selection aid practical?

8. *Uses*   How can it be used—as a buying guide, a reference tool, to construct bibliographies, as a primary resource? Can it be used to complement other selection aids? Who would use it—the acquisitions librarian, reference librarian, cataloger, or patron?

9. *Special features*   Does it contain articles of interest? Does it give procedures on how to locate information? Does it give suggestions on

possible different ways it can be used? Does it contain advertisements? What kinds of indexing are used? Does it provide lists of suggested acquisitions? Does it use photographs or other graphic devices? Does it include actual passages from items it has selected?

10. *Cost*   Is the cost reasonable when compared to the price of similar selection aids? Are there discounts for multiple copies? Is the library required to purchase a subscription? Are replacement copies available, and if so, at what cost? Is it available in microform, and if so, at what cost?

All the foregoing considerations are helpful in determining and justifying the inclusion of a selection aid in the librarian's collection of professional tools and in assuring that the selection aid will be a useful and valuable one. These 10 components are not only useful in evaluating a selection aid; they are also basic considerations in library referencing, and, as such, should become an integral part of the fundamental knowledge of all professional librarians.

Major Criteria Used in Comparing and Complementing Selection Aids

As previously described, the components of a selection aid can be assessed in determining its particular value to the librarian. Obviously, it is impossible for any one selection aid to be all things for all librarians; but the librarian can determine the value of the aid by the degree to which it satisfies his or her particular needs. Being aware of what each component can contain, there are three major criteria to consider when assessing how well a particular selection aid suits the necessary requirements. Attention must be given to (*a*) completeness, (*b*) datedness, and (*c*) evaluation.

Completeness

Once the librarian has determined his or her needs, the first consideration will be that of completeness, which incidentally can have two different meanings. It can mean that an aid provides as much information as possible about a particular item, or it can mean that the aid lists every item available in a particular genre, topic, or area. The former characteristic is invaluable in investigating the merits of a particular item; the latter is indispensable as a locator. Here is obviously a situation in which a combination of selection aids used in conjunction with each other, one for locating a particular item quickly and efficiently, and the other to give detailed information about it, is ideal. Although it may be best to have both in combination, this often cannot be properly achieved: The proliferation of materials being produced daily would result in a rather large, unwieldy selection aid. Even selection aids published in multiple volumes ultimately reach a point of diminished returns. It becomes analogous to using an encyclopedia; exactly how much information does the librarian really need at his or her fingertips. Perhaps the most complete sources of information on particular items are publisher's catalogs; however, they are obviously biased and do not provide critical review data. There are many selection aids that attempt to list every item available in a particular genre, topic, or area. Examples are *Books In Print* for book titles and *NICEM Index to Motion Picture Films* for educational films.

Datedness

It is essential in selecting library materials that the librarian be kept informed of current releases. The possibility always exists that what he or she is looking for is currently available in a more recent edition, a new revision, or even a whole new treatment. In the case of an item like a novel, the content of which obviously would not change, there may be recently released supplementary materials available (e.g., films, readings) that would greatly enhance the book. Also, an awareness of what is recent may lead the librarian to modify what he or she is planning to acquire for the collection. At the opposite end of the datedness continuum are selection aids of out-of-print materials that may now be available only in microform; the right selection aid is invaluable in locating an out-of-print item you may desperately need. An excellent tool for keeping abreast of what is currently available in books is *Books in Print,* which list all books currently being published. This selection aid is an annual publication; therefore, old copies can be used for locating books that are out of print. The possibility of a book being out of print does not mean it is not available, and a selection aid like *Books on Demand* would indicate if the information is available in microform.

Evaluation

The third criterion to consider in selection aids is evaluation. Librarians are not omniscient about the different types of information a library may acquire; even if they were, they would not have the time to preview all the materials available. Hence, the librarian must rely on evaluations to assist in acquisition decisions. Evaluations vary greatly in scope: One may be nothing more than a simple annotation telling what the item is about; another may be a review conducted by a single critic; another an appraisal performed by a select group using some type of objective criteria; or still another a subjective evaluation performed by people from various walks of life and compiled by a central agency.

Regardless of what form the evaluation takes, it is essential to know the credentials of the evaluator; these are the best measure of the evaluation's validity and reliability. Furthermore, an evaluation should be clear, precise, and succinct. As an added feature, evaluations should have some type of uniformity. They should all be constructed in the same way so that the librarian does not have to decipher the format and approach of each evaluation in order to glean the information he or she seeks. The Educational Film Library Association (EFLA) provides respected evaluations on educational films, and there are a host of periodicals that review new and forthcoming book releases, (e.g., *New York Times Book Review, Booklist, Book Review Digest*).

Through the use of these three criteria—completeness, datedness, and evaluation—selection aids can be acquired that complement and enhance each other. All that is needed is for the librarian to develop the professional skill of utilizing them to their optimum potential. To this end, the librarian should continually ask, "Are the selection aids I am using keeping me completely informed in the most efficient way possible?" It would be ideal if the librarian could design his or her own unique selection-aid format whereby only the exact information needed would be immediately accessible. Perhaps in the not too distant future, such information will be stored in a computer that will not only provide the information needed, but also make all the selections for any particular library. In the meantime however, the librarian needs to have access to the right combination of selection aids, which, in the hands of a knowledgeable professional, become the tools for doing an excellent job in the area of acquisitions.

Evaluation Grids for Examining Selection Aids

To determine which selection aids are needed for your particular task, a system should be devised that permits an easy, accurate analysis of any group, genre, or combination of selection aids. An easy method for achieving this is to construct grids that can be used to plot the values of selection aid characteristics being examined. Separate grids for completeness, datedness, and evaluation provide a graphic assessment. Furthermore, the grids, once completed, can be used in the future when different combinations of selection aids may be needed for different acquisition purposes. The result is an evaluation, in graphic form, of all selection aid tools presently available in the library, which can then be used for (*a*) determining what if any additional types of selection aids are needed; (*b*) assessing the strengths and weaknesses of selection aids; (*c*) deciding which combinations of selection aids are needed for a particular task; (*d*) providing a method of introducing a new librarian to the value and purpose of a particular selection aid; and (*e*) establishing a method of evaluating any newly produced selection aids against current selection aid holdings.

There are no particular standards for selection aid grids. Therefore, the librarian must design a grid that best serves the needs of the particular library in which he or she is working. The form may be designed in a variety of ways, from a series of numerical values to a plotting of subjective statements. The grid becomes a personal type of tool and should reflect whatever works best for the librarian who designed it. Tables 3.1 and 3.2 are two different types of grids that may be used as a guide by the librarian interested in constructing a selection aid grid.

With the type of rating system used in Tables 3.1 and 3.2, a selection aid can be assessed according to specific criteria and it is the librarian's decision as to which criteria should be assessed. Incidentally, if a selection aid should happen to score very low on a particular criterion, this would not necessarily be justification for rejecting it; rather, it may be an indication that there is a need for another selection aid to be used in conjunction with it. For example, with regards to treatment, the *NICEM Index to Educational Overhead Transparencies* provides little information on individual transparencies, but it does list what is available. When used in conjunction with a publisher's catalog, it provides location information as a complement to the selection information provided by the publisher's catalog.

The overall rating gives the general value of the selection aid, but identical scores could very well have been achieved on entirely different criteria. The librarian may also assign, a priori, a cut-off number on the overall rating, and any selection aid receiving an overall score below a specified number would automatically be rejected.

The selection aid grid in Table 3.2 provides space for comments that can be extremely helpful in ascertaining why a particular score was assigned to a feature of the selection aid. The last column, "Notes," provides space for comments that are perhaps not applicable to a particular criterion. This grid also involves a weighting system for use when it is determined that different aspects of a selection aid are not equally important. In the case of this grid, scope has a weighting of 5,

Table 3.1 General Selection Aid Grid

Selection aid	Scope	Arrangement of information	Special features	Treat-ment	Author-ship	Format	Overall rating
A	5	4	3	3	4	5	24
B	5	3	5	5	5	5	28
C	2	3	0	2	4	1	12
D	2	4	4	2	5	3	20
Y	4	4	3	2	3	4	20
Z	3	5	4	5	5	3	25

Rating criteria[a]	Rating (points)
Scope	
Are the materials included relevant for library use?	1
Is the aid comprehensive enough to give the selector an adequate picture of what is available?	1
Are the materials listed recent enough to be useful?	1
Are materials in all different media listed?	1
Does the aid cover the necessary subject areas?	1
Arrangement of information	
Is information arranged concisely?	2
Is information cross-indexed?	2
Are easy symbolic devices used (e.g., stars, asterisks)?	1
Special features	
Does it contain informative, interesting articles?	1
Does it contain advertisements?	1
Does it give suggestions on methods of selecting?	2
Does it list special collections?	1
Treatment	
Does it provide enough information to justify acquisition?	1
Are bibliographic data complete?	2
Does it refer to other bibliographic sources?	1
Does it include footnoted information?	1
Authorship	
Are the authors reputable?	3
Are critical reviews signed?	1
Does the aid use expertise of librarians in the field?	1
Format	
Is the aid easy to use and handle?	2
Is the print easy to read?	1
Is the page layout convenient?	1
Are the binding and paper durable?	1

[a] The maximum number of points for any particular category is 5.

Table 3.2 Selection Aid Grid for Selection Aids Dealing with Nonprint Materials

Selection aid	Criterion and weighting[a]					Score	Notes
	Scope (5)	Price (1)	Arrangement (4)	Annotation (3)	Authorship (3)		
A	Reviews hardware and software — 3	$12/yr — 4	Index of reviews — 2	Very little but complete — 2	Official publication — 4	45	
B	Reviews of all media; directory of producers and distributors — 5	$5.50/yr for subscribers — 5	Each medium appears in table of contents; items arranged by medium — 4	Reviews are critical and give extensive information — 5	All critical reviews are signed — 5	76	Exceptionally good price; print is too small
C	Reviews motion picture films only — 2	$8/yr — 5	Poor table of contents — 1	Description of most media not critical — 2	Editorial board — 5	30	
D	Lists films only — 1	$14; has quarterly supplement — 5	Arranged by curriculum subject, which is cross-indexed by author and title — 4	Descriptions too brief — 2	Many consultants — 5	47	Revised quarterly
Y	All media extremely comprehensive — 5	$150/5 vols. — 1	Multiple listing with crossreferences — 5	No annotations, simple line entry — 1	Editorial board — 2	55	Contains reference to primary aids for further information
Z	All media — 5	$40/2 vols. — 3	Confusing — 0	No consistent format — 1	Field editors — 2	37	Revised yearly

[a] Weighting range is from 1 (low) to 5 (high); values are shown in parentheses following criterion.

but price a weighting of only 1. The score for selection aid A, therefore, is 15 (3 × 5) for scope, 4 (4 × 1) for price, 8 (2 × 4) for arrangement, 6 (2 × 3) for annotation, and 12 (4 × 3) for authorship—yielding a total score of 45 (15 + 4 + 8 + 6 + 12).

Both grids achieve the same purpose; that is, they provide a tool for assessing selection aids. The grid in Table 3.1 uses a point system for each category with a possible maximum of 5 points. With this system, it is possible to vary the point system so that a particular category could have a total of more than 5 points if indeed one category had a higher point value than another. The grid in Table 3.2 achieves this result by assigning weighting values to each category. Either method achieves the same result, and the librarian should use the type of grid that seems to be the most efficient. As stated earlier, the librarian should actually design his or her own unique grid; the two grids presented here are only examples of the many possibilities.

Using selection aids properly is not a haphazard process of collecting all the selection aids available. Rather, it is a process of acquiring those needed for a particular professional application, based on a knowledge of the exact capabilities of each. It must be remembered that selection aids are professional tools designed to assist the librarian in accurately and efficiently providing the materials that best serve the library's patrons.

Selected Bibliography

Broadus, Robert N. *Selecting Materials for Libraries.* New York: H. W. Wilson, 1973.
Bonk, Wallace John, and Magrill, Rose Mary. *Building Library Collections,* fifth edition. Metuchen, New Jersey: Scarecrow Press, 1979.
Evans, G. Edward. *Developing Library Collections.* Littleton, Colorado: Libraries Unlimited, 1979.

Selection Aids

Alternatives In Print: An International Catalog of Books, Pamphlets, Periodicals, and Audiovisual Materials. New York: Neal-Schuman, 1980.
Audio Visual Equipment Directory. Fairfax, Virginia: National Audio-Visual Association, 1953–.
Directory of Directories, first edition. Detroit: Gale Research, 1980–.
Educator's Purchasing Guide, sixth edition. Philadelphia: North American Publishing, 1974–.
Hart, Thomas L., Hunt, Mary Alice, and Woolls, Blanche. *Multi-Media Indexes, Lists, and Review Sources: A Bibliographic Guide.* Books in Library and Information Sciences, Vol. 13. New York: M. Dekker, 1975–.

International Bibliography Information Documentation (IBID). New York: Unpub, 1973–.

MacLaury, Jean. *Selected Federal and State Publications of Interest to Planning Librarians: No. 9*. Monticello, Illinois: Council of Planning Librarians, 1977.

Rufsvold, Margaret. *Guides to Educational Media*, fourth edition. Chicago: American Library Association, 1977.

Wall, C. Edward, and Northern, Penney B. *Multi-Media Reviews Index*. Ann Arbor: Pierian Press, 1970–.

4

Systems Approach to Selecting Materials

Overview

Selecting materials for the library is a major task, and the complexity of choosing the right item continues to increase. More information is being produced than ever before, which results in a corresponding increase in the diversity of patrons' requests. The librarian, to perform efficiently in material selection, is almost compelled to follow some type of systems approach. Actually, using some type of system for selecting materials is not new to the librarian, for this task always requires some type of procedure. Unfortunately, this procedure far too often evolves through trial and error and the efficiency, and the effectiveness of the process is never challenged. A systems approach is predicated on a detailed analysis of the process to ensure that all the elements that influence it are examined and refined for the ultimate purpose of using the best means to get the right materials.

Need for a System of Media Selection

It is impractical for the librarian to think that books, even though they are presently the mainstay of a collection, should receive prime acquisition consideration and that all other media should therefore be of secondary importance. Selecting any one medium for acquisition is in itself a complex task if done properly, but when an entire range of media is involved, performing the task successfully can become all but impossible. The librarian must not assume that selection of media can be achieved by some subjective inner feeling for what a library should acquire; attention must be given to a host of variables. The librarian must know all the intricate characteristics of the various media and their effectiveness in fulfilling the library patron's needs. Cost-effectiveness factors must be considered. Availability of information from all sources has to be analyzed. The means by which the media are utilized is also an important factor. Finally, a decision on what is to be selected must be predicated upon its effect on the library's program. All these tasks require an orderly, efficient procedure of investigation.

The problem confronting the librarian is the development of a procedure for materials selection that can be performed objectively, function clearly for all involved, and result in the building of a well-balanced collection. When it comes to selecting among various media, their interrelationships must be assessed. A particular kind of information might be available in many media, but the challenge is to select those that best serve the library collection. A hard bound book can be used conveniently by an individual and is quite durable; a paperback book containing the same information is less durable, but also less expensive. A motion picture film, on the other hand, though more expensive, has the advantage of sound, color, and motion, and can be used with large audiences; but a motion picture requires projection equipment to make its information accessible. However, if motion is not vital to presenting a certain kind of information, then a sound filmstrip should perhaps be chosen instead. But the problem remains as to how the librarian is to perform selection responsibilities time and again, accurately and speedily. Actually, what is needed is some method or system in which the task of material selection is a formalized procedure. The formulation of such a procedure must be based on the library's philosophical goal in selecting information and must also reflect the policy of the institution. To satisfy these needs successfully, the librarian must have an operational knowledge of the systems approach.

Advantages of a Systems Approach

A systems approach is an activity involving the orderly, scientific analysis of all the components that can be identified with a functioning entity or contribute to its maintenance. This entity, or system, can be as microscopic as the electron or as macroscopic as the entire universe. *The American Heritage Dictionary of the English Language* (1976) defines a *system* as "a group of interacting, interrelated, or interdependent elements forming or regarded as forming a collective entity." Specialists involved in using the systems approach as a scientific method identify their activity with a host of synonyms: systems analysis, operations research, operations analysis, systems evaluation, operations evaluation, systems research, and management science. Regardless of the synonym used, the function remains the same—the scientific investigation of the functioning of a system.

The systems approach is a worthwhile endeavor, for in any system, the conduct of any element invariably has an effect on every other element and on the system as a whole. Some elements may be so insignificant that detecting their effect on the system is difficult, but a sufficient quantity of them could ultimately have a profound effect on the efficiency of the system. By using a systems approach, one initiates a methodical search to identify and assess significant interactions among the multitudinous variables that effect the entire system.

The scientific method requires that each discrete component or procedure in the system be identified, its purpose described, and its contribution evaluated. Alternative components or procedures are considered in an effort to evolve the most efficient system possible. The task of systems analysis involves: (*a*) formulating the problem; (*b*) constructing a model, formula, or equation; (*c*) deriving a solution; (*d*) predicting the impact of the solution (solutions involving several alternatives are individually evaluated as to their consequences to the system); (*e*) simulating the solution(s) on a model of the system; (*f*) analyzing results; (*g*) making recommendation for course(s) of action; (*h*) evaluating the effect on the system.

The systems approach is worth the time and effort, for too often when a problem exists, those responsible either become oblivious to it or assume the obvious and miss the subtleties causing the problem. Too often the problem is not obvious; rather, it is an array of complex subtleties, and a heuristic approach is used to help discover precisely what is happening. The librarian using the scientific method afforded by systems analysis no longer has to rely solely on subjective judgment in determining solutions to problems. Rather, decisions can be made based on empirical evidence accumulated by identifying, isolating, and testing every facet of the problem. It is a comprehensive approach that considers all the interrelated factors and generates results that are objective, quantifiable, and measurable.

The Systems Approach
Applied to Library Operations

Because the systems approach is an orderly, scientific method of analyzing the components of any system, it can certainly contribute to improving the efficiency of a library operation. Before we proceed to its application to the library, a word of caution is warranted. Too often, people reading about the systems approach for the first time treat the term as a euphemism for practical thinking. They claim that when a problem arises in the library it is discussed, thought over, and resolved, and that the discussing and thinking are essentially a systems approach. Such a simplification could not be further from the truth; it is for just such reasons that a systems approach is needed. The systems approach is a research and development tool that can help improve library operations. Furthermore, its application is not restricted to management of the library as a whole institution, but in fact is perhaps most serviceable when used with the myriad of components or subsystems within the library.

Libraries are perenially struggling with problems of shortages of funds, staff, space, facilities, and materials. These problems are further compounded by ever-increasing demands for services both in kind and in quantity, and they can no longer be resolved in a piecemeal fashion. The traditional method of resolving a problem as an isolated entity may yield only artificial results; it is analogous to attempting to cure symptoms without regarding the disease. It would be well for the entire library professional staff to be skilled in using the systems approach. As a consequence, all the subsystems are analyzed, and the results are resolved within the context of the larger system that they ultimately affect. In reality, every subsystem is a component of a larger system, which in turn is itself a subsystem of a still larger system. It is characteristically a pyramid concept, with each layer supporting that which is above it. Through the systems approach, not only is the subsystem itself analyzed, but its effect on the rest of the system is ascertained as well. An accrued benefit is also realized: Communications are greatly improved, for now the staff has a better understanding of how their respective components function and how they relate to every other component within the system. No longer are subsystems competing for budget priorities; instead, needs are determined by how well they contribute to the operation of the entire system.

The library as a system is becoming ever more complex. The individual library building is becoming more diversified with regard to materials and services. Coupled with this is the increasing trend for local libraries to function as part of a state library system that is part of a national library, which is in turn a subsystem of an international library system. With the continuing astronomical accumulation of information and the use of electronic data banks for its control, the era of isolated operations is rapidly disappearing.

Computer programs are available to assist in systems design and research. The librarian unskilled in computer technology can still apply some of the computer processes in resolving smaller subsystem problems. Concern must be given to voids or duplication of materials, breakdowns of operations, and bottlenecks in service. Plotting these problems and analyzing their causes and effects will help to remedy shortcomings in the subsystem. Although ideally, these problems can best be handled by computer, the library without one can begin to use systems procedures and prepare for the time when a computer becomes available. It is not that the library cannot function without the aid of a computer; it is just that the computer can process data much more efficiently.

The first step in considering the library as a system is to identify the types of services or functions it performs; next, to generate a list of activities necessary to perform these services and functions; and finally, to prepare procedures for conducting these activities. The procedures, activities, services, and functions are diagrammed for purposes of analysis and decision making.

To illustrate the analytic potential of the systems approach more graphically, we can choose one of the library types included in Figure 4.1, for example the city library, and see that we can proceed upward and investigate how the library contributes to a larger system; proceed laterally and examine its function as part of a regional network of libraries; or proceed downward and examine the subsystems that affect its operation. It is suggested that the subsystems be the first area of investigation; for in the pyramid concept, it is best to start at the bottom and work up. If each small component is doing the job properly, then there is an assurance that the entire system is generally healthy.

Each library type, as a system, is responsible for administering to the information needs of a particular community. The major subsystems involved in achieving this objective are acquisition, processing, storage, retrieval, and circulation. Within these particular subsystems there are in turn another set of subsystems, some of which are common to all of them. For the purpose of this discussion, we will examine only the area of acquisition.

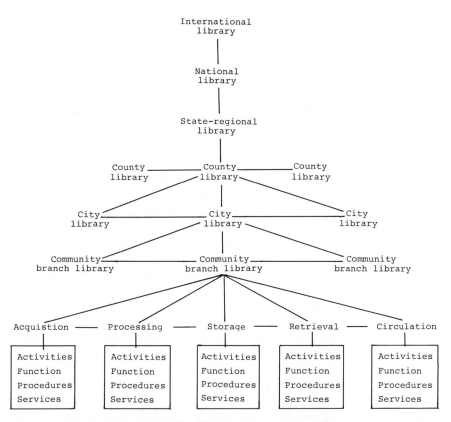

Figure 4.1 Diagram of a public library system (does not include interface with other types of libraries such as academic, medical, industrial, private).

Library Systems

The operation of the library as an information institution can be conceived of as the performance of five interacting systems. They are (*a*) administration, which is responsible for supervising operations; (*b*) acquisitions, which selects and acquires materials; (*c*) processing, which controls the cataloging and storing of bibliographic information; (*d*) circulation, which controls the flow and movement of library materials; and (*e*) the reference system, which is involved with the retrieval and transfer of information requested by the user. Each of these systems contributes to the goals and objectives of the institution. Although they are not discrete entities, each system has a sphere of authority, responsibility, and functions that can be categorized into a group or class. The spheres of influence of each system obviously overlap, but the overlaps are not competitive or redundant; rather, they are a means of cooperating to get a job done. Similarly, within each of the major systems are series of subsystems that are created to perform specific functions. The entire system's performance at an optimal level depend(s) on how each system is developed and refined, as the library's operations change and evolve.

Within any system and subsystem, there are essentially four elements: input, storage, reaction, and output. The manner in which these four elements interact to maintain homeostasis in a heating system is analogous to their operation in a library material selection system. First, a comfortable temperature range is determined which requires the collection of *input*. The thermostat is then set to maintain this range; that is, the knowledge is *stored*. If the temperature strays from this set range, the thermostat must *react* by elliciting an increased or decreased output from the furnace, thereby reestablishing the proper temperature range. A thermostat is an example of a subsystem of a heating system in that it is responsible for collecting input, processing that input in relation to information currently stored, and reacting by elliciting the appropriate increase or decrease in output.

In the library, *input* in the form of patron need assessment and media availability and evaluation is collected. The proper balance between patron need and the library holdings is determined by considering various criteria—selection policy, budget parameters, library circulation records. This balance is then *stored;* it becomes the thermostat-like subsystem of the material selection system. It *reacts* to an upset in the balance by acquiring new materials and/or reevaluating and redefining the impact of current library holdings; therein generating *output,* that is, making these materials available to the patron via technical processing, circulation, and the reference system.

In determining what is needed or wanted (input), the library needs feedback, and the librarian should solicit patron requests for and evaluation of materials. In school libraries, faculty often have total control of the funds used for acquiring materials, with the possible exception of reference and replacement materials. Often, in special libraries, it is the library staff, knowing the institution's needs, who selects materials. Public libraries try to encourage patron requests. The librarian responding to these requests needs to have professional selection aid tools in order to know what is available.

The storage component requires that the librarian must operate within the library policy. The policy should be a printed statement that is precise and detailed enough to allow selections to be based on an intelligent knowledge of what the library ought to acquire, not just a "feeling" about what the librarian thinks the library needs. The budget is a specific figure, and from it, the librarian knows what expenditures are possible. The librarian knows what is already in the collection and uses this information also to make selection decisions.

Reacting, the act of acquiring the material, involves knowing where to order materials and how to process orders for delivery to the library. This function is primarily clerical in nature, requiring the processing, recording, and controlling of data, but must be carried out in a well-organized fashion because it usually involves a considerable flow of data and materials to and from vendors. Although it does not require extensive decision making, it does require the maintenance of detailed accounting records.

Finally, the output component insures that when the selected material arrives, it is promptly sent to the next library subsystem, technical processing, and then to circulation and reference. Each subsystem in turn performs its input, storage, processing, and output functions.

The success of the system ultimately rests on the critical analysis of feedback. Properly analyzed, feedback leads to a knowledge of how well the materials were selected and how successfully they contribute to the library's goals: Does a particular acquisition indeed answer the patrons' needs (i.e., is it being used)? Is the format appropriate? Is there sufficient quantity to satisfy patron demand? Is it cost/effective?

Following a systems approach is not limited to any particular size of library or library function. Regardless of the size of the library or the amount of material involved in the selection process, the librarian needs to follow some type of intelligent systems process. Therefore, the librarian must develop a procedure (system) for selecting materials, and the means of setting up, organizing, and analyzing the effectiveness of a system is flowcharting.

Basic Flowcharting

To facilitate the synthesis of a procedure for selecting materials, the systems analyst uses the technique of flowcharting. Flowcharting is a process of diagramming all the components of a particular activity; the result is an easy-to-read, understandable, visual display. It replaces the cumbersome, inefficient narrative procedure, which is solely verbal, tends to be rather extensive, and does not utilize easy to comprehend visual symbols—which aid in the verification of decision making. All that is required of the user in flowcharting is an understanding of how to use some basic visual symbols.

The elements of the activity are diagrammed in a logical progression. The flow of activity can proceed either from top to bottom (vertical flow) or from left to right (horizontal flow), depending on the analyst's preference. Additional symbols are also used. In *Library Systems Analysis Guidelines* (1970), Edward Chapman provides a more detailed treatment of flowcharting. However, the basic symbols described in Figure 4.2 are sufficient for the development of a primary flowchart.

Flowcharting provides an orderly, disciplined approach to analyzing. library procedural activities. It also provides an easy-to-read, visual plotting that can be critically analyzed for any omissions or redundancies. Through its use, not only are existing procedures analyzed, but

Terminal: Beginning or end of procedure under analysis.

Process: Activity that must be performed.

Input–Output: Material or information introduced to or sent out of the procedure.

Decision: A point in system where a yes-no decision must be made in order to continue.

Connector: Indicates an entry or exit to another part of the flowchart. Aids in eliminating lengthy lines to other parts of the flowchart. Usually a letter appears inside the symbol to indicate the part of the chart to which the symbol refers.

Offpage connector: If the flowchart is on more than one page, offpage connector serves as a referent and locator as to where the flowchart connects.

Arrow: Used when the flow of activity is not in the same direction, or part of the general central line of the flowchart.

Predefined process: Involves several steps, but is represented as a single statement.

Figure 4.2   Basic flowchart symbols. (Data from Edward Chapman, *Library Systems Analysis Guidelines* © 1970, John Wiley & Sons, Inc., New York. Pp. 86–98.)

new procedures can be scrutinized prior to their implementation. New personnel in a library can follow flowcharts as a training aid or a checklist of the prescribed functions of an activity or procedure.

The novice to flowcharting may initially regard it as a cumbersome conglomeration of nonsensical doodles that poorly represent a schematic for intelligent thinking. Perhaps this is true, but even the most intelligent thinker must be able to communicate thought if it is to be of any benefit to the institution. The flowchart provides a precise, efficient means of communication and a method for analyzing it.

For example, consider the film-selection flowchart provided in Figure 4.3: Are there any redundancies or omissions? Is it easy to read and understand? If the same information were in verbal form only, would it be as easy to analyze? Finally, does it define the procedure in detail and provide a succinct decision-making process. Figure 4.3 is essentially a decision-making flowchart; similar charting can be used for workflow design, organization of operations, time (clock–hour) procedures, and job function networks. It also has the added feature that the various components are demonstrated visually, thus facilitating the simplification, elimination, rearrangement, combination, or expansion of any of the activities of the decision-making process illustrated in order to improve the system as a whole.

Selection of Multiple Media Forms

The major concerns in making the proper or best selection of information in a particular medium can be ascertained by making the following inquiries: (*a*) Is the information suitable and presented in the best medium? (*b*) Is the information in the best medium, considering the patron(s) who will be using it? (*c*) Are facilities, if needed, available and equipped to make the information accessible?

Determining which medium is best for a particular type of information requires that the characteristics of the information be carefully examined. An obvious example is music; which is best presented in an audio form (audiotape or disc recording) rather than in a motion picture or videotape format. There are situations in which different media have more subtle differences with regard to information content. Should a speech by a famous person be in printed form or audio form? Any decision regarding any kind of medium must be predicated on knowledge and not preference. The most effective method of making this type of decision is to identify all the media formats applicable to a particular piece of information, list them in order according to how well they

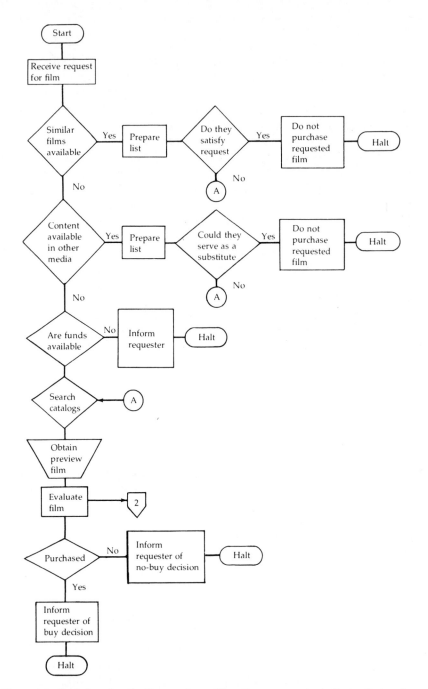

Figure 4.3 Basic flowchart for film purchase. (The offpage connector indicates that evaluation procedures are charted on page 2.)

present the information, and find if indeed the information is available in the forms identified. This task requires a knowledge of the characteristics of various communications media (see Chapter 5).

After the best media forms and their availability are determined, the next step is to identify the most likely ways in which the patron(s) will use the information. It could be for independent use, small or large group use, cultural enrichment, entertainment, supplementary information, reference, research, or extensive study; the information may be used either inside or outside the library facility; the information, by virtue of format, could be of short- or long-term value (e.g., perhaps a film would be viewed only once by a particular patron, whereas a book might be consulted on repeated occasions).

The final consideration in selecting a medium is to examine how accessible it is to the patron. The library has a facility and a policy of how the facility is to be used that defines conditions for the use and extent of use for each medium. A medium is of little use if it is inaccessible to the patron. A book is ready to use straight off the shelf, but a film requires projection equipment. Conversely, a book can be read by only one person at a time, whereas a film can be viewed by one person or an audience of hundreds. Closely linked to accessibility is convenience of use; (i.e., which medium would the patron prefer).

These three characteristics—suitability of medium, patron utilization, and accessibility—are not investigated as discrete entities; rather, they are used as a means of determining which medium should ultimately be selected. This selection can best be achieved by developing a flowchart that provides a vehicle for logically, sequentially, and efficiently determining the merits of the various media being considered. The use of flowchart techniques ensures that the best decisions are made and that the selection process is accomplished by precise, thorough measurement. Because the emphasis in this textbook is on selection, greater stress is given to the use of systems analysis for acquiring materials; this is not, however, intended to negate the equally important areas of accessibility and utilization. Ultimately, all the factors of selection, accessibility, and utilization and their respective systems analysis are interfaced into an even larger system.

A Priori Considerations to Flowcharting

The flowchart method developed earlier in this chapter introduced a procedure for selecting materials to make the selection process more accurate and efficient. It is also a method whereby any flaws or shortcomings can be easily detected and eliminated. In a situation involving the selection and consideration of more than one medium to satisfy an informational need, the process of flowchart analysis can make an enormous contribution. The flowchart will provide the valid visual proof necessary to substantiate a selection decision involving more than one medium.

When it has been determined that a need exists for information available in various media, the media can be processed through the flowchart to determine their contribution to the library collection. The procedure involves a flowchart for each type of medium. Incidentally, the media flowcharts, once constructed, will be applicable in selection of a particular type of medium regardless of circumstance. In essence, the flowchart is a visual diagram of the library's selection policy, acquisition procedures, and utilization demands. Once it is prepared, flowchart revisions will be necessary only if changes occur in those areas. The construction of flowcharts for each medium is predicated on well-defined criteria. Obviously, there will be a replication of many parts of the flowchart for all media, and it is unquestionably in the replicated areas that a one-to-one comparison can be made. In flowchart areas not replicated in other media flowcharts, information is discovered regarding unique traits of a particular medium that further justifies its acceptance or rejection for acquisition.

Essentially, the flowchart for each medium will be based on criteria that allow selection policy, acquisition procedures, and utilization demands to be properly analyzed. This is achieved by listing in sequence the criteria for each area as they apply to a particular medium and then plotting the criteria onto a flowchart. The following is an example of criteria a city library might formulate for 16-mm film selection.

Cloverdale City Library's Procedure for 16-mm Film Selection

Selection Policy

1. Film should not be readily available from any other public institution (e.g., schools, local museum).
2. Film should not be of the genre presented over broadcast television.
3. Film should culturally benefit library community.
4. Film should not cost more than 30 times the same type of information available in book form.
5. Film should not cost more than 3% of the total film-purchasing budget.
6. Film must be requested or recommended by a patron and a librarian.
7. Film should not be in an area representing more than 30% of library's current holdings.

Acquisition Procedures

1. All film titles pertaining or relevant to request must be listed.
2. Applicable titles shall be previewed.
3. Film evaluation committee must be unanimous in its decision to acquire the film.

Utilization Demands

1. Anticipated usage must be five times a year for a minimum of 5 years.
2. Must be applicable to an identifiable need of a particular community group that makes use of the library (e.g., elderly, hobbyists, vocational groups).

From these criteria, a flowchart can be constructed that will depict the activities and processes necessary to select a film. The development of flowcharts for other media acquired by the library will result in a highly refined selection apparatus that is ready to assist in the selection process on demand. When an information request is received for an item available in more than one form, it is subjected to the meticulous scrutiny of the flowchart. How well it survives the rigors of inspection will determine which medium is selected. It is possible to have a requested item accepted or rejected in all media available. Whatever the decision, it is justified by a well-established, systematized selection process.

Selected Bibliography

Benton, John B. *Managing the Organizational Decision Process.* Lexington, Massachusetts: Lexington Books, 1973.

Bingham, John E., and Davies, Garth W. P. *A Handbook of Systems Analysis,* second edition. New York: Halsted Press, 1978.

Boillot, Michael H., Gleason, Gary M., and Horn, L. Wayne. *Essentials of Flowcharting,* second edition. Dubuque, Iowa: William C. Brown, 1979.

Chapin, Ned. *Flowcharts.* Auerbach Computer Science Series. New York: Van Nostrand Reinhold, 1971.

Chapman, Edward A. *Library Systems Analysis Guidelines.* New York: Wiley, 1967.

Churchman, Charles West. *The Design of Inquiring Systems and Organization.* New York: Basic Books, 1971.

Cohen, Leo J. *Operating System; Analysis and Design.* New York: Spartan Books, 1970.

DeGennaro, Richard. "Library Administration and New Management." *Library Journal* 103(Dec. 15, 1978):2477–2482.

Evans, G. Edward. *Management Techniques for Librarians.* New York: Academic Press, 1976.

FitzGerald, John M., and FitzGerald, Ardra F. *The Fundamentals of Systems Analysis.* New York: John Wiley & Sons, 1973.

Hicks, Warren B., and Tillin, Alma M., eds. *Managing Multimedia Libraries,* second edition. New York: R. R. Bowker, 1977.

5

Selecting the Proper Medium

Overview

In Chapters 1–4, I have attempted to identify, categorize, and characterize how various information media can be selected and utilized. Ultimately, situations will arise in which it must be determined what indeed is the proper medium. Granted, there are many circumstances in which there is no choice; the information is only available in one media format or, because of use criteria, only one media format can be considered. But, in order to have a library in which the right medium is available in the proper format for the best use conditions, a systems approach and a careful examination of selection and use criteria are required.

Bearing in mind the media alternatives discussed thus far, an approach to selecting the proper medium should entail the following: (*a*) a formulation of a policy and program of equipment selection, (*b*) selection of the medium that best satisfies a particular need, (*c*) categorization of the media into a hierarchy or taxonomy of characteristics, (*d*) consideration of the conditions under which the information will be used, and (*e*) development of a set of basic criteria for selecting equipment. By following this systems approach, the librarian can knowledgeably determine the way the library should maintain, develop, and achieve its goals of information acquisition and utilization.

Designing a Policy and Program of Equipment Selection

Media selection for the library cannot be a haphazard process. It must be predicated on a specific policy that takes into consideration patrons' needs, budget, physical space, personnel requirements, and philosophical goals of the library. Once formulated, the policy for media selection will have to be examined periodically and perhaps revised to reflect utilization trends and technological developments.

Patrons' needs, both real and perceived, regarding media utilization must be carefully identified. The ultimate success of the media selection policy will certainly be measured by the extent to which media are actually used. It is therefore essential to develop a profile of user characteristics and to determine propensities toward any particular types of media. However, this should not preclude consideration of a medium not presently in the library collection, because such a medium could be well received by patrons once it is in the collection. Frequency, location (e.g., inside or outside of the library), and conditions (e.g., individual or group use) of patron use must be assessed.

It is a hard reality, but one that cannot be ignored that the library operates on a budget. The criteria for selecting media must conform to budget constraints. The flexibility lies in determining how much of the budget will be allocated for each type of medium. Of course, no librarian ever has a large enough budget to buy everything that should be acquired. Obviously, limits must be set; and a good librarian can design a justified set of priorities that conforms to the budget and makes the best contribution to the library program. Without well-developed media selection criteria, it is difficult to justify the purchase of one $400 film rather than 40 books or 30 periodical subscriptions. Operating within budget requires that the library develop a balanced collection with regard to types of media and kinds of information required. It is much too easy, and perhaps too safe, for example, to expend the greatest portion of the budget on books of a particular genre and ignore completely other media needs. Such an approach will result in the provision of a rather narrow or limited service and will never achieve the full potential of serving all the information needs of the library community. Increasing media service to patrons might even result in obtaining larger budgets. The librarian must determine which media are capable of fulfilling a particular information need and then employ the systems approach discussed in Chapter 4 to determine which media will yield the greatest cost benefit.

Physical space necessary for media storage and use, though not usually a great concern, should nevertheless be considered. It is ironic that that an inverse ratio usually exists between the cost of an item and the storage space it requires. (A $400 film requires less storage space than 40 $10 books.) If there is a shortage of storage space weeding can provide considerable relief. It should be mentioned at this point that the library should have a prescribed policy for weeding out media as well as selecting it. Weeding is, afterall, a process of *selection*—in this case, selection of those media that should be removed from rather than added to the collection—and as such is subject to the same concerns. With regard to space necessary for utilization, some space allotments (e.g., reading area, carrels, learning centers) can provide the appropriate use setting for a variety of media. However, some media have particular space requirements—some require the use of equipment that makes additional demands on space requirements; some are most advantageously viewed in a group settings, which makes a different kind of demand on available space. It is indeed regrettable when media are acquired and there are inadequate provisions for their use. The librarian must consider the characteristics and peculiarities of space requirements of media being considered for acquisition in order to determine if the library has the capacity to provide for patron utilization of that media to its greatest advantage.

Personnel requirements for maintaining media involve a variety of skills. The collection requires maintenance; for example, books must be kept in good repair; periodicals must be bound, films cleaned and inspected, and equipment maintained. In smaller libraries, one person might handle all maintenance responsibilities whereas in larger libraries, several individuals might be hired, each of whom would be responsible for a specific maintenance task. In either case, it is an inescapable fact that maintenance chores must be performed. The librarian must be cognizant of the maintenance needs of the various types of media being considered for selection in order to determine if the library has the capacity to satisfy these needs.

To be meaningful, the library's philosophical goals should not be regarded as a collection of nebulous euphemistic phrases. They should be respected as the guides and procedures by which the library is to serve its community. If the library's philosophical goal is to serve as a depository of information for private citizens, then perhaps its media needs may differ from those of a library for which the goal is to provide information in its most usable form. Philosophy is not sacrosanct; when it is no longer useful or consistent with the needs of the community it serves, it should be modified. However, until that time, it should be strictly adhered to; for without it, the library has no mission or sense of direction. When media are selected in agreement with philosophical goals, the library maintains the posture of a dynamic, growing institution providing a valuable service to the community.

Any policy and program of media selection should cover an extended time period. It is recommended that the policy and program be projected for 5-year periods. This means that any media being selected should fit into a 5-year acquisition plan. For example, the librarian should project how many films the library anticipates acquiring over a period of 5 years, and then acquire films within the projected figure. The purpose of this projection is to keep a balance within the collection and also to perform within the library's goals. This does not imply that in the case of films, 20% should be acquired each year, but that the total number of films acquired should comply with the 5-year projection. If all the films for the 5-year period are acquired within the first year, no additional films will be acquired for another 4 years. With a 5-year policy, budget planning is greatly facilitated; the library can perform much better within its budget; and media acquisition goals can be more realistically realized.

Concomitant with material selection is the acquisition of any equipment necessary to utilize media formats. Here again, a 5-year projection plan can greatly facilitate selection, because equipment is continually being modified and improved. There has to be a continual concern with obsolescence, for the possibility always exist that some newer, better, less expensive, or more efficient piece of equipment may be developed. Equipment standardization must also be a concern; it can be confusing for the patron if several different kinds of equipment (e.g., different kinds of tape recorders), each requiring the patron to learn a different operation procedure, are used for the same purpose. The librarian should select equipment with the assumption that it might be used for up to 10 years. If a piece of equipment receives extensive use and is properly maintained, 10 years is a reasonable life expectancy, after which it can be replaced by a newer model.

A 5-year planning program, once instituted, should be examined annually and revised if necessary, in light of changes not anticipated at the time of the original projection. Such revision should not alter the media selection program, but result either in shortening or lengthening the period of realization, or in incorporating a change because of technological developments or patrons' demands.

Selecting the Medium That Best Fills the Need

A recurring theme throughout this text is that whatever materials the librarian acquires for the collection, their ultimate value must be measured by how well they serve the needs of library patrons. It must also be firmly understood that library patrons are not just those people who actually use the library, but also the vast numbers of other people who are entitled to use it but perhaps never, or rarely, do so.

In ascertaining patrons' needs, the task of the librarian is to (*a*) identify the specific community the library serves; (*b*) list the general or predominant traits of the community, which include the various activities its members persue (e.g., vocations, avocations, interests, leisure time activities); (*c*) indicate the educational, cultural, political, and social attitudes possessed by the community; and (*d*) determine what services can be provided both to serve and to attract people to the library. It is essential that the librarian be cognizant of these needs, for nothing can be more frustrating than to know that a bond issue has failed or the budget has been cut because of public indifference. It is discouraging, for example, for the librarian to be informed that more people visit the local zoo than the public library. These unfortunate circumstances result when the community does not see a need for its library. Moreover, many libraries are continually competing with other public services for tax dollars. Although governments are currently in a situation in which tax bases are severely diminishing, the public still expects the same level of service that it received when it was supplying more dollars to support the operation of government.

The specific community that the library serves is readily apparent, for it is determined by whoever provides the finances, whether it be the taxpayer or the tuition-paying student. Information regarding community traits, in the case of a public library, can easily be obtained from the chamber of commerce; for educational libraries, the information can be gathered from faculty. It is considerably more difficult to obtain information regarding the educational, cultural, political, and social attitudes possessed by the community. Valid and reliable data can best be obtained by conducting a survey.

The survey, to be valid, must obtain responses from both users and nonusers of the library. User response can be easily obtained by having the patron fill out a survey form in the library. Surveying the nonuser is a bit more complicated, but it can be done by telephone, mail, or door-to-door canvassing. The telephone survey is less expensive to administer than door-to-door canvassing and yields a higher return than a mail survey. All methods are costly; it is for the individual library to decide which method it prefers to use and which is most suitable to the type of information it is attempting to gather. The objective checklist survey form is easier to administer, tabulate, and analyze than a subjective, essay, or short-answer form. Furthermore, a checklist survey takes the least time to answer.

The librarian must keep the survey form as brief and succinct as possible, asking only those questions that provide information regarding user and nonuser needs for services that the library can provide. The following are items to be considered for inclusion in a survey.

1. *Vital information about the individual responding* sex, age, occupation, level of education, frequency of library use
2. *Information about acquisition habits* what kind of newspapers and periodicals are read, how many hours per day are spent viewing television, number of books read, frequency of film viewing
3. *Information preferences* scholarly, scientific, avocational, vocational, artistic
4. *Information needs* reference, enrichment, enjoyment, leisure
5. *Areas in which the library can improve service* more communication to potential users, special programs, special services

Figure 5.1 is a suggested form that incorporates the above items.

The survey will provide the librarian with a profile of library patrons, both actual and potential, their information habits, and what the library means to them. The respondents to the survey should be a cross-sectional representation of the community; and, as mentioned earlier, the local chamber of commerce can provide information regarding the composition of the community.

Services that can be provided both to serve patrons and attract them to the library can be partially ascertained by examining Part V of the survey form in Figure 5.1. Displays, booktalks, bookmobiles, special events and activities, etc. are the means by which services can be implemented. The survey will indicate the type of medium most frequently used (or preferred), what type of information patrons expect to obtain from the library, and the extent to which patrons require library materials. The librarian, with the information obtained from the survey, is now ready to try a pilot program to test the reliability of the survey. A campaign that provides patrons with materials in formats for which preferences are indicated can be launched. The patrons are informed of the availability of these media and the librarian observes the results. If the survey is properly conducted, it will be safe to hypothesize that materials selected will receive greater use by more patrons during the campaign than prior to it. It is very important, however, that the patrons be informed that their perceived needs have been acknowledged and that something has been done about them. When patrons become aware that they are providing actual input regarding the types of materials being acquired by the library, they undoubtedly will feel they are not just using materials selected by unidentifiable librarians, but rather are involved in the development of the library collection. This process of

In an effort to improve the library's service to you please respond to the following:

I. Sex: Age: Level of Education:
   ☐ Female   ☐ 3–12   ☐ K–8
   ☐ Male   ☐ 13–19   ☐ 9–12
                          ☐ 20–35   ☐ College
                          ☐ 36–55
                          ☐ 56+

   Occupation: Average frequency of library use:
   ☐ Professional   ☐ Once a month
   ☐ Producer   ☐ Once a year
   ☐ Distributor   ☐ Once in 5 years
   ☐ Service   ☐ Never
   ☐ Unemployed

II. How do you acquire information?

Daily newspapers	Number read	1	2	3+
Magazines, and periodicals	Number read weekly	1	2	3+
	Number read monthly	1	2	3+
Television	Hours of daily viewing	1–2	3–4	4+
Books	Number per year	1–3	4–10	10+
Motion picture films (not on television)	Number per year	1–3	4–10	10+

III. Types of materials read, viewed, listened to:
     ☐ Education
     ☐ Pleasure
     ☐ Vocational
     ☐ Hobby
     ☐ Other _____

IV. Purpose of getting information:
     ☐ Reference
     ☐ Enrichment
     ☐ Enjoyment
     ☐ Leisure
     ☐ Other _____

V. How can the library improve its service to you?
     ☐ Inform you of services and material available
     ☐ Offer special interest programs and services
     ☐ Group activities (e.g., book talks, films, seminars)
     ☐ Other _____

Figure 5.1   Survey of community needs for library service.

informing patrons that their requests are acted on requires a good follow-up public relations program, which should involve the cooperation of local channels of mass communication (newspaper, radio, television) in providing adequate news coverage and interesting byline human interest stories about the patrons and their library.

Environments in Which Media Are Used

Knowing the use characteristics of various media is important, but the librarian must also know something of the physical environmental requirements for using them properly. Viewing a film in a room that cannot be properly darkened can be frustrating to the viewer and severely reduce the quality of the message transmitted by the film.

When the environments for using media are assessed, it is immediately apparent that physical spaces in the library can accommodate a variety of media, and, in some cases, accommodate them simultaneously. Some of the newer equipment designed expressly for individual use can be adequately used in an ordinary room without inconveniencing either the user or other occupants of the room who are using other types of media. For example, a patron can view and hear a slide and tape presentation on a small unit with rear screen projection, using a set of headphones. This allows the patron to view the slides without the need for room darkening, and the headphones allow the patron to hear the program without disturbing, or being disturbed by, anyone else in the room.

In Table 5.1, media characteristics are charted in relation to their required physical environments. The information assessed in each column of Table 5.1 is as follows:

1. *Number of users* How many people can actually use the material at one particular time? This can be a complex assessment, because some material, depending on the equipment being used, can be used both individually and in groups. When a particular medium can be used either way, it is repeated in the *Medium* column, and its characteristics are charted for both independent and group use. A *group* is defined as four or more people.

2. *Requires equipment* Is a device needed in order to gain access to the information?

3. *Requires light control* Must the room be adequately darkened in order to view the material?

4. *Requires noise control* Must the room be free from sound (noise) distractions?

Table 5.1 Media Characteristics and Environmental Requirements

Medium	Number of users	Requires equipment	Requires light control	Requires noise control	Makes sound	Utilized in one sitting	Carrel beneficial	Requires private room
Printed page	1	No	No	No	No	No	No	No
Microforms	1	Yes	No	No	No	No	Yes	No
Slides or filmstrips silent	1	Yes	No	No	No	Yes	Yes	No
Slides or filmstrips silent	Group	Yes	Yes	Yes	No	Yes	No	Yes
Slides or filmstrips sound	1	Yes	No	No	Yes	Yes	Yes	No
Slides or filmstrips sound	Group	Yes	Yes	Yes	Yes	Yes	No	Yes
Audio recording disc and tape	1	Yes	No	No	Yes	Yes	Yes	No
Audio recording disc and tape	Group	Yes	No	Yes	Yes	Yes	No	Yes
Motion picture films silent	1	Yes	No	No	No	Yes	Yes	No
Motion picture films sound	1	Yes	No	No	Yes	Yes	Yes	No
Motion picture films sound	Group	Yes	Yes	Yes	Yes	Yes	No	Yes
Television	1	Yes	No	No	Yes	Yes	Yes	No
Television	Group	Yes	No	Yes	Yes	Yes	No	Yes
Flat visuals (e.g., maps, charts, pictures)	1	No	No	No	No	Yes	No	No
Flat visuals	Group	No	No	No	No	Yes	No	Yes
Overhead transparencies	Group	Yes	No	No	No	Yes	No	Yes

5. *Makes sound* Does the material itself make sounds that would disturb nonparticipants?

6. *Utilized in one sitting* Is the material designed to be consumed in its entirety in less than 2 hours?

7. *Carrel beneficial* Would it be more advantageous if the material were used in a carrel or private, individual space?

8. *Requires private room* To be properly used, is a private room necessary?

As indicated in Table 5.1, a variety of media can be used simultaneously in the same physical environment. It is the duty of the librarian selecting media for in-library use to make provisions for the right kinds of space and environmental controls. When material is charged out of the library, problems of a different kind are generated. In such cases, the concern is not for space, but for making certain the patron has access to the necessary equipment (hardware). For some media, equipment must be made available. If it is provided by the library, it needs to be light-weight, portable, relatively easy to operate, and durable enough to withstand the rigors of frequent movement. Perhaps even more difficult is the situation in which the patron uses his or her own equipment. The librarian really has no way of knowing the condition or quality of the patron's equipment. A disc recording played on a record player with a badly worn phonograph needle will be returned in poor condition. If 16-mm sound film is played on a double sprocketed silent-only projector, it will completely destroy the sound track. It is advisable for the library to provide the patron who will be using his or her own equipment with a list of dos and don'ts for using media. Many libraries, in anticipation of occasional destruction of material, charge patrons a use fee, which is in effect a type of insurance to help defray expenses for replacing damaged material. The librarian should verify a patron's ability to use equipment before he or she takes mediated material out of the library.

Basic Criteria for Selecting Equipment

Selecting the right piece of equipment for library use is no easy task. Too often equipment is acquired that, for any number of reasons, receives little or no use, and the anticipated use and value of such equipment is never realized. Decisions for selecting equipment must be based on an intelligent investigation. With the plethora of brands and types of equipment on the market, making the ultimate decision of which equipment to acquire, as well as which to reject, necessitates the use of a basic set of selection criteria. The librarian will find that a positive correlation exists between the degree to which the criteria are developed and used for selecting equipment and the eventual value of the equipment to the library.

The criteria of equipment selection are purpose, cost, extent of usage, skill of patron (difficulty of usage), life expectancy (amortization), standardization, maintenance, and new developments (obsolescence). Some librarians develop a psychological aversion to equipment and prefer not to be involved in its selection. This kind of thinking is archaic as well as detrimental to the progress of the library. Any librarian with a less than positive attitude toward technological media should make a sincere attempt to adopt a more objective perspective about these media and cultivate at least a basic skill in their operation and utilization. A positive approach will inevitably result in a positive attitude. If the librarian lacks experience in equipment selection, he or she should contact other agencies in the community that are using audiovisual equipment to obtain input and direction as to which types, models, and brands are best suited for a particular application. It is also important to bear in mind that once the equipment is in the library, the staff will have to be accountable for providing instruction to patrons for its operation and general use, and for periodic maintenance. With this kind of responsibility, only a positive attitude and commitment toward the media should prevail.

Purpose

Purpose is not an evaluative criterion; rather, it is used to delineate precisely what it is that is needed. It takes heed of such questions as (*a*) What is the equipment needed for? (*b*) What kinds and quantity of materials are in the library collection that require its use? and (*c*) Where and how will it be used? These are obvious questions, but often it is by overlooking the obvious that poor decisions are made. For example, if the librarian is considering acquiring a microform reader, the answer to Question *a* (need) is obvious: to magnify and read the microforms in the collection so that the patron will be able to read them. But is it necessary to make it as readable as information projected on a screen or printed on paper? Kind in Question *b* (kinds and quantity of material) refers to format; in our example, if the microforms are in microfiche and microfilm formats, the purpose may be to gain access to more than one format; quantity refers to the actual amount of materials in the collection (buying two less expensive pieces of equipment might be better than buying one expensive and refined model). Question *c* (where and how it will be used) addresses the need for space and portability. Again, to use the example of selecting a microform reader, if it is to be used in a brightly lighted, busy room, the brilliance of the projected image and quietness of operation become paramount. If it is expected that the microform reader will be moved around frequently or even charged out of the library, it is essential that it be lightweight and compact.

Cost

Every librarian must and should be concerned about cost. Although libraries are not intended to be profit-making institutions, the librarian must nevertheless work within a budget and is judged by how well he or she manages it. Actually, the best way to measure cost is on a comparative basis; which make or model is least expensive, and, more importantly, exactly why does it cost less? Here the librarian should actually use and compare different models in the environment in which they will be used and question the sales representative as to why one model costs more or less than another. (A reputable salesperson will willingly provide this information).

Extent of Usage

Usage is synonomous with wear. The librarian should project anticipated usage. There are two variables that should be considered here: quantity of use and frequency of use. It is important to anticipate the quantity of use because if a piece of equipment will receive only infrequent use, perhaps the acquisition of a less expensive model is justified. The librarian should also have an idea of how many times a piece of equipment must be used before it has paid for itself. When projecting the frequency-of-use the librarian must consider not only the frequency, but also when the frequency occurs. Knowledge of the frequency variable will help to ascertain how many pieces of a particular type of equipment should be acquired.

Skill of Patron

Not to be overlooked is the patron's ability to operate or use equipment. If the library staff is to operate the equipment, patron operation is of no concern, but attention must be given to making staff available for equipment operation. The selector of equipment to be operated by patrons must take into consideration whether patrons will be occasional users or frequent and repeated users of the equipment. If equipment is difficult to operate, staff assistance will have to be an integral aspect of patron use. If this is the case, it might be best to opt for more expensive automatic equipment. Also to be considered is the possibility of an inexperienced patron doing damage to the equipment, to the informational materials, or even to him or herself.

Fortunately, much of the audiovisual equipment designed for individual use is relatively simple to operate. In selecting such equipment, it is advisable to have a truly inexperienced person try to operate it in order to determine if it is simple to operate. In situations in which a particular piece of information will conceivably receive a considerable amount of use in a given period of time, it is recommended that the material be permanently loaded in the machine so that using it requires merely pressing on and off buttons.

Life Expectancy

Although libraries are seldom allowed to set up plans for amortization of equipment, the librarian should set up some type of plan for depreciation, in order to provide for eventual repair or replacement. There are two main aspects of life expectancy to be considered: frequency of use and the actual number of years the equipment should be expected to perform. No piece of equipment can be expected to last forever, and the perceptive librarian will make life expectancy projections at the time of selection.

A piece of equipment should be selected with a maximum life expectancy of 10 years. By the end of that period, most equipment will have received enough use and wear to warrant replacement, either with the same model or, if the model has become obsolete (which in all probability it will have), with a more up-to-date model. Granted, there are pieces of equipment that, either because of limited use or extreme durability, may last longer than 10 years; however in most cases, this is the exception rather than the rule. Librarians and administrators must cease subscribing to the myth that equipment, once it is purchased, will last forever.

Standardization

If more than one piece of a particular type of equipment is to be acquired, standardization is a prime consideration. Finding a multitude of different kinds of equipment can be confusing to the patron, who may be expected to operate all of them. Added to this is the problem of maintaining an inventory of basic replacement parts for the various types of equipment. The only justifiable reasons for changing the type of equipment being used are that a newer and significantly better model has become available, that a considerable dollar savings would be realized, or that the current model has been discontinued. This criterion must be given considerable thought; for once the decision on standardization is made, the librarian should be able to be satisfied with it for some time. Furthermore, it will eliminate the need for an extensive study every time an additional piece of a particular type of equipment must be acquired.

Maintenance

Practically every piece of equipment requires some maintenance. When selecting equipment, the librarian should determine whether he or she can be responsible for its maintenance or whether the services of a trained technician will be required. If a trained technician is required, the librarian must decide whether that person should be employed by the library, or whether it would be best to have the equipment serviced by a representative of the company that sells it. An important factor to consider regarding the latter option is whether such service is readily available in the library community. Nothing is more frustrating than having to wait many days before a piece of equipment in need of repair can be serviced. It is also important to investigate the possibility of service maintenance contracts—exactly what they entail and how much they cost. If simple maintenance can be done by the librarian, it is necessary to determine how often components will have to be replaced, whether they can be installed by an untrained person, how much replacement parts cost, how extensive the replacement part inventory should be, and whether other special tools will be required. Of course, a primary consideration should be the quality of the construction of the equipment; it should be sturdy and durable.

New Developments

With the accelerating rate of technological developments, it is necessary to be aware of obsolescence. It is certainly disappointing to purchase an expensive piece of equipment that is expected to receive many years of service and find shortly thereafter that a far superior model is available. If the state of the art for a particular piece of equipment has been investigated thoroughly, a valid commitment can be made to use that piece of equipment for a specified period of time, regardless of technological developments occurring in the interim. Incidentally, it is just as foolish to take an ultraconservative stance and decide to wait for something better to come along. This is analogous to riding a horse and buggy while waiting for the ultimate form of automobile. The librarian must be aware of what is happening, attend conferences at which the latest equipment is displayed, and check with other libraries in an effort to determine their equipment plans.

These eight criteria for selecting equipment discussed in the preceding are not all of equal value and can vary in value among different libraries. However, each deserves careful consideration. If a large amount of expensive equipment is to be purchased, it is a good idea to engage the services of a qualified consultant. Even in this case, the eight criteria stated here should be considered carefully. Ultimately, the burden of decision rests with you. Do not skirt the criteria or try to disguise their implications. Be objective; it is really a case of "To thine own self be true."

Conclusion

The librarian must know the advantages as well as the disadvantages of each particular medium and then proceed to select a medium according to its availability in various formats, the needs and utilization skills of patrons, and the conditions and frequency of use. The library must be a dynamic, growing institution, with the librarian controlling the degree and direction of development. It is good to take advantage of the expertise and recommendations made by interested outside agencies (general public, information designers, media companies, reviewers, and institutions using or serving the library), but ultimately it is the librarian who must decide and justify the way that the library is to evolve. In this age of continuous and rapid technological change, the library must not only keep pace with information demands, but must also be in the vanguard of information utilization.

Selected Bibliography

Boyle, Deirdre. *Expanding Media*. Phoenix: Oryx Press, 1977.
Broadus, Robert W. *Selecting Materials for Libraries*. New York: H. W. Wilson, 1973.
Brown, James W., Lewis, Richard B., and Harcleroad, Fred F. *AV Instruction: Technology Media and Methods*, fifth edition New York: McGraw-Hill, 1977.
Davis, Robert Harlan, Alexander, Lawrence T., and Yelen, Stephen L. *Learning Systems Design: An Approach to the Improvement of Instruction*. New York: McGraw-Hill Book Co., 1974.

Ford, Stephen. *Acquisition of Library Materials*. Chicago: American Library Association, 1978.

Futas, Elizabeth. *Library Acquisition Policies and Procedures*. Phoenix: Oryx Press, 1977.

Goudket, Michael. *Audiovisual Primer*, revised edition. New York: Teachers College Press, 1974.

Haney, John B., and Ullmer, Eldon J. *Educational Communications and Technology*. second edition. Dubuque, Iowa: Wm. C. Brown, 1975.

Klein, Frances M., and Miller, Richard I. *About Learning Materials*. Washington, D.C.: Association for Supervision and Curriculum Development, 1978.

Nadler, Myra. *How To Start an Audiovisual Collection*. Metuchen, New Jersey: Scarecrow Press, 1978.

Prostano, Emanuel T. *Audiovisual Media and Libraries: Selected Readings*. Littleton, Colorado: Libraries Unlimited, 1972.

Rosenberg, Kenyon C., and Doskey, John S. *Media Equipment: A Guide and Dictionary*. Littleton, Colorado: Libraries Unlimited, 1976.

Treasure Chest of Audiovisual Ideas. Plainville, Connecticut: Kalart Company, 1976.

Selection Aids

Audiovisual Equipment Directory. Fairfax, Virginia: National Audiovisual Association, 1953–.

Audiovisual Market Place 1979: A Multimedia Guide, ninth edition. New York: R. R. Bowker, 1979.

Chisholm, Margaret, ed. *Reader in Media, Technology and Libraries*. Englewood, Colorado: Information Handling Services/PDS Hard Copy Publishing, 1976.

Educator's Purchasing Guide, sixth edition. Philadelphia: North American Publishing, 1974.

Komoski, Kenneth, ed. *Educational Products Information Exchange*. New York: EPIE, 1967–.

Library Technology Reports. Chicago: American Library Association, 1965–.

Sive, Mary Robinson. *Selecting Instructional Media: A Guide to Audiovisual and Other Instructional Media Lists*. Littleton, Colorado: Libraries Unlimited, 1978.

6

Motion Picture Films

Overview

Motion picture films are an important part of the library collection. However, because they require the use of rather sophisticated projection equipment, some librarians and patrons tend to be reticent in using motion picture films. The need to use what is considered to be complicated equipment and the need for special viewing areas have caused the motion picture collection to be developed as a discrete entity within the library's overall collection. Usually, motion picture films are housed in one area of the main library, and a librarian knowledgeable in the medium is assigned to maintain the collection. Branch libraries do not ordinarily house films, but obtain them from the main library on patron request.

Generally, 16-mm films comprise the largest part of the motion picture collection and are most often used outside the library by groups. Individual use generally takes place in the library, quite often for the purpose of previewing with the intent of using the film at a later time for a group activity. A second motion picture format found in libraries is the 8-mm film, many of which are silent. The 8-mm films usually are entertainment films (e.g., oldtime movie shorts), or what are called single concept films. Both 16-mm and 8-mm motion picture films make a unique contribution to the library collection; and, once the apprehension most people have about using them is allayed, they become an enjoyable and highly informative medium.

Motion Picture Film in the Library

The motion picture film makes a unique contribution to the library collection as a medium of entertainment, education, and cultural enrichment and as an art form. It is essential for the librarian to be aware of why motion picture films are currently the most prevalent form of sound–visual–motion media in the library, and, perhaps more important, to appreciate how motion picture films in general are capable of enhancing information effectiveness.

Motion picture films are presently predominantly available in three formats, 8 mm, 16 mm, and 35 mm (mm stands for *millimeter,* a measurement of the actual physical width of the film). Eight-millimeter film is produced in both standard 8-mm and Super 8-mm formats. Eight-millimeter films are extremely popular with the amateur or home moviemaker, and commercially produced 8-mm films are being acquired by libraries to satisfy information requests limited to individual or small group viewing. At the other extreme of motion picture film formats is the 35-mm film. This format is intended only for professional use for theater or large audience viewing. The cost of production and production equipment limits the feasibility of 35-mm film to film producers who aim their productions toward large audiences in order to insure a return from their considerable investments. In an ever-increasing search for better quality, producers are making film spectaculars in 70-mm format. The costs of producing 70-mm films are obviously even greater than those of producing comparable 35-mm films. Needless to say, the acquisition of films in 35-mm (or larger) formats is well beyond the range of the library in both cost and need.

Sixteen-millimeter film format is the mainstay of the library collection. There are four main reasons why this is so: (*a*) historical development; (*b*) cost; (*c*) capabilities of 16-mm film, and (*d*) availability of titles.

Historical Development

Motion picture film development began in 1894, with the invention of Thomas Edison's Kinetoscope and the first motion picture and continued through the advent of the sound motion picture film, which by 1930 was hailed as a new form of entertainment. This period witnessed major cinematographic milestones; for example, the nickelodeon; *The Great Train Robbery,* which set filmic standards for shooting and editing films that are still used today; *Birth of a Nation,* which is recognized as one of the first successful feature length films ever made; and the evolution of the movie mystique, which includes Hollywood, motion picture stars, and the recognition of motion pictures as a legitimate art form. Early motion picture films were made of a highly flammable nitrate material, and because of several disastrous fires, legislation was passed requiring motion picture films to be projected from within specially designed fireproof projection booths. With the eventual development of safety or fireproof film, the path was clear for films to be used in a nontheater setting. It immediately became evident that the nontheatrical film was being viewed by a considerably smaller audience than that which viewed theater productions. This sparked development of 16-mm film, which, if limited to small audience viewing, produces results in quality of projection comparable to those of a 35-mm film projected to a large audience. Early developments of 16-mm film were rather slow; productions were primarily short, one-reel (11 minutes approximately) cartoons, recreations of historical events, and travelogues. The 1940s saw a growth in the demand for educational films, which gave the 16-mm filmmaker the necessary impetus for producing films. Sixteen-millimeter films were recognized as a valuable means of presenting information. They contained sound–visual–motion information in the only format available to schools and libraries that was both manageable and economically feasible. As a result of this acceptance, 16-mm films are currently the sound–visual–motion format that offers the greatest number and variety of available titles, which in turn makes them the mainstay of the library for information in this format.

Cost

The consideration of cost as a reason for libraries to become predominant users of 16-mm films was originally a help, but now may be a hindrance. The beneficial aspect is evident; the hindrance aspect is a factor each librarian must carefully evaluate. First, to consider the beneficial aspect of 16-mm films, the equipment used to produce 16-mm films is far less expensive than 35-mm equipment and permits more people to film more low-budget films, which libraries can afford to buy. There is also a significant savings in the actual cost of 16-mm film in comparison with 35-mm film. When 16-mm film became the standard for the nontheatrical film market, 16-mm projectors were massproduced at a fraction of the cost of 35-mm theatrical projectors. This resulted not only in less expensive projection equipment, but because of the competition in the American free enterprise system, many improvements were made in projection equipment. Today, 16-mm motion picture projectors project brilliantly sharp images, reproduce sound of highly acceptable fidelity, are compact and lightweight, function quietly, and are extremely easy to operate, and new improvements continue to be made—for example, refinements are still being made on the self-threading projector. Because of these cost factors, the 16-mm format is the standard sound–visual–motion medium of libraries.

With regard to cost being a hindrance, many librarians presently believe that for the largest portion of their sound–visual–motion projection requirements, Super 8-mm film more than adequately fulfills their needs. For small audience viewing (20–30 people) or individual viewing, Super 8-mm film performs as well as 16-mm film. Both Super 8-mm film and its projection equipment cost less than 16 mm. However, because libraries have invested heavily in 16-mm films and equipment, they are committed to them, and any gradual transition to Super 8-mm film is neither practical nor economically feasible. For the Super 8-mm format to penetrate the library collection requires "plateau decisions." For example, the first plateau would be that all films to be viewed primarily by one individual at a time should be acquired in the Super 8-mm format only. The next plateau would be to determine if there are many groups of audiences in the 20- to 30-person range served by the library; and if so, films for these groups should also be in Super 8-mm format. The final plateau would be to become aware of new technological developments in both Super 8-mm and television projection that could make 16-mm films truly obsolete. Many film distributors now provide the librarian the option of purchasing materials in either Super 8-mm, 16-mm, or videotape format. Sixteen-millimeter film has the virtue of providing the librarian a means of acquiring a sound–visual–motion medium, but the prudent librarian should know to what extent to become involved and when to make the necessary transition to a new and better format.

Capabilities of Motion Picture Films

Other information forms have some of the characteristics of motion picture film, but they do not blend all the characteristics of the motion picture film, that is a visual image with the combined effects of sound, motion, and color that is projected onto a screen for small or large group viewing. The expert combination results in films that can provide a common experience; films from which viewers with a wide range of abilities and interests can benefit; films that require the use of such techniques as montage, timelapse, slow motion, flashback, microphotography, and animation. Besides entertaining, 16-mm films are capable of educating, informing, persuading, and testing the viewer. Many contemporary social issues such as drugs, ethnic problems, ecology, and vocational planning are finding an effective vehicle of expression in the 16-mm film. Although these issues are more than adequately developed in print form, the 16-mm film serves as a catalyst for small group identification, discussion, persuasion, and reaction.

Availability of Titles

Of all the sound–visual–motion formats, the 16-mm film has the greatest number of titles commercially available to the librarian. Coupled with this are free films distributed by government, nonprofit institutions, and industry that are presently available only in the 16-mm format. A brief perusal of the three volume *NICEM Index to 16-mm Films* or the *Library Of Congress National Union Catalog of Films and Other Materials for Projection* immediately reveals the number of subjects and titles available to the library. Because of the vast number of titles available in 16-mm format compared to other film formats, the library is almost obligated to invest money in this medium. This being the case, the librarian is responsible for investigating the 16-mm medium to understand better how it can be used to its best advantage and truly to profit from its fullest potential.

Advantages of Motion Picture Films

When audiences are asked, after the showing of a fine motion picture what impressed them most about the film, the typical replies are to extol the film's realism, mention total involvement with the film, claim complete understanding of the film, and cite a genuine identification with the film's content. These comments are not platitudes; they are sincere expressions of the feelings a truly fine film can evoke in the viewer. Undoubtedly, the key to classifying these comments is in the word *feelings,* for of all information media, motion pictures are capable of providing the *observer* with the greatest vicarious experience. The word observer is italicized to categorize an entire body of information media in which the consumer is an observer rather than a participant. This category includes all types of print media (books, art prints, photographs, graphics), slides, filmstrips, and tape and disc recordings. By definition, the consumer of information is an observer because he does not actually handle, manipulate, or construct the information being consumed; in short, he or she is not performing or doing. Of all the items in the observing category, the motion picture film is the least abstract, or, stated positively, provides the most concrete experience. By virtue of its concreteness, it is also the most real. Considering the elements of the motion picture film, this is easy to understand: It can contain visuals (print and nonprint), motion, sound, and, in many cases, color. The other media in the observing category contain at most only two of these elements.

The librarian must critically analyze and synthesize the motion picture's basic elements, visuals, sound, motion, and color, as a means of identifying its unique advantages in order to ascertain if it is a truly fine production. The motion picture is described as a medium that emphasizes picture primacy, and perhaps in most cases this is true. However, it is necessary to avoid the pitfall of becoming overly absorbed with picture and not maintaining an acute awareness of sound. Again it must be stressed, the librarian must attend to all the elements of the motion picture and be certain that they are meaningfully orchestrated into a truly fine production. The elements of the motion picture become the means with which the successful communication of its unique advantages can be carefully scrutinized.

There are several unique advantages to motion pictures. They can record, document, or preserve events in the most realistic form possible. These film events can be the actual occurrence or a dramatization of it. The event can be staged or filmed on actual location. As a result, the past can be recreated, and the future acted out. Because films involve motion, they provide a continuity of action; the viewer knows not only what is happening, but how it is happening. Motion pictures do not require a high degree of intelligence or verbal ability in order to be understood. It is said that they provide a common experience from which all levels of intelligence can derive something of benefit. It is the librarian's task to determine whether the advantage of common experience is suitable for the patrons for whom it is intended. It is conceivable that even if a film is intended for a specific audience, for example, viewers of high intelligence, when viewed by such a group, the range of ability within the group will cause some to get more out of the film than others even though all will understand the film to some degrees. Motion picture films remove the barriers of time, distance, size, and visibility. Time can be compressed, expanded, turned backward or forward, or held still. Distance is never a problem; the film can take the viewer to the other side of the earth or the far side of the moon. The smallest of objects can be microphotographed, or an entire planet can be seen in motion. Nothing is invisible to the motion picture film. The real invisible world can be seen by magnification, cutaway, or animation. The abstract, invisible world of the human mind can be viewed using such techniques as the flashback or superimposition; that is, the viewer is able to see what the actor is thinking. Motion picture film has the unique advantage of providing a bird's eye view of the events being depicted. The viewer is "there," right in the heart of the action. Again, bear in mind that these unique advantages of the motion picture are achieved by the filmmaker's skillful combination of the elements: visuals, motion, sound, and color. The techniques the filmmaker uses when working with these elements are what makes the motion picture an art form.

Making a Motion Picture Film

Motion pictures involve more than a technique of recording moving visuals on photographic film. Motion picture film is truly an art form, and it would be well for the librarian to be cognizant of how the film production crew employs the medium to achieve desired results. This cognizance can be invaluable when the occasion arises to select a motion picture for the library collection. The librarian needs a critical evaluative eye for motion pictures and should know not only if the film message is achieved, but also how it is achieved.

Producing a motion picture film is an art, and the filmmaker has at his disposal three techniques or devices through which to create his product. They are (a) camera manipulation, (b) sound recording, and (c) film editing. Narrowing our explanation of motion picture production to three major techniques allows us to discuss the process in sufficient detail for our purposes here, but it must be borne in mind that filmmaking is a highly complicated art form. It is the filmmaker's knowledge, ability, and skill to work successfully with the components of each technique that results in a great motion picture.

Camera Manipulation

By careful selection of lenses, camera position, and camera movement, the filmmaker can capture on film precisely the information required from the script. Lenses can make objects appear near or far away, large or small; and scenes can have infinite degrees of focus. Zoom lenses can take the viewer into or out of a scene without a change in perspective. Lenses can also distort spatial relationships in an effort to achieve desired effects. Camera position can range from a very high to a very low level, can be very close to or very far from the subjects and scenes being photographed. Again, it all depends on the effect that the filmmaker wants to create; for example, a low camera very close to a subject, with the camera shooting up from a low angle, will make the subject appear to be huge and monstrous, whereas the opposite setup will make the subject appear small and diminutive. Camera movement creates a feeling in the viewer of moving through the scene being filmed (remember the camera lens serves as the eye of the viewer when the film is being shot). The camera can be moved up or down (tilt), rotated on a fixed axis (pan), moved in or out of a scene (dolly), moved across a scene (truck), or any combination thereof. Camera movement is said to be successful when the viewer is unaware of its occurrence, that is, the technique should not detract from the content. One of the most essential elements of all camera manipulation, however, is lighting, in fact, producing proper lighting conditions should be considered as a major technique in and of itself.

Sound Recording

Too often, the viewer takes sound for granted because, as discussed earlier, motion picture film relies on picture primacy. Nonetheless, if sound is poor, the film's message could become lost or obscured. Sound techniques employ such devices as music, either dominant or in the background, to create a mood or heighten visual effects; sound effects to add realism to the film; voiceover or voice narration, that is, an offscreen voice describing what is being viewed; and live voice recording (lip synchronization), that is, a sound track that is actually recorded while the scene is being filmed. The combination of sound with the visual and the action (motion) can result in the overall success or failure of the film. Although the emphasis of picture primacy has been stressed, it is nevertheless a fact that the viewer is less tolerant of poor sound than of a poor picture.

Film Editing

After the film has been shot, it is the film editing that puts the polish on the film by the skillful combination of all the scenes that were filmed. Many filmic effects are achieved in the editing room. Scenes are cut and tailored to appropriate lengths, and transitional devices are used to join scenes together. These include cuts, fades, dissolves, and special effects such as the montage, iris, and wipe. The cut is the straight splicing together of two scenes to direct the viewer to another scene occurring at the same place or at the same time. In a fade, one scene fades out to black and the succeeding scene fades in from black. This, in effect, denotes a change in time or place between scenes, the amount of change being controlled by the length of the fade. A dissolve, similar to a fade, occurs when two scenes overlap each other and conveys a gentle and easy transition from one scene to another; again, the effect achieved is dependent on the length of the dissolve. Special effects embellish the quality of production. A montage is a series of usually short but not directly related scenes which, when edited together, form a picture statement. It is analogous to a collection of words forming a sentence. An iris occurs when two scenes are superimposed, with the main scene occupying the bulk of the screen and the secondary or superimposed scene appearing within a circle or iris, usually in the corner or center of the screen. A wipe occurs when one scene is replaced by another by sliding it across the screen on either a horizontal or vertical axis; in other words, as one scene is being "wiped" off another scene is being "wiped" on.

There are many other components to these three major techniques, but even from our somewhat simplistic discussion here it should be clear that filmmaking is a highly technical art form. The librarian would do well to become knowledgeable in the techniques used in order to better understand and evaluate motion picture films. (A good basic film on the topic is *Basic Film Terms: A Visual Dictionary*, Santa Monica, California: Pyramid Films, 1970.)

Cost/Effectiveness of Motion Picture Film

After the librarian has determined that film is the appropriate information medium to answer a particular patron need, the next consideration is which film(s) should be acquired and whether there are any acquisition alternatives (e.g., which particular film on a particular topic should be acquired). In order to make this decision, the librarian must take into account several criteria.

Perhaps the first factor to be considered in the acquisition process should be that of cost/effectiveness. More succinctly stated, will the 16-mm film return more value per dollar than any other media format? There is no question that 16-mm film is currently the single most expensive information item that the librarian acquires. It is unfortunate to purchase a $10 book that receives little or no use, but it is just short of catastrophic to purchase a $500 film that receives little or no use. Indeed, it is reasonable for a budget administrator to challenge a librarian's request for a $500 film when the same information is available in a $10 book. An answer to such a challenge must be predicated on a thorough knowledge of the capabilities of information media forms and, in this case, of the particular capabilities of 16-mm motion picture film.

A 16-mm motion picture can be viewed by an individual or by a large audience. When it is viewed by an audience, there is a commonality of experience—everyone is seeing it at the same time, and they can respond and react to it together. Presenting information to an audience accomplishes an objective more efficiently than the use of individual books. If the library were to buy 50 books (50 × \$10 = \$500), they would still only accommodate 50 people; a film can accommodate several hundred people at one time. A further comparison of the cost/effectiveness of a \$500 film compared to a \$10 book is that if each time the film is used it is viewed by an average audience of 50 people and the film is used 25 times, then the cost of the film is \$.40 per person [\$500 ÷ (50 people × 25 uses) = \$.40]. Using the \$.40-per-person film cost and applying it to the \$10 book, the book too must be used 25 times [\$10 ÷ (25 people × 1 use) = \$.40]. If the sole criterion for selection is per patron cost, then the purchase of the film or the book can equally be justified. Other criteria must also be considered in making a media selection determination, however.

As regards the actual cost of a film, it is best to use the 5–5 rule, which, when applied to the purchase of a 16-mm film, is interpreted to mean that in order to justify the purchase of a 16-mm film, it must be used a minimum of 5 times a year for 5 years. Otherwise, it should be rented instead of purchased. The 5–5 rule can be quickly validated by examining the catalogs of companies that rent and sell films. It immediately becomes apparent that the cost of 25 rentals (5 × 5) usually approximates the film's purchase price. Incidentally, many libraries have a policy of only renting films. The 5–5 rule still applies, and such libraries would do well to examine their rental records and determine whether their film rental policies are in need of modification.

In addition to the factors of actual costs and numbers of patrons, the film presents its message in a fraction of the time it would take to obtain it from a book. Furthermore, the 16-mm motion picture film has the capability of providing for individual differences, in that both the slow and fast learner can benefit from it. Several factors become evident. For the slow learner, viewing a film is not predicated on an ability to read. Also, any vocabulary used in a film is augmented and reinforced with moving images; the viewer sees as well as hears how the vocabulary is used. On the other hand, the fast learner, or more knowledgeable person who comprehends the spoken word, is able to perceive visual subtleties that further enhance the understanding of the film's message.

Much research indicates that our society is gradually becoming functionally illiterate (i.e., approximately 22 million Americans are unable to read a classified ad or fill out a job application). In inverse ratio to the decline in reading literacy is a growth in visual literacy. More people now acquire information via audiovisual channels, such as, television and motion pictures. This does not mean that the librarian should condone reading illiteracy, but rather that having films available could be a means of furthering the cause of reading literacy. The film will provide information that the functional illiterate can handle, and will get such a person into the library (which is still an environment conducive to reading); and the film could serve as a bridge to books. It could well be a case not of deciding which of media should be acquired, the book or the film, but rather that both the book and the film should be acquired.

As regards time, 16-mm motion picture films in library collections usually range from 10 to 60 minutes in length, and therefore they do not require a long attention span. The film can be viewed in one sitting, which eliminates the need to retain information over an extended period of time. The film's message is presented succinctly in motion, sound, and color and does not require the timeconsuming use of cues or lengthy descriptors. Film offers a concreteness and reality of experience that enhances retention of information. Because the film is a timesaver, it is possible for an individual to view it more than once for different reasons (e.g., introduction of information, appreciation, review).

Along with the intellectual advantages of film are the psychological attributes. By providing a vicarious experience, motion picture film is able to shape behavior and attitudes. When a film is well done (an excellent documentary, for example), it can cause the viewer to react by wanting to do something. While being projected, the film requires the attention and demands complete control of the viewer's auditory and optic senses. Since the film is projected in a darkened room, the viewer is not distracted by the real environment and becomes immersed in the world of the film. When this occurs, the viewer "feels" the film, and the resultant psychological impact can be tremendous. To substantiate this, the reader need only view a film such as the classic documentary, *Harvest of Shame*. It is indeed a rare person who is not affected by this film and does not feel the experience of the futile plight of the United States migrant farmworker. *Harvest of Shame* is an excellent, moving documentary film, but the librarian in selecting a film needs to develop an objective perspective. It must be remembered that the filmmaker lets the camera and audio recorders "see and hear" only what he or she wants them to "see and hear." Nevertheless, when properly used, the 16-mm film captures a sense of realism unachievable by any other information media form. It would be truly wonderful, for example, if the signing of the Declaration of Independence had been recorded on film. (Note: Television producers use basically the same techniques as the filmmaker.)

If the rationale described in this section leads to the decision to acquire films, the librarian can attend to the task of which films to acquire. For this purpose, it would be well to have some kind of understanding of the types or classifications of films.

Feature, Educational, and Art Films

There are many ways to categorize films in the library collection, but it is recommended that they be assigned to three major categories: the feature film, the educational film, and the art film. The reason for this classification is to provide the librarian with a means of ascertaining what proportion of the film collection is generally devoted to entertainment, information, and cultural enrichment. These three categories are not mutually exclusive, and a film could possibly be assigned to more than one category. To be able to utilize the three categories properly, it is necessary to have a working definition of the three terms.

To be classified as a *feature film,* a motion picture must display the following characteristics: It is usually a theatrical or dramatic production, and, when compared to educational and art films, it has a much longer running time—averaging 90–135 minutes. Its purpose is to entertain and provide viewers with an opportunity to escape, if only for a short while, from their own daily routine existences. A feature film is usually associated with the Hollywood type of production; it has a story to tell. Feature films usually have well-developed plots and tend to focus on people and the events in their lives.

The *educational film* should contain a learning objective. It is viewed for the specific purpose of learning something, whether a process, factual information, or an attitude. Although it can be entertaining, the purpose of the entertainment is only a vehicle for the learning that is expected to occur. The educational film makes extensive use of voice-over narration that informs the viewer of what is taking place and directs viewers' attention to what should be observed. To be properly used, the educational film should entail pre- and postviewing activities, and many educational films are accordingly accompanied by teacher guides or instructional pamphlets. It is beneficial to the viewer when the learning objectives are explicit, but too often they are only implied. In either case, the learning objectives should be well developed in the film and should not be many in number. As a result, educational films average 10–30 minutes in length, a practice which serves two purposes: (*a*) it is an adequate time to present a limited number of learning objectives and (*b*) since the film is often used in a classroom setting, it allows for pre- and postfilm activities during a normal class period. To be truly effective, the educational film should be made with the intention of providing the viewer with the best way to achieve a particular learning objective. On occasion, the educational film will supplement, or be supplemented by, other forms of information media. The educational film will not replace the textbook, but it can certainly enhance it.

Without becoming mired down in a definition of art, let it suffice to say that the *art film* uses technique to depict a creative experience. The viewer sees the genesis of an idea evolve into a creative experience. By skillful use of camera, light, color, and sound, the filmmaker produces a work of cinematic art. Incidentally, an art film is not to be confused with a film about art, which is classified as an educational film. Rather, an art film uses the motion picture medium to convey its message, which in a pure sense means the film is the message. An art film cannot be translated to another media form without a tremendous loss of the total esthetic experience. Of the three types of films, the art film is usually the shortest, ranging from about 5 to 20 minutes of playing time. Art films are extremely popular in public libraries; they provide patrons with films that are unavailable from any other source. Furthermore, public librarians are assuming the role of purveyors of art films, citing as justification that the library is the only community organization attending to art film masterpieces.

These, in summary, are the definitions of the three major categories of films. Subsumed under the categories of feature, educational, and art film are a host of film types: history films, science films, cartoons, mystery films, horror films, comedy films, biographical films, etc. These types obviously need not be defined, as the title of the type is in fact a definition of content. As stated earlier, a film or film type can be assigned to more than one of the three major categories, but fundamentally a feature film entertains, an educational film informs, and an art film provides an esthetic experience.

16-mm Motion Picture Selection Aids

Once you have made the decision to acquire a film or a particular type of film for the library collection, the next task is to find what films are available in any given genre. The knowledge acquired in the preceding sections of this chapter can now be applied to the actual selection process. The task of selecting a film is a demanding one, but in terms of both the film's relatively high cost and the number of film titles available for selection, it is a worthwhile endeavor. Thousands of 16-mm films are currently available, and each year hundreds of new films are produced that would enhance a library's film holdings. Unfortunately, there is always a financial limit on the number of films a library can acquire. Certainly, if the valid constraint of cost/effectiveness is prudently applied, it is a skillful librarian who knows when to acquire the particular film that is just right for the library. To assure that the film search is properly conducted, the librarian needs to have access to the proper 16-mm film selection tools. Here again it is the professional responsibility of the librarian to know which selection aids are available and what information they provide.

Making a decision as to which selection aids to use becomes a case of knowing exactly what information is needed to make film selection decisions. A good film selection aid has some unique feature that makes it valuable, and perhaps several selection aids will need to be consulted in order to determine which films need to be previewed and ultimately acquired for the library collection. The unique features that may be provided in selection aids are lists of all films available, films of a particular genre, new films, and free films, as well as vital statistics (e.g., producers, cost, length, date), evaluations and reviews, annotations, and cross-indexes. Obviously, no one selection aid could do justice to all these aspects in an easy-to-manage format; hence, several aids may need to be used in combination.

As an aid in determining which selection aids to use, Table 6.1 provides a cross section of film selection aids, listing the predominant feature of each. Some of the titles of the selection aids are self-explanatory. Many selection aids provide more information than is indicated in the table; however, they are considered excellent aids for the purpose(s) indicated.

Table 6.2 lists periodicals that contain information helpful in film selection. Some of the periodicals are devoted entirely to film selection, whereas others contain articles or sections devoted to film selection. The library involved in film selection should subscribe to some of these periodicals—they provide the best way to keep pace with new film releases.

Selecting 16-mm Motion Picture Films

Motion picture selection aids tell the librarian what is available and something about the films, but criteria must be established in selecting a

Table 6.1 Motion Picture Selection Aids

Title	Location[a]	Evaluation[b]	Review[c]	Selection[d]	Notes
Educational Film Locator of the Consortium of University Film Centers and R. R. Bowker Co.	X				For organizing collections
Educator's Guide to Free Films	X			X	
Educator's Purchasing Guide	X				
Feature Films on 8mm, 16mm, and Videotape	X	X			
Film Literature Index	X				
Film and Video Review Index			X		
Film Review Annual			X		
Guide to Free Loan Films: About Foreign Lands	X			X	
Guide to Free Loan Government Films	X			X	
Guide to Free Loan Sport Films	X			X	Special topic
Guide to Free Loan Training Films	X			X	Special topic
Guide to Free Loan Films: On the Urban Condition	X			X	
Index to Critical Film Reviews			X		
Library of Congress Catalogs: Films and Other Materials for Projection	X			X	
Media Review Digest		X			
Multi-Media Reviews Index	X		X		Annual of AVI reviews
NICEM Index to 16mm Educational Films	X		X		
North American Film and Video Directory	X				
United Nations 16mm Film Catalog	X				Special topic
United States Government Films for Public Education Use	X				

[a] A location tool is one that provides information about the availability of films on a particular topic.

[b] Evaluation tools provide evaluations of films.

[c] Review selection aids are sources of film reviews. In many cases, simply the fact that a film is reviewed in these publications is indicative that it is deemed worthwhile by the editors.

[d] Selection aids that focus particularly on selection provide objective information and data about films, (e.g., bibliographic entry, cataloging information, subject heading, précis).

Table 6.2 Periodicals Helpful in Film Selection[a]

Title	Loca-tion	Evalua-tion	Review	Selec-tion	Notes
AV Guide Newsletter				X	
Booklist		X			
Film News	X			X	
Films in Review			X	X	
Film and Video Review Index	X		X		
Instructional Innovator			X		Instructional films
Media and Methods			X		Instructional films
New Cinema Review	X		X		
Preview			X	X	
Sightlines		X		X	Instructional films

[a] See Table 6.1 for an explanation of the terms used here.

motion picture. Film selection must be accomplished in an orderly, systematic fashion that justifies acquiring certain titles and rejecting others. In the final analysis, the question must be asked, "Considering my library, did I purchase the right film?"

When establishing criteria for film selection, it is best to identify main areas of consideration and their effect on the selection process. Three main areas are (*a*) the library, (*b*) the film, and (*c*) the patron. Within this broad delineation criteria can be developed to insure that proper attention is given to each of the areas. It is only by utilizing a systematic investigation through the use of specific criteria that the librarian will be assured that films being selected are the best for the library's film program. The following criteria, though not exclusive, are worthy of consideration when selecting a motion picture film.

The Library

Before any film selection can be made, the librarian must know the library's philosophy, policy, budget, and current holdings.

1. *Philosophy*   What does the library regard as the purpose of having films? What kind of collection does the library want (e.g., feature films, educational films, art films)? What are the plans or goals of the library for its film collection?

2. *Policy*   Who can use the films? When and where can films be seen (e.g., in the library only or can they be charged out)? What are the provisions for making projection equipment available?

3. *Budget* How many dollars are available for purchase, rental, maintenance, repair? Does the patron pay a fee? Are any funds allocated for a special genre of film? Is it better to buy a long, expensive film or several short ones?

4. *Current holdings* Is there a good balance in the collection? Do certain areas need rejuvenation with second editions or updated topics? How large is the collection? To what extent are the films being used?

The Film

Criteria developed for the actual selection of a film deal with the specifics of the film and are concerned with obtaining films of the highest quality. If the right film is selected, it will be in agreement with the library's program and worthwhile to the library patron.

1. *Content* Does it have something to say and know how to say it?
2. *Authenticity* Is it truthful and accurate?
3. *Objectivity* Is it biased or prejudiced? Does it present propaganda, or is it selling something?
4. *Subjectivity* Does it let the audience "get close" to the story?
5. *Relevance* Does the film have any relevance to the patron?
6. *Specificity* Does the film make a point, and does it do so effectively? Is film the proper medium (e.g., could it be better done as a filmstrip)?
7. *Technical quality* How good are the photography, color, sound, lighting, continuity and organization of scenes, and camera technique? What is the picture primacy (i.e., the emphasis in a film should be on the visual and not the audio)? What is the rate of development or sequencing?

The Patron

The librarian must be aware of the patrons' needs. The best film, in complete compliance with the library's policy, is of no value if the patron does not use it.

1. *Groups* Are there any special interest groups or institutions that would make use of the film?
2. *Programs* Is there a library film program that the patron would attend to view the film?
3. *Interest* Do patrons have the background, need, or interest to want to see the film?
4. *Other resources* Can the film be seen elsewhere (e.g., local theatre or on television)? Is the film available in another medium (e.g., book)?

Although these criteria are assigned to the three main considerations, it is only by using them in combination that the best results can be obtained. Too often, librarians place great concern on the second consideration and disregard the library and the patron. When this occurs, great films are undoubtedly acquired, but unfortunately they are of little value to the library and of less value to the patron. By giving equal concern to all considerations and employing all the criteria to accomplish the selection process, one employs a procedure that guarantees acquiring the best film for a particular library. Using the criteria as a guide, the next logical step is to develop a film evaluation form that will expedite the selection process and be congruent with the library's goals and objectives.

16-mm Film Evaluation Forms

When placed on a continuum, film evaluation forms can range from the highly subjective to the highly objective. A highly subjective form would contain very few questions and leave much space for narrative and subjective comments from the evaluator. At the other end of the continuum, a highly objective form would only provide opportunity for the evaluator to circle numbers or make appropriate checkmarks, which would make it more like a rating form. Either type of film evaluation form can be respectable, valid, and reliable. The emphasis on a subjective form is to obtain qualitative information (i.e., to learn precisely what the evaluator thinks of a particular film). Unfortunately, subjective remarks are often difficult to quantify; each evaluator makes judgments based on an individual value system, and does not necessarily assign the same meaning or value to words. Perhaps one evaluator, who says a film is "terrific" or "great," in extolling its virtues, is using the terms somewhat hyperbolically and in reality merely means that the film is OK. Another evaluator, who may use only short, terse remarks that do not reflect a high degree of preference for the film, may consider the film very worthy of acquisition. The task of the librarian, in assessing remarks on a purely subjective film evaluation form, is to quantify the remarks of various evaluators and try to make valid interpretations as to whether the film should be acquired.

On the other hand, a highly objective film evaluation form can ask many more questions about the film being evaluated, but the respondent can only check off those remarks that appear to be closest to his or her reaction to the film. The objective form limits answers to yes or no or to some variation of a rating scale (e.g., excellent, good, fair, poor). No provision is made for subjective remarks. A purely objective form is easy to quantify—all that is required is to total all the check marks and average them out. Unfortunately, there may be some characteristic about the film on which the evaluation form did not focus and the evaluator is therefore unable to provide a subjective insight which, in fact, may give an indication of the film's true worth. Therefore, most film evaluation forms employ a combination of subjective and objective statements. It is the librarian's responsibility in constructing a film evaluation form to determine what information is needed from the evaluator in order to make an acquisition decision and which types of statements, subjective or objective, best achieve this end. In the final analysis, the librarian who ultimately makes the buy–no buy decision should work with the combination of subjective and objective information that is most useful in making that decision.

The librarian will need to determine how the form will be used and make appropriate arrangements for its use. If the form is to be used by a committee, the librarian will have to identify, recruit and/or select committee members; arrange for meeting times; give directions to the group vis-à-vis its specific responsibilities; establish procedures for evaluating or moderating any necessary discussion; and collect and collate the evaluation forms. Depending on the extent of desired involvement, the librarian can either chair the committee and be an active participant, or allow the committee, once a meeting is requested, to operate independently. If, on the other hand, a film is to be sent to an individual evaluator, a brief explanatory cover letter should accompany the evaluation form so that the evaluator will be able to use the form properly. It also helps to know something about the evaluator's credentials; it can be very beneficial if the evaluator has some knowledge or expertise in film technique, content, and use. If the librarian does not know the evaluator's skill, such information should be requested on the evaluation form; this can be achieved simply by asking for the person's name and position. For situations in which the evaluator is not identified (e.g., the librarian encloses an evaluation form with the film), it must be realized that this is, in a sense, soliciting information from an unknown person. When this procedure is followed, the form needs to be extremely brief, perhaps asking only for the user's occupation and checkmarks to pertinent "yes–no" questions. To assure some degree of response, it is suggested that the form be in relatively large print and taped to the outside of the film container.

Other factors in addition to the evaluator's expertise are important; for example how much time he or she can devote to filling out a form, how frequently he or she will be using the form, and whether or not he or she is familiar with evaluation procedures. If, for example, the evaluator is a professional librarian with facility in using evaluation forms, there will be little or no need to explain the evaluation process; whereas if the evaluator is a patron with little or no experience in such matters, an explanation will be necessary. Regardless of respondent's background, however, it is a good idea to use terms that are simple enough so as not to require explanation or interpretation.

Another consideration which can prove to be a distinct advantage in obtaining a valid and informative evaluation is brevity. Regardless of the length of the form, there is one cardinal rule: Ask a question only if you actually intend to use the information. Often, an elaborate form is used, and the only question the librarian looks at is the yes–no question on whether to acquire the film. If this is the case, save the evaluator's time and ask only one question: Should the film be purchased, yes or no?

The use to which the form will be put is another consideration in developing a film evaluation form. Is it to aid in selection and purchase; to develop a précis; to provide information to the potential viewer; or to be used for special classes of films? Whichever the case, the form must be designed for its particular application.

Basically, there can be six parts to a film evaluation form:

1. vital information, or bibliographic entry, which should include title, producer, running time, color or black and white, cost, copyright date, and distributor
2. content information in the form of a 75-word précis
3. content evaluation, which examines how well the information is presented
4. technical evaluation, which examines the cinematic qualities of the film
5. application; that is, how, by whom, and for what purpose the film can be used
6. a summary statement that should include, whether implied or specifically stated, a yes or no conclusion

The film evaluation forms shown in Figures 6.1 and 6.2 provide examples of purely subjective and purely objective forms, respectively, that can be used as a basis for constructing forms for any institution. Depending on the needs of a particular library, the forms can be combined or modified in any way necessary that would move them away from the subjective–objective extremes of the continuum. But it must be

Date:

Title of film:

Annotation:

Content quality:

Technical quality:

How can film be used:

Conclusion:

Name of evaluator: Position:

Figure 6.1   Subjective film evaluation form.

kept in mind that only questions that will actually be used should be asked. In both forms, the bibliographic information and possibly the annotation can be modified, depending on the viewpoint of the individual librarian, or even filled in by the librarian rather than the evaluator, since this is not evaluation information per se.

An interesting aspect of the objective form is the number under each evaluative category. To carry objectivity to its extreme, the librarian should also be objective in analyzing the evaluator's response. This can be achieved if the librarian develops numerical accept–reject standards for each category, prior to looking at the evaluator's response. For example, if the librarian makes a decision a priori that in order to be accepted, the film must achieve a score of 21 in the content section; and the evaluator checks excellent three times ($3 \times 4 = 12$), good twice ($2 \times 3 = 6$), and fair twice ($2 \times 2 = 4$); the total score is 22 ($12 + 6 + 4 = 22$), and the librarian must accept the fact that the content is worthwhile. If this objective scoring system is followed throughout the entire form, decisions will not be influenced by the librarian's bias. Conversely, with the subjective form, the librarian must qualitatively score the evaluator's value statement him or herself, and it is very difficult in such cases to eliminate bias totally.

One should not claim that one form is better than another. The only good form is the one that works, and where this lies on the subjective–objective continuum is a decision only the librarian can make. It is to be hoped that the information in this chapter will result in intelligent, well thought out decision making in developing the library's motion picture film collection.

Evaluator's name: Position: Date:

Title of film: Distributor:
Producer: Date: Running time:
Color_____ Black and white_____   Cost:

Annotation (75 words or less):

Content:	Excellent 4	Good 3	Fair 2	Poor 1	Not applicable
Authentic					
Biased					
Accurate					
Propaganda					
Up-to-date					
Enough information					
Length					
Technical quality:					
Photography					
Editing					
Continuity					
Sound					
Cinematic technique					
Uses:					
Introduction					
Overview					
Stimulation					
Review					
Demonstration					
In-depth study					
Audience:					
Preschool					
K–6					
7–9					
10–12					
College					
Adult					
Does film:					
Achieve its objective?					
Keep viewer's interest?					
Tell its story successfully?					
Have cross-discipline use?					

Do you recommend that this film be acquired for the library collection?
Yes_____ No_____

Figure 6.2   Objective film evaluation form.

Physical Features of Motion Picture Film

The 16-mm motion picture film is so named because the width of the film is 16 millimeters. Silent 16-mm film has sprocket holes along both edges and travels through the projector at a speed of 18 frames per second. Sound 16-mm film has sprocket holes only along one edge; the sound track is recorded on the opposite edge. Sound 16-mm film operates at a speed of 24 frames per second.

When standard 8-mm film was originally designed, it was actually 16-mm silent film cut in half. For many years, standard 8-mm film was the only type of 8-mm film available. Unfortunately, the sprocket holes were designed for 16-mm film and equipment, and it became apparent that 8-mm film actually did not need such large sprocket holes in order to function properly. Hence, Super 8-mm film was designed with much smaller sprocket holes, and the extra space resulted in a 50% increase in the size of the picture area.

From careful examination of Figure 6.3, we can see that both standard 8 mm and Super 8 mm are the same width, but the size of the sprocket holes of standard 8 mm (3 mm) is twice as wide as that of Super 8 mm (1.5 mm). We can also see from Figure 6.3 that on standard 8-mm film, the sprocket holes are located where the frames meet, whereas on Super 8-mm film the sprocket holes are adjacent to the middle of each frame. Finally, the Super 8-mm film frame is approximately 50% larger in area than the standard 8-mm film frame. When projected, the Super 8-mm film produces a clearer, sharper picture than the standard 8-mm film; and when used for small group projection (20–30 people), it projects an image comparable in quality to that of a 16-mm film. As a result, the standard 8-mm film is considered obsolete and is no longer acquired by libraries. Currently in some libraries where motion picture films are used only for small audiences, Super 8-mm films are being purchased in lieu of 16-mm film, because both the film and related projection equipment are less expensive.

Physical Features of Optical and Magnetic Sound Tracks

Sound tracks are of two varieties, magnetic and optical. The magnetic sound track has a very thin strip, or stripe, of magnetic tape placed on the edge of the film. If you are shooting your own film, the magnetic stripe can be purchased on the original film or placed on the film after it has been exposed and processed. A major advantage of magnetic striped

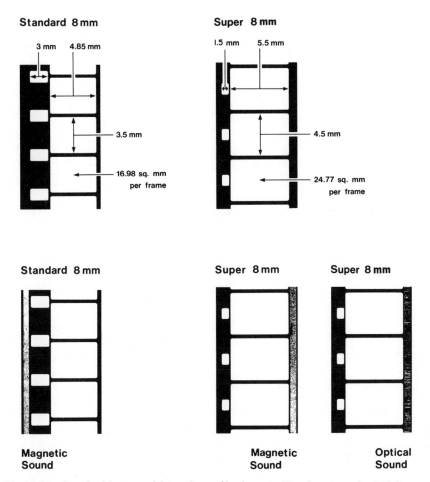

Figure 6.3 Standard 8-mm and Super 8-mm film formats. Note location, physical dimensions, and shape of sprocket holes, and location of frame lines and sound tracks.

film is that with inexpensive equipment, anyone can narrate or edit his or her own sound tracks. An obvious disadvantage is that information can be accidentally erased quite easily.

Putting an optical sound track on a film is a professional procedure. Because the optical sound track is produced by a photographic process that does not require additional striping for each film copy, production and processing costs are reduced. An optical sound track is permanent and cannot be altered or edited. It is interesting to note that the majority of 8-mm films use magnetic sound tracks, but with 16-mm film optical sound tracks are overwhelmingly prevalent. This occurrence is attributed primarily to the fact that 16-mm films are used mostly by professional filmmakers, whereas 8-mm film is the domain of the home filmmaker.

If we examine again the sound tracks in Figure 6.3, we can observe that the magnetic sound track is an extremely thin piece, or stripe, of magnetic tape, whereas the optical sound track is photographed right on to the film and appears as variations of clear, transparent areas. If one were to actually touch a piece of magnetic sound track film the additional thickness of the magnetic tape, would be apparent.

8-mm Film Containers

With 8-mm films, concern must be given to the type of container used to store the film (see Figure 6.4). The two most important considerations are (*a*) How easy is it to use? and (*b*) How well does it protect the film? When choosing between these two factors, it is sometimes necessary to make compromises.

The open reel is obviously the least complicated. The end of the film is slotted into the hub and wound on to the reel. But the film must be handled when it is threaded on a projector. Also, an open reel is more susceptible to collecting dust. (All film, regardless of container, however, should be stored in a closed package.)

Figure 6.4   8-mm film containers, left to right: open reel, Technicolor loop cartridge; Fairchild loop cartridge, and Kodak cartridge.

Technicolor and Fairchild containers are similar in that the film is housed in an almost closed container, the only opening being a small aperture through which the film comes in contact with the projector to drive the film and reproduce sound. The end of the film is spliced to the beginning, creating an endless loop. Both Technicolor and Fairchild containers are called loop cartridges. (Other companies make similar cartridges for use in their respective projectors.) The film in a loop cartridge receives no physical handling, but if you examine it carefully when it is in a projector, you will observe that the film loops rub against each other. Although the film has a special lubricant to minimize friction, it is very important to prevent dust collection because any dust that collects on the film will act as an abrasive as the loops of film rub against each other. This highlights the need to keep a cartridge in a closed container when it is not in use to prevent dust from entering the aperture. Both cartridges are sealed, and a special tool is required to open them if film repair becomes necessary.

The Kodak cartridge, which is not a loop, allows the user to load film easily. The cartridge actually houses a regular open reel that can be opened without special tools or skills. This cartridge has more open spaces than loop cartridges and is more susceptible to dust; but, on the other hand, it does not have the friction problem caused by film loops rubbing against each other.

Assessing the pros and cons of 8-mm film containers, one finds that the open reel is least expensive but requires that the film be handled in threading and rewinding; it is also the most susceptible to dust. The loop cartridges are the easiest to use and have the smallest apertures, for minimal dust exposure, but any dust entering will act as an abrasive; the film cannot be rewound (i.e., if the viewer does not wish to see the entire film, the film still must be projected in its entirety in order for the next viewer to see it from the beginning), and a special tool and skill are required to repair damaged film. The Kodak cartridge loads easily, using an open reel; the film can be rewound at any time during viewing; and repairs are easily made; but it has a comparatively large opening that allows dust to collect; and the machine on which it is used is slightly more complicated than a loop projector, because the film must go through an automatic threading phase before it is ready for viewing.

Selecting Motion Picture Projection Equipment

The decision on which motion picture projector to buy must be predicated on intelligent reasoning and factfinding, not solely on the recommendation of a salesperson. This is not a criticism of salespeople; actually they can be most helpful. But ultimately it is the librarian's decision, and once it is made, he or she has to live with it.

Before the librarian even starts to think about equipment, he or she must first consider the patron. Is the patron skilled in operating projection equipment, a first-time user, or is it even necessary that the patron operate the equipment at all? (e.g., many institutions have trained projectionists available, and the viewer does not even touch the film)? Will the film be viewed in the library building, or does the patron have to borrow the equipment as well as the film? (If the latter, portability is a concern.) Will the film be viewed by one person or a large group?

The first consideration is ease of operation. Is the projector a manual threader, a self-threader, or, as in the case of a loop cartridge, does it require threading at all? With a manual threader, the threading path should be simple and easy, not a maze requiring that film be inserted into places accessible only to fingers shaped like tweezers. The requirements of self-threaders vary from merely putting the cartridge loaded with film onto a feed spindle to using an open reel requiring that the film be inserted into a slot in a special way and, after the film is threaded, slotted into the projector before turning on the projector.

The quality of the projected image should be examined to ascertain whether (a) the image is stable and does not vibrate on the screen, (b) the image is bright enough for the conditions under which it will actually be used, and (c) the lens is easy to focus and is in focus over the entire screen (some projectors have such critical focusing that if the lens is moved just slightly, the image will be out of focus).

Some projectors come equipped as complete units with built-in rear projection screens. These projectors are designed for independent viewing. The librarian should make sure that the controls are conveniently accessible, that the unit can be set up in an area within the library where there will not be any glare on the screen from light in the room, and that the screen does not have any hot spots (i.e., one area of the screen that is brighter than another).

It is also very important to listen to the projector. Does it sound like a cement mixer, or is it smooth and almost noiseless? This is an important consideration if there will be a half-dozen independent units being used in the same room at the same time. While listening to the projector in operation, it is also a good idea to look at it to see if any areas are putting excessive wear on the film.

Finally, any additional features the projector may have should be listed, and the librarian should determine whether these features are needed or can be used. (The librarian must remember that he or she is paying for these features.) Some examples of additional features are stop motion, reverse, sound (magnetic or optical), high- as well as low-beam lamps, capability of projecting both standard 8-mm and Super 8-mm films.

Other features to consider are (*a*) size or compactness (an independent viewing unit should be as small as is practicable); (*b*) weight (it should be easy to carry); (*c*) durability (a strong, lightweight metal will take more abuse than a thin, brittle plastic); (*d*) cooling system (the fan should adequately, and quietly, disperse the heat generated by the lamp); (*e*) ease of maintenance (e.g., lamps should be easy to replace); (*f*) availability of a local dealer to service the unit; and (*g*) cost (it should be worth the price).

Keeping all these criteria in mind, the best way to select a projector is to field-test it with a side-by-side comparison. Any reputable dealer would be more than pleased to consent to this type of evaluation.

Using Motion Picture Film

Although the motion picture film is mostly used in group situations, the librarian should encourage individual use as well. The task of the librarian is to have the right film for the patron whenever he or she wants it, and to offer an environment that allows the viewer to be totally involved with the medium so that he or she can be transported vicariously to the place, time, or event the film depicts. This kind of viewing experience may appear to be somewhat idealistic, but it can be achieved to some extent through proper use of the motion picture film.

Using film requires a systems approach. The first task of the librarian, after the film has been acquired, is to inform the patron that it exists. With films, this is usually done by preparing a film catalog, which quite frequently is in book form. The advantage of a book form is that the catalog can be circulated throughout the library community. It is also wise to send catalogs to groups and organizations who would be interested in using films and might, in turn, promote the library's film holdings. Periodically, it will be necessary to distribute supplements to the catalog (perhaps annually or when a large quantity of films is acquired). After a few years, it may be necessary to prepare an entirely new edition of the catalog. Any special awards or evaluations received by a particular film should also be included in the catalog description to aid the patron in selecting films for viewing. Along with the book catalog of films, it is recommended that a card for each film be placed in the library's main catalog, and the card may even be colored coded to attract attention. The library should also advertise through public information channels any new films that have been acquired or any film programs that are being planned. Film programs should be prepared and organized to obtain optimum benefits, (e.g., preparing film programs to coincide with special events, holidays, and cultural affairs that affect the community served by the library).

The library needs to formulate procedures with regard to who is allowed to charge out films and whether certain use restrictions are necessary. Because films are expensive, only properly trained patrons should be allowed to use them independently. It is advisable that anyone who will be operating a motion picture projector be required to demonstrate competency and be issued a certificate of proficiency that allows him or her to charge out films. The certificate should also include a statement that the user will not transmit any film via television, charge a fee, or use the film to promote a service or product without prior written permission from the librarian. In this way, the library is protected against copyright infringements.

When a patron selects a film from the catalog, it must be reserved for his or her use. Although some patrons will want to see a film immediately, on the library premises, most patrons use films in group situations and want to reserve a film so that it will be available when the group convenes. Every film has to be cleaned, inspected, and properly wound for each use. For this task, it is recommended that the library acquire an electronic film-inspecting machine that requires very little technical skill to operate. Any damage to the film discovered during inspection can be repaired so that the film is in good condition for its next use. Most film companies sell replacement footage for repairing damaged film, and usually such information appears in their catalog. When extensive damage does occur, the library must determine who is to absorb the cost of repair. Many public libraries charge the patron insurance or a small fee for using a film, so that there will be a reserve fund to cover the cost of repairs. In this way, if a film is extensively damaged, the patron will not be burdened with an expensive repair charge.

If the librarian is responsible for showing the film to a group, particular attention has to be given to projection techniques. The room used should be able to be adequately darkened, properly ventilated, and conducive to good sound amplification. Attention must be given to any ambient light or sound that may distract the viewer. With regard to ambient light, it is well to remember that a color film requires more room darkening than a black and white film. The film should be set up and ready to project before the audience arrives. The bottom of the projected image should be at least 1.2 m (4 feet) from the floor so that everyone in the audience can have an unobstructed view of the screen.

The seating arrangements should be such that the closest viewer is at least two image widths from the screen and the farthest viewer no more than six image widths away. The viewing angle, depending on the projection surface, should be approximately 25–40 degrees from a line that is perpendicular to the screen; and, in any case, should not exceed an angle that would result in the viewer seeing a deteriorated image (i.e., the projected image must be brilliant and sharp). Ideally, the speakers should be located alongside the screen, so that picture and sound emanate from the same place. However, this may require running a speaker cord from the projector in the rear of the room to the screen in the front of the room, which could be a potential hazard in that someone in the audience might trip over it. As a result, many projectionists prefer to keep the speakers in the back of the room, adjacent to the projector. If a room is to be permanently assigned for film use, then it may be advisable to have built-in speakers, with concealed speaker cords connected to the projector.

If the film is being shown in conjunction with a special event or is part of a film program, it may need an introduction. Any introduction should be brief, to the point, and motivate the audience to want to see the film. Information may be given on the writers or producers of the film, unique cinematic techniques employed, the shooting location of scenes, or facts about the content that serve to heighten interest. Do not tell the audience what the film is all about, because then there would be no need to view it. Above all, do not insult the intelligence of the audience by stating information that becomes obvious when the film is viewed. If the films being shown require nothing in the way of introduction, it is strongly recommended that there be a short intermission between films during which time the audience could discuss or assimilate the information just viewed and relax for a few moments before viewing the next film. This break also gives the projectionist ample time to set up the next film for projection. At some time, either between each film shown or at the conclusion of the program, it might be a good idea to solicit comments from the audience on their reaction(s) to the film(s), their film literacy, and their film preferences. This would also be a good time to provide information about other media in the library that the audience can use to supplement or enhance the film(s) viewed. This, in a sense, gives the viewers an opportunity to have a saturated experience, for not only do they see a film that was properly shown and discussed, but also they have the occasion to explore it further in other informative media forms.

The library should also have facilities for the independent viewing of films. *Independent* as it is used here refers to a single individual or a small group of two to six people. There are commercially available rear projection units in which the film is projected on the back of a special type of screen about twenty-five inches wide. The rear projection unit allows the film to be viewed in a normally lit room, so that the film does not have to be viewed in darkened private spaces, and can be seen in regular rooms in areas of minimum traffic. The viewer wears a headset so that the sound from the film does not disturb other patrons in the room. In lieu of using rear projection units, small viewing rooms may be used for independent viewing. The librarian must decide which method of independent viewing is best for his or her particular library. The patron, whether viewing the film as an individual or in a small or large group, should be able to do so in undisturbed comfort, under conditions that will enable him or her to hear and see all the qualities of the film.

The motion picture film is a unique information media form that vicariously engulfs the viewer in the message through the skillful use and combination of visuals, color, motion, and sound. It is important to bear in mind that most viewers have had extensive experience viewing film and therefore have the ability to judge a film's strengths and weaknesses. If the librarian, by judicious selection, gives the viewer the best films that can be obtained and presents them under the best possible conditions, the film will provide an enjoyable and informative experience for all who view it.

Selected Bibliography

Boyle, Deidre, ed. *Expanding Media*. Phoenix: Oryx Press, 1977.

Burke, John Gordon, ed. *Print, Image and Sound: Essays On Media*. Chicago: American Library Association, 1972.

Eidsvik, Charles. *Cineliteracy: Film Among the Arts*. New York: Random House, 1978.

Film Library Quarterly. New York: Film Library Information Council, 1967–.

Instructional Innovator. Washington, D.C.: Association for Educational Communications and Technology, 1956–.

Jones, Emily Strange. *Manual On Film Evaluation*. New York: Educational Film Library Association, 1967.

Rehrauer, George. *The Film User's Handbook: A Basic Manual For Managing Library Film Services*. New York: R. R. Bowker, 1975.

Sightlines. New York: Educational Film Library Association, 1967–.

Selection Aids

AV Guide Newsletter. Chicago: Educational Screen, 1922–.

Booklist. Chicago: American Library Association, 1905–.

Educational Film Locator of the Consortium of University Film Centers and R. R. Bowker Company, first edition. New York: R. R. Bowker, 1978.

Educator's Guide To Free Films. Randolph, Wisconsin: Educator's Progress Service, 1941–.

Educator's Purchasing Guide. Philadelphia: North American, 1969–.

Film and Video Review Index. Pasadena: AudioVisual Associates, 1978–.

Film Literature Index. New York: R. R. Bowker, 1973–.

Film News. New York: Rohama Lee Film News, 1939–.

Films in Review. New York: Films in Review, 1950–.

Gaffney, Maureen, comp. and ed. *More Films Kids Like: A Catalog of Short Films for Children*. Chicago: American Library Association, 1977.

Guide to Free Loan Films: About Foreign Lands. Alexandria, Virginia, Serina Press, 1975.

Guide to Free Loan Films: On the Urban Condition. Alexandria, Virginia: Serina Press, 1976.

Guide to Free Loan Government Films, fourth edition. Alexandria, Virginia: Serina Press, 1978.

Guide to Free Loan Sport Films, second edition. Alexandria, Virginia: Serina Press, 1976.

Guide to Free Loan Training Films. Alexandria, Virginia: Serina Press, 1975.

Instructional Innovator. Washington, D.C.: Association for Educational Communication and Technology. 1956–.

International Index To Multi-Media Information. Pasadena: AudioVisual Associates, 1968–.

Landers Film Reviews: Source Directory. Escondido, California: Landers Associates, 1956–.

Library of Congress Catalogs: Film and Other Materials for Projection. Washington, D.C.: Library of Congress, 1948–.

Limbacher, James L., comp. and ed. *Feature Films on 8 mm, 16 mm, and Videotape: A Directory of Feature Films Available for Rental, Sale, and Lease in the U.S. and Canada: With a Serial Section and a Director Index*, sixth edition. New York: R. R. Bowker, 1979.

Media and Methods. Philadelphia: North American Publishing, 1965.

Media Review Digest. Ann Arbor: The Pierian Press, 1970–.

New Cinema Review. New York: New Cinema Review, 1969–.

New York Times Film Reviews, 1913–1974, (8 vols.) New York: Arno Press, 1974.

NICEM Index to 16mm Educational Films, sixth edition, (3 vols.) Los Angeles: University of Southern California, 1979–.

North American Film and Video Directory. New York: R. R. Bowker, 1976.

Schrank, Jeffrey. *Guide To Short Films*. Rochelle Park, New Jersey: Hayden Book Co., 1979.

Sightlines. New York: Educational Film Library Association, 1967–.

7

Filmstrips and Slides

Overview

Filmstrips and slides are a rather special medium because the public has to become accustomed to their use. Patrons readily accept print information and are more than familiar with audio and motion picture forms; but when it comes to filmstrips and slides, patron exposure has quite often been limited to candid photography. There is a whole body of information that lends itself to the filmstrip–slide medium. This is information that is enhanced by virtue of being projected, but does not require the more expensive, elaborate, and sophisticated processes involved in the motion picture format. Filmstrips and slides have found ready acceptance in elementary school libraries and art collections, but unfortunately are not being used to their maximum advantage in other types of libraries. Silent filmstrips and slides are most prevalent in elementary school and art libraries, but both these and other libraries are gradually building their sound–filmstrip and sound–slide collections. The inclusion of a sound recording enhances the value of filmstrips and slides for individual viewing and, as such, is beneficial for all classes of libraries.

Filmstrips and slides are inexpensive media when compared to motion pictures. With the incorporation of sound a new dimension of communication is added in that a still projected image is accompanied by an audio message. The librarian, by judicious selection, can build a filmstrip and/or slide collection that provides information in an easy-to-use format. There are many titles available, especially in filmstrips, and by properly using these media, as well as orienting the patron to their use potential, they become still another means of increasing the library's effectiveness and efficiency in information dissemination.

Filmstrips and Slides: Physical Characteristics

The fundamental difference between filmstrips and slides is that filmstrips contain a *group* of still pictures on a continuous piece of transparent film, whereas slides are *individually* mounted, still visuals on separate pieces of transparent film. Both filmstrips and slides can be made in the same camera, use the same kind of film, and contain exactly the same information. Again, the difference is that a filmstrip is a series of still visuals on one physical piece of film, whereas slides are cut and mounted to be used as individual still visuals.

Filmstrips and slides each have special advantages and disadvantages. A filmstrip is easier to control physically because all the visuals are on one continuous piece of film that is usually stored in a plastic or metal canister. When checking a filmstrip in or out of the library, the librarian can quickly and easily determine whether it is complete and intact. Slides are more difficult to control because each visual is an entity and must be stored, labeled, and distributed separately. On the other hand, filmstrips, because they are on continuous pieces of film, must be used in a prescribed order; whereas slides can be arranged in any order the user deems necessary, and it is possible to shuffle, add, delete, and update a series of slides. In this sense, a slide presentation can be tailormade to the needs of the individual user. In defense of fixed filmstrip sequences, they are photographed, and therefore intended to be presented, in a prescribed, logical sequence; and the user would never need or want to rearrange this sequence. Filmstrips are usually less expensive than slides, because slides are twice as large and require additional materials and labor for individual mounting. An average filmstrip costs about $.40–.60 per frame, whereas a slide frame costs about $1, or approximately twice the price of a filmstrip frame.

Most commercially produced and locally produced filmstrips are photographed on 35-mm film. Some producers have considered the feasibility of using 16-mm film, but to date, very little has been produced. Sixteen-millimeter filmstrips are somewhat cheaper to produce (the cost is about one third of the cost of producing 35-mm filmstrips) and occupy less storage space. But they require 16-mm still projectors for viewing, and the fact that few libraries have such projectors is the main reason why the format has been very slow to gain acceptance.

Librarians should keep abreast of 16-mm filmstrip developments, however, for they could prove to be an economic boon.

Thirty-five millimeter filmstrips are available in only two formats: single frame and double frame. Single-frame filmstrips make up well over 99% of available 35-mm filmstrips. The differences between the single- and double-frame formats are illustrated in Figure 7.1. The visuals of a single-frame filmstrip are photographed on a vertical plane and that the ratio of picture (or frame) height to width is approximately 3 to 4. The double-frame filmstrip is photographed on a horizontal plane, and the height–width ratio is 2 to 3. This means that a librarian selecting a filmstrip projector must know what types of filmstrips are to be projected. If the library has only single-frame filmstrips, there is no need to purchase a projector capable of projecting double-frame filmstrips, and the additional capability obviously increases the cost of the projector. Conversely, if the library has only single-frame filmstrip projectors, it should not consider purchasing double-frame filmstrips. (If information is available in double-frame format only, and the library does not have double-frame filmstrip projection equipment; the filmstrip can be purchased and the visuals cut and mounted as individual slides. This procedure requires no special equipment or skill, and any local camera shop has cardboard mounts available.) As we can see from Figure 7.1, the overall dimensions of two single frames are exactly equal to those of one double frame. This explains why they are called single frame and double frame; some librarians call them half- frame and full frame. But whichever way they are named, the ratio is still 2 to 1.

Slides are available in various sizes, the 2- × 2-inch (5.1- × 5.1-cm) size being the most prevalent. Its overall dimensions, including the mount (or frame) measures 2 inches wide by 2 inches high. The 2- × 2-inch mount can contain 35-mm half- (or single-)frame film, 35-mm full- (or double-)frame film, or 127 size film (see Figure 7.2). Because these three sizes of film all have the same size mount, they can be viewed using the same type of projection equipment. Other size mounts are the relatively new 110 size, the $2\frac{1}{4}$- × $2\frac{1}{4}$-inch (5.7- × 5.7-cm) mount used with 120 film size, and the $3\frac{1}{4}$- × 4-inch (8.2- × 10.1-cm) mount. Each of these sizes in turn requires viewing equipment that is adaptable to its respective size. As a result, commercial producers and libraries have adopted the 2- × 2-inch format as a standard. However the librarian should keep abreast of new developments. The new 110 ($1\frac{3}{16}$- × $1\frac{3}{16}$-inch [3.0- × 3.0-cm]) size is rapidly gaining in popularity. A further consideration is that technically, the larger the film, the better is its quality of resolution and image when projected. As a result, many art, architecture, and medical visuals, which demand extreme clarity of detail, are

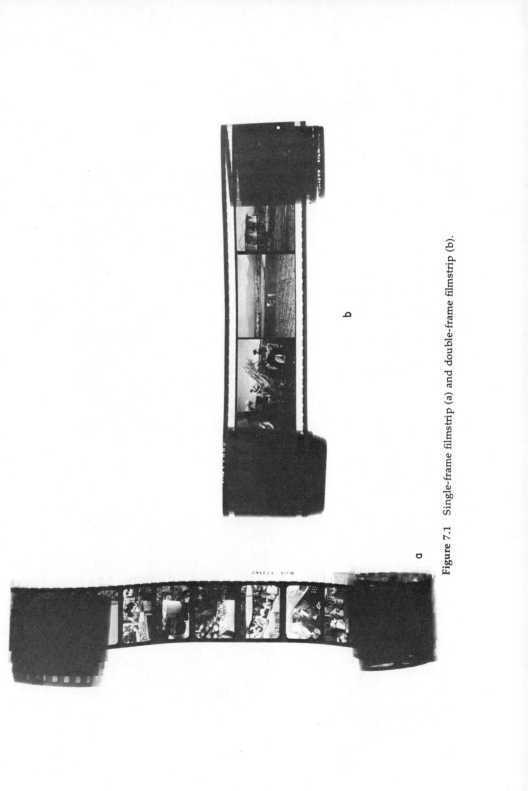

Figure 7.1 Single-frame filmstrip (a) and double-frame filmstrip (b).

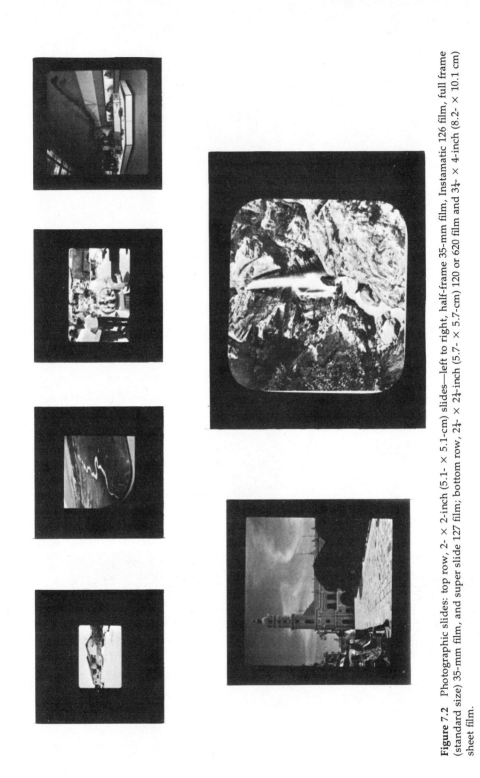

Figure 7.2 Photographic slides: top row, 2- × 2-inch (5.1- × 5.1-cm) slides—left to right, half-frame (standard size) 35-mm film, full frame 35-mm film, Instamatic 126 film, full frame (standard size) 35-mm film, and super slide 127 film; bottom row, $2\frac{1}{4}$- × $2\frac{1}{4}$-inch (5.7- × 5.7-cm) 120 or 620 film and $3\frac{1}{4}$- × 4-inch (8.2- × 10.1 cm) sheet film.

photographed with larger size films. In fact, many commercially available visuals for art, architecture, and medicine are available on 35-mm full-frame (2- × 2-inch) slides, or on 3¼- × 4-inch slides rather than the more common half-frame filmstrip.

A final type of transparent still film is the stereoscopic slide, which projects a three-dimensional image. Most stereo equipment is intended for individual viewing. Because stereo slides require the simultaneous viewing of a pair of visuals or slides, they must be mounted in juxtaposition in order to give the three-dimensional effect. Some companies mount the visuals on cardboard wheels; other companies mount them on rectangular cardboards. Again, it is critical when selecting stereoscopic visuals to consider the format (wheel or rectangular card) because each requires its own type of viewing equipment, and the two are in no way interchangeable.

Advantages of Filmstrips and Slides

Photographic film provides the most brilliant and realistic reproduction of graphic or pictorial information possible. A picture in a book communicates well, but a slide or filmstrip, when projected, adds a depth and vitality unobtainable from a paper print. Also, the slide or filmstrip, although it can be viewed by an individual using a slide or filmstrip viewer, can be projected on a large screen. This permits many people to view it at the same time, which is not possible with visuals in a book. Compared to large prints or photographs, slides and filmstrips cost much less, are easier to manage and store, and are less susceptible to damage. Still another consideration for using filmstrips and slides is that if the information to be viewed does not require motion, a filmstrip or slide is far less expensive than a motion picture film.

Filmstrips and slides have a distinct advantage over motion pictures in that viewers can pace the viewing of information at their own rate of speed. They can have a visual projected for only a fraction of a second or leave it projected for as long as they want to look at it.

Used by a competent librarian for group presentations, filmstrips and slides can compel attention, generate discussion, and involve followup activity, such as reading books for further information. When the librarian provides filmstrips and slides to children and young adults, the results are usually most gratifying. They tend to stimulate an interest in the library, and most filmstrips and slide sets, since they can be viewed in one sitting, do not require a long attention span. This makes them a great motivational device for culturally deprived patrons who are not inclined toward reading. It is quite probable that the reticent reader, after viewing a few filmstrips, may be less reluctant to attempt to read a book and may feel that if the library has enjoyable filmstrips, it might also have some equally enjoyable books. For the good reader, accessibility to filmstrips and slides is a means of obtaining supplementary and enrichment materials to embellish the experience of reading a book. Actually, the task of the librarian is to select the right information, in the proper medium, that best suits the needs of the patron.

Many filmstrips contain visuals accompanied by captions. The librarian should know how best to use the captions in group presentations. If they are used with a young group, the librarian or individuals in the group may read them aloud. It is suggested that, when necessary, captions be further discussed, for they usually give only basic information. When captions are used with literate adults, it is advisable, as a rule of thumb, to read each caption silently twice, and then proceed with any necessary discussion or advance to the next visual. This type of pacing provides an opportunity for slower readers to read the entire caption, but does not bore fast readers with a slow, dragging presentation.

An ever-increasing number of sound filmstrips and sound slide sets are being produced. Although these do restrict the flexibility of viewing because the visuals must be shown at the pace dictated by the sound commentary (of course, the sound source can be stopped to allow for prolonged viewing), sound does add a new dimension to filmstrips and slides: The viewer can be given more information than would be feasible on a caption, and the use of music, real sounds, and sound effects greatly enhances communication of the visual information. The sound is provided on either a disc record or an audio tape. The addition of sound gives filmstrips and slides the scope of a sound motion picture film, and when motion is not essential, a sound filmstrip or sound–slide set can do the job just as well, at a fraction of the cost.

A librarian should spend some time perusing filmstrip and slide selection aids to get an idea of the extremely wide range of information available. With a comparatively small expenditure of funds, a good collection can be acquired. The librarian can investigate an almost infinitely wide range of titles, concentrate on a particular topic, or even consider the acquisition of a series. Incidentally, series add the dimension of continuity to the experience of viewing a filmstrip or slide program in that many patrons will want to view more than one filmstrip or slide set of a particular series.

Filmstrips and slides enhance the viewing quality of a visual, can be viewed individually or in groups, are more economical than motion picture films, and are easy to manage. Each visual can be viewed for as long as desired, which stimulates further interest. They can be either captioned or accompanied by sound. A breadth as well as an in-depth range of titles and topics is available.

Local Production of Filmstrips and Slides

Because cameras are fairly inexpensive and do not require professional photographic training to use, librarians can produce their own filmstrips and slides. Often, there is information of local interest that is not available on a commercially produced filmstrip that can be photographed easily by the librarian. If patrons have a particular need for information that is not available in a filmstrip or slide format or must be uniquely photographed or arranged, local production is justified. Local production can never be justified on the basis of economy, for it will be immediately apparent that even if the estimated cost of labor is as low as $1 per hour, the eventual cost in time expended will usually far exceed the cost of purchasing a commercially produced filmstrip or slide set of comparable quality.

Examples of filmstrips or slide sets that might be locally produced include those that provide the viewer with instruction on how to use the local library facilities, that supply information regarding local library programs, that offer promotional packages advertising the library and its services for the purpose of informing or encouraging patrons to use the library, that request additional funds, or that provide a community service. Filmstrips and slide sets are also useful as inservice training devices. Local production provides an opportunity to photograph information that the viewer can readily identify. Another ideal use for a locally produced filmstrip or slide set could involve a field trip to a community resource. The viewer can learn and observe specifics prior to the field trip, or the need for the field trip might even be eliminated. If the field trip is taken, the filmstrip or slide set becomes more meaningful, and it can also be viewed later as a followup activity.

There are several basic considerations to be resolved when producing a filmstrip or slide set. Assuming that the necessary equipment is available for both photographing and projecting the information, it must first be determined whether the end product is to be a filmstrip or a slide set. Filmstrips, as explained earlier, are less expensive and easier to manage than slides. They require a bit more technical skill to produce than slides. It is strongly advised that a half-frame camera be used to produce a filmstrip, since this is the overwhelmingly prevalent format. The visuals for a filmstrip must be photographed in a prescribed sequence. Although a filmstrip can be spliced—which means visuals (frames) can be added, deleted, or rearranged—this is not recommended. Filmstrip splices have a tendency to jam in a projector, and they are usually a weak link in the physical durability of a filmstrip. This means that if, after a roll of film is processed, some of the visuals are not satisfactory and must be rephotographed; it is best to reshoot the entire filmstrip. In photographing slides, the problems are not so acute. The visuals can be photographed in any sequence that is convenient, unsatisfactory shots can be deleted and replaced with more satisfactory shots, and the finished slides can be arranged or rearranged whenever and however desired. The end result when viewed, be it filmstrip or slides, will be same; it is just that filmstrips allow less margin for production error.

When the decision has been made whether to make a filmstrip or a slide set, the next consideration is the type of material to be photographed. If the material can be photographed with a hand-held camera or a camera mounted on a tripod, there is no problem. However, if material is to be copied from a book or is comparatively small, then a copystand must be employed. This is not an insurmountable difficulty—a copystand like the Kodak Visualmaker allows slides to be made by those having no photographic skills whatever, and with the complex cameras with interchangeable lenses or lens attachments available today extremely small objects can be photographed. A copy of a slide can be made with a slide copier, which can be either a simple camera accessory or a copy camera like the Repronar. In fact, if copying slides is not a frequent occurrence, it would be best to have it done at a local camera shop.

Because making them is rather difficult and timeconsuming, captions are hardly ever used in the local production of filmstrips and slides, which leads to the next consideration: Whether to include sound. If sound is to be included, a script must be prepared and the sound must be recorded with a taperecorder. If the finished product is to be viewed independently, the tape must be cued. If the library equipment has a feature that automatically advance the filmstrip or slide on electronic cue or signal, the electronic cues must be put on the tape. If automatic equipment is not available, then audible cues must be put on the tape. The problem with audible cues is to make them sound pleasant and not distracting. Some people use bells, clickers, or "cricket" devices; others strike water glasses or create other sounds. (The author's experience has been that a device that produces a C-sharp tone, for example, a child's xylophone, is best and can be purchased in a music store. Also good for generating a tone is a code practice oscillator with variable volume and tone control, which can be purchased in an electronic equipment store.) Unfortunately, the end result is often far from what is desired and can turn an otherwise fine production into a fiasco. If the package is to be used only for group presentations, it is better to provide the projectionist with a printed script, with which he or she can advance the projector while listening to the tape and reading the cues from the script, than to use audible cues.

When the librarian has become adept at producing filmstrips and slide sets, he or she might want to consider a *multiimage, multimage,* or *multiscreen* presentation. The foregoing terms are synonomous and simply mean a presentation using more than one projector simultaneously. Although the presentation requires more work, patience, and perhaps just a bit more skill, the results can be gratifying. Again, depending on skill, production time, and equipment, the multimage presentation can range from a simple affair using 2 manually operated projectors to a complex, automated, computerized production using 30 or more projectors. Multimage adds a refreshing dimension to slide presentations by keeping things "happening" on the screen. Picture statements can be presented on one screen and counterpointed on another screen, or visual statements can expand or contract before the viewers' eyes. A multimage presentation is not the standard fare available in libraries; rather, it is something the librarian considers using for a special purpose or occasion to impress patrons with a special message. Because the average person does not have much occasion to view multimage productions, he or she very often finds them interesting, exciting, and entertaining, as well as informative.

Another consideration is that of making multiple copies of a production. As mentioned previously, this can be achieved with special equipment (e.g., a Repronar copy camera), but for most libraries, the local camera shop is a more likely source for multiple copies. One word of caution: The quality of the copy will never be as good as that of the original; something is always lost in the succeeding generations (e.g., realism of color, sharpness). Therefore, each copy should be examined carefully to insure that it meets the minimum standard of quality.

Related to the consideration of multiple copies is that of copyright. Legally, when information is copied out of a book or anything else that is copyrighted, it is necessary to have permission from the rightful owner. Ignorance of this law is not an excuse; and as a professional, the librarian (or his or her institution) is responsible for any violations of copyright.

These considerations are basic to the actual local production of a filmstrip or slide set. There are others of a more technical nature that are beyond the scope of this text. The purpose here is to provide information about what is basically involved in producing a filmstrip or slide set. It can be done, it is not difficult, and it can be rewarding, because it provides your library with material unobtainable from any other source.

Selecting Filmstrip and Slide Projection Equipment

A recurring theme in this textbook with respect to audiovisual equipment is that it is of value only if it is being used. Is it truly worth the price paid for it, and does it do everything it was expected to do at the expected level of performance? These concerns serve as primary guidelines in assessing filmstrip and slide projection equipment.

When selecting filmstrip and slide projection equipment, the first consideration is the size of the library's filmstrip and slide collection and how it is being used. The size of the collection will help determine how many pieces of equipment are needed. Of course, there are libraries with large collections that receive so little use that very little viewing equipment is needed. Where this is true, it indicates an extremely poor system—a large collection not being used is a sure indication of poor selection procedures. If the collection is extensively used, an analysis must be made to determine how many patrons use it (i.e., number patrons using projection equipment during peak utilization periods). This will give an indication of the number of projectors needed. The next factor to consider is how the patrons are using the equipment (i.e., large group, small group, individual viewing) and where it is used (i.e., in the library or in a remote location that would require it to be light and portable). Having determined the when, how, and where particulars of equipment use, it is now necessary to consider these in light of the library's budget, and to decide how much should be allocated to purchase any particular type of equipment. The librarian may even find that the library can afford something better than what he or she had originally intended to purchase, or you may have to make compromises in order to satisfy your needs. Bear in mind that equipment can range from simple, hand-held, manually operated viewing equipment for individual use to automated electronic equipment for large group use. With such a wide range of selections and prices, it is essential that the equipment receive its intended use.

If sufficient equipment use can be justified, then it is best to select equipment designed for a specific type of use; if not, equipment with greater versatility should be selected. As an example, if individual viewing is the most extensive use of the filmstrips and slides in the library, a small aircooled projector with its own rear projection screen built into the cabinetry of a viewing carrel should be considered; but if both outside-the-library and in-library use are expected, a lightweight portable unit with a self-contained viewing screen should be selected. If the same piece of equipment has to be used for both individual and small group use, a still different set of selection criteria will have to be considered. There is no one piece of viewing equipment that can satisfy all needs. Many questions for each type of use must be answered when selecting filmstrip and slide equipment. The Educational Products Information Exchange (EPIE), P. O. Box 620, Stony Brook, New York 11790, is an excellent resource to assist in slide and filmstrip projection equipment selection. This organization evaluates and prepares reports on various types of audiovisual equipment.

Individual Use

Depending on your particular type of library, you may want to select filmstrip or slide projection equipment that is permanently installed into a learning carrel, as well as portable equipment capable of being used both inside and outside the library. With permanently installed equipment, thievery problems are eliminated, since it is virtually impossible to steal a projector when it is built into a large piece of furniture. But there are some problems inherent in this type of set up as well; for example if the projector needs repair, it will have to be removed from the furniture it is built into, and if repair is to take some time, a replacement unit will have to be installed in its place. Built-in equipment also has the dual advantage of not cluttering a working area and being esthetically more attractive.

A prime concern for filmstrip and slide viewing equipment for individual use is ease of operation. The equipment should be simple enough to operate that even a school-age child can use it with little or no instruction. If the patron has to load and unload the projector, it should not have a difficult and complex loading or threading mechanism. If the equipment is permanently loaded, it should have a procedure for cycling or rewinding so that every patron can view the presentation without having to spend time trying to find the beginning.

If the equipment has audio capabilities, audio cassettes are strongly recommended because they are easier to operate and are more compact than either open audio reels or disc records. Also, with audio combination systems, attention should be given to the quality of headsets that are to be purchased; they should be acoustically good, comfortable to wear, and hygienically safe. If the library can afford it, it is recommended that equipment that automatically responds to inaudible electronic cues be purchased in preference to manually operated equipment because automatic equipment eliminates the task of having to advance the filmstrip or slides, thereby freeing the user to enjoy and concentrate on the information presented.

Because projection equipment for individual use does not require a large projection lamp, many projectors do not require fans to cool the lamps. If the library budget allows, these are obvious advantages to purchasing such a projector: the noise that would be generated by a fan would be eliminated, the projector use less electricity, and the absence of a fan means there would be one less part of the equipment in need of maintenance. However, before an air-cooled projector is purchased, it should be tested under conditions exactly like those under which it will be used in the library: The librarian should leave the lamp on and the projector loaded with a filmstrip or slides for an extended period of time (several hours if necessary) to observe whether any damage is done to the filmstrip or slides and whether the projector does not become so hot that it cannot be handled safely or becomes a potential fire hazard.

The viewing surface or screen must also be considered. It should be large enough to provide sufficient magnification for even the smallest caption to be read without eyestrain. The screen should also be evenly illuminated and not have any bright (hot) spots; it is very irritating to view a projected image that is blindingly bright in the center and rapidly falls off to a dark, shadowy image toward the edges.

Small Group Use

For purpose of definition, a small group would consist of 2 to about 10 people. If viewing groups will rarely exceed 2 or 3 people, consider selecting equipment that is intended for individual use, but has a viewing screen large enough to be used by a group of 3 as well. If the group is going to be larger (4–10 people), and front-projection equipment is to be used, it will be necessary to use a viewing room that can be darkened. (Front projection occurs when a projector at rear of room projects an image on the *front* surface of the screen.) Presently, there are some excellent rear projection screens for small group viewing that can be used in a normally lighted room. (Rear projection occurs when a projector, usually using a front surface mirror, is placed behind a translucent screen and the image is projected on the *rear* of the screen). In either case, the image should be of adequate size and quality to be properly viewed by everyone in the group. Ideally, seating arrangements should be such that the person closest to the screen is no closer than the equivalent of two screen widths from the screen, and the furthest person no more than six screen widths away.

It is recommended that equipment have some type of remote control device that permits a member of the group to advance or stop the presentation without actually being at the projector. Oftentimes small groups become involved in discussion as the presentation proceeds, and the remote control device makes operating the equipment much more convenient in such situations. Although small group equipment tends to be larger than individually used equipment (i.e., projector, screen, sound system), concern should still be given to acquiring equipment that is portable and easy to assemble and disassemble.

Large Group Use

A prime concern in selecting projection equipment for large group use is that the lamp wattage be adequate to illuminate the screen properly. The best way to determine this is actually to try out the projector under the severest use conditions imaginable. The equipment should be relatively quiet, but less concern about complexity of operation is needed, because in large group presentations, a qualified person usually operates the equipment. Lenses should be properly selected for the size of the screen and for the distance between the projector and the screen (see Table 7.1). For a multiplicity of projection situations (e.g., large screen–small room ranging to small screen–large room), a zoom lens with a variation of lens sizes should be acquired.

Combination Projection Equipment

For a library with a limited budget or equipment that will receive limited use, combination equipment should be considered. Some projectors project both filmstrips and slides; can be used for both front and rear projection (individually as well as by a large group, with or without sound), have detachable sound systems that can be used independently (either with or without headsets) and can be operated manually, with a remote control device, or automatically.

Storage Equipment

Although not a part of utilization, storage of filmstrips and slides warrant consideration. Storage equipment should be compact and not wasteful of space, designed for modular addition or expansion, and impervious to light, dust, and humidity. Slide storage should require minimal handling of slides, provide proper separation so slides do not rub together, and allow for accession numbering. As an added feature, some slide storage cabinets permit viewing of slides in large quantities

Table 7.1   Lens and Screen Selection Chart

Lens focal length (inches)	Projector-to-screen distance (feet)								
	Width of screen								
	40 inches	50 inches	60 inches	70 inches	84 inches	8 feet	9 feet	10 feet	12 feet
2- × 2-inch slides									
3	7	9	11	13	16	18	20	22	27
4	10	12	15	17	21	24	27	30	36
5	12	16	19	22	26	30	34	37	45
6	15	19	22	26	31	36	40	45	54
35-mm single-frame filmstrips									
3	11	14	17	19	23	27	30	33	40
4	15	19	22	26	31	36	40	44	53
5	19	23	28	32	39	44	50	56	67
6	22	28	33	39	47	53	60	67	30
7	26	32	39	49	55	62	70	78	93

Lens focal length (cm)	Projector-to-screen distance (m)								
	Width of screen (m)								
	1.02	1.27	1.52	1.78	2.13	2.44	2.74	3.05	3.65
5.1- × 5.1-cm slides									
7.6	2.13	2.74	3.35	3.96	4.87	5.48	6.10	6.71	8.23
10.2	3.05	3.66	4.57	5.18	6.40	7.32	8.23	9.41	10.97
12.7	3.66	4.88	5.79	6.71	7.92	9.14	10.36	11.28	13.72
15.2	4.57	5.79	6.71	7.93	9.45	10.97	12.19	13.72	16.46
35-mm single-frame filmstrips									
7.6	3.35	4.27	5.18	5.79	7.01	8.23	9.14	10.06	12.19
10.2	4.57	5.79	6.71	7.92	9.45	10.97	12.19	13.41	16.15
12.7	5.79	7.01	8.53	9.75	11.89	13.41	15.24	17.07	20.42
15.2	6.71	8.53	10.06	11.89	14.33	16.15	18.29	20.42	24.39
17.8	7.92	9.75	11.89	14.94	16.76	18.90	21.34	23.78	28.35

without physical handling or removal from the cabinet. This is expedient when the librarian has to select each slide from a large collection.

Selecting Filmstrips and Slides

There is no universal form for selecting and evaluating filmstrips and slides. Depending on its purpose, a library could perhaps have need of more than one type of filmstrip and slide evaluation form. The criteria used to evaluate are fairly standard; the variation arises in determining how many criteria should be used; the degree or depth to which the criteria will be examined; who is to do the evaluating with regard to knowledge, interest, and amount of time that can be devoted to the task; and the purpose for conducting an evaluation in the first place (e.g., acquisition, deletion, special programs, abstracts).

The following standard criteria can be used as a guide in constructing a filmstrip and slide evaluation form. Each criterion is defined in the form of a question and should be developed (i.e., contracted, expanded, combined, or deleted) so that it fulfills its intended function for the particular library.

1. *Proper medium*   Is the filmstrip or slide medium appropriate for communicating the topic or subject in question?

2. *Content*   Is it accurate, truthful, up to date, authentic, and complete? Is it applicable to more than one subject or topic area? Is it an overview or an in-depth investigation?

3. *Bias*   Does it contain propaganda? Does it present a point of view that is extremely or even slightly one sided?

4. *Appropriateness*   Is the method by which the information is presented appropriate for the intended patron?

5. *Organization*   Are components integrated? Is there continuity of information, serious gaps or omissions, or overcondensation?

6. *Photography*   Is the exposure, color, and composition of the photographs, art work, and graphics good? Do visuals effectively communicate the intended message? Are orientation devices included when needed?

7. *Captions*   Do captions provide sufficient information? Are they easy to read and succinct? Are attention-getting devices used (e.g., italics, underlining, capitalization of key words, color)? Is the vocabulary suitable?

8. *Sound*   Is the fidelity good? Does it relate to and enhance the visuals? Are interesting sound techniques used (e.g., music, sound effects, background sound, fades, dissolves)? Is sound necessary? Does it heighten interest?

9. *Special features*   Does it contain numbered frames, an introductory frame, or a summary frame? Are guides or supplementary materials available?

10. *Series*   Is the filmstrip or slide presentation part of a series? If so, can each filmstrip or slide set be viewed as an entity or in random order, or must they be viewed in a prescribed sequence?

11. *Patron reaction*   Will the patron identify with the material? Is it challenging and compatible with the intelligence of the viewer? Does it promote discussion or further investigation?

12. *Related materials*   Can it be used to complement other materials (e.g., books, motion picture films)?

Again, the preceding criteria should be developed according to the needs of the particular library. The arrangement, style, and detail of the evaluation form will depend on how much information is needed and the skill of the people using the form. The evaluation form can be either subjective (i.e., the respondent writes in comments to questions) or objective (i.e., respondent makes check marks in appropriate places). The preceding criteria can be incorporated into an evaluation form in the following suggested arrangement:

1. *Vital statistics*   bibliographic information (title, producer, cost, number of frames, color or black and white, series, sound, and price)
2. *Précis*   short description of what the material is about
3. *Content information*   criteria 1, 2, 3, 4, and 5
4. *Technical quality*   criteria 6, 7, 8, and 9
5. *Possible uses*   criteria 10 and 12
6. *User*   criteria 4 and 11
7. *Evaluator*   name and credentials of the evaluator
8. *Summary*   overall yes–no statement or reaction to the material

A final consideration in developing criteria for evaluating filmstrips and slides is the time factor. Any evaluation of filmstrips or slides should be done efficiently. It is rather foolish to spend an hour evaluating a 30-frame filmstrip, when there are so many filmstrips that must be previewed by a library that is building a collection. As has been stressed repeatedly in this text, the evaluation criteria and corresponding evaluation form should solicit only information that the librarian intends to use, and the form should be structured in such a way that the evaluator can fill it out and the librarian can extract information from it quickly.

Using Filmstrips and Slides

For large group viewing, it is best to accompany filmstrips and slides with a running commentary by someone knowledgeable in the topic being presented. The commentator must be careful to avoid talking excessively and to discuss only the visual being projected. Unless it is a really remarkable visual, it is recommended that it not be held on the screen for more than 30 seconds. It can also be rather monotonous when all visuals are projected for the same length of time. To give some snap to the presentation, it is advised that the pace of projection be varied anywhere from a second or two to the full 30 seconds. Ideally, group presentations should be about 15–20 minutes long, and additional time should be allowed for discussion, reaction, and assimilation before showing anymore filmstrips or slides. As discussed previously, captioned filmstrips and slides can be used successfully with primary and intermediate grade children, but when used with literate adults, it can be somewhat demeaning when someone reads the captions aloud; conversely, it can be equally deadly when there is nothing but silence during the presentation.

It would be a good idea to share these suggestions about filmstrip and slide presentations with the novice presenter who wishes to use the library to make a presentation to a community group. The novice must also bear in mind that the viewer might not share the same degree of enthusiasm about the information being projected. The presentation must be kept interesting and it has a better chance of being so if it is brief.

Most utilization of filmstrips and slides in the library will be by individual patrons using a small filmstrip and/or slide viewer. Some filmstrip and slide viewers are nothing more than a device that illuminates the visual and projects it through an 8× magnifying glass. The resultant image is rather small, but nevertheless, clearly legible. Patrons seem to prefer viewing filmstrip and slide images on a rear screen unit, which projects a larger image than the magnifying glass method. On a rear screen unit the size of the projected image can range from about 10.1 × 15.2 cm (4 × 6 inches) to 22.8 × 22.8 cm (9 × 9 inches). It seems that with individual viewers, filmstrips and slides that have sound accompaniment are preferred to those that are silent. The librarian should also seriously consider acquiring equipment that automatically advances the visuals. This frees the user from having to advance the visual every time an audible tone or beep is heard, which in and of itself is a distraction. The automatic equipment responds to an inaudible signal and the user hears only the commentary, which makes the presentation more enjoyable. However, the user of automatic equipment must be instructed on how to cue the presentation since the visuals and the audio recording are discrete entities. If it is not properly cued, the entire presentation will be out of synchronization and confusing, if not meaningless. Cueing up the presentation is really not that difficult: The recording must be started at the very beginning, and the filmstrip or slide must be set on the first, or cue, frame.

The user will need a comfortable headset to hear the audio and should view the material in an area with minimum distractions. A carrel with low partitions on three sides works well in that it reduces distractions and gives the user a sense of privacy. If the equipment is built into the carrel, the patron will have additional space to take notes and use supplementary materials. It is recommended that the equipment be permanently placed in the carrels or viewing areas and that patrons be assigned to a particular space. In school libraries, it may even be feasible, if a particular presentation is to be viewed by many students, to have a learning station set up with a complete package of materials that need not be charged out for each use. Materials that are charged out should be at least cursorily examined for damaged or missing components when they are returned. A filmstrip is easy to examine; for missing parts, because if it is not in one piece or is otherwise damaged, that damage will invariably be visible. Missing or damaged slides, are not as easy to detect. It is recommended that slides be distributed in the container that will be used on the projector (e.g., a Kodak Carousel tray), which can be quickly examined for missing slides. Having the slides in a container has the added advantage of preventing physical handling by the user thereby lessening the chances of the user getting fingerprints on the slides, and assuring that they will not be projected upside down or backwards, which is a rather annoying distraction for the viewer.

Many filmstrip and slide packages are accompanied by a printed guide, script, or description of content. This can be of considerable value to the user in the selection of a particular presentation and as a reference after viewing the presentation. The librarian can also use the material to make detailed recommendations to patrons desiring to know more about what is available in the collection.

The librarian needs to be cognizant of the unique qualities of the sound filmstrip and sound slide. These allow the user to view still visual graphic information while receiving verbal information about what is being looked at and its significance via an audio recording. If the same visual were to be examined in a book, the user would have to read the printed information and then look at the visual, but could not do both at the same time. This alternation from the print to the visual can be tiresome, and it is certainly inefficient. If the visual does not require motion—thereby eliminating the need for the more expensive motion picture film—and if the librarian can provide the proper environment and orientation necessary to use filmstrip and slide packages, these two media can provide an extremely informative and enjoyable experience.

Selected Bibliography

Boerner, Susan Lee. "Fundamentals of the Slide Library." *ERIC* ED 140 858:1–37, (June 1977).

Haney, John B., and Ullmer, Eldon J. *Educational Communications and Technology: An Introduction,* third edition. Dubuque, Iowa: William C. Brown Co., 1980.

Irvine, Betty J. "Slide Classification: A Historical Survey." *College and Research Libraries* 32(January 1971):23–30.

Irvine, Betty J., and Fry, Eileen P. *Slide Libraries: A Guide for Academic Institutions, Museums and Special Collections,* second edition Littleton, Colorado: Libraries Unlimited, 1979.

Selection Aids

De Laurier, Nancy, ed. *Slide Buyer's Guide,* second edition Kansas City, Missouri: University of Missouri, Kansas City, 1974.

Educator's Guide to Free Filmstrips. Randolph, Wisconsin: Educator's Progress Service, 1949–.

Hart, Thomas L., Hunt, Mary Alice, and Woolls, Blanche. *Multimedia Indexes, Lists, and Review Sources: A Bibliographic Guide.* Books in Library and Information Sciences, vol. 13. New York: M. Dekker, 1975–.

Library of Congress Catalogs: Films and Other Materials for Projection. Washington, D.C.: 1948–.

NICEM Index to Educational Slides, fourth edition Los Angeles: University of Southern California, 1980.

NICEM Index to 35mm Educational Filmstrips, (3 vols.) seventh edition Los Angeles: University of Southern California, 1980.

Rufsvold, Margaret I. *Guides To Educational Media,* fourth edition Chicago: American Library Association, 1977.

8

Audio Recordings

Overview

All too often when thinking of audio recordings, the librarian primarily has music in mind. No doubt, the most appropriate medium for music is the audio recording, but there are many types of information besides music that can be expressed through this medium. Lectures, debates, speeches, musings of famous people, poetry readings, booktalks, and interviews are quite appropriate to the audio medium. These types of recordings can be most enjoyable to listen to, as well as extremely informative. The individual recorded can be a famous person delivering his or her own message, or a person with a professionally trained speaking voice. On an audio recording, the message can be delivered with a style, emphasis, intonation, and character that are virtually impossible to achieve in print and that would not be embellished or enhanced by producing it as a motion picture film or video tape recording, which would also be more expensive. Old radio programs are presently experiencing a renaissance and are even popular with people from the "television generation," who never really listened to radio or audio recordings for anything other than music.

The task of the librarian is to select audio recordings that are best suited to the medium and are the kind that the patron either needs, wants, or appreciates. With the new technology available, the quality of the audio recording is continually improving, while at the same time, audio equipment is becoming less expensive and easier to operate.

Audio recordings need no longer be considered as being for music only or as supplementary to the print collection. Rather, they should be seen as appropriate channels of information acquisition and as vital to the library collection. Also, the library patron needs to be informed of the advantages of using this valuable medium.

Advantages of Audio Discs

The audio recording was one of the first nonprint media to be incorporated into the library's repertoire of information services. Undoubtedly, the growth of the audio recording industry has been paralleled by a similar growth in library record collections. Libraries have been quick to respond to new developments in audio recording technology. It is quite common to visit all types of libraries and see vast arrays of audio software and hardware. Often, entire rooms are allocated to audio listening stations where patrons can listen to disc or tape recordings, either independently or in groups.

The reason for the popularity of audio recordings is quite obvious. There is a whole body of information that can best be appreciated or acquired only in an audio form. The information most characteristically preserved by audio recording is music. Although there are films and videotapes on music, the patron will ultimately request an audio recording because it is such a convenient medium, and, even more importantly, the fidelity of the reproduction is invariably far superior.

Perhaps the predominant audio form is the disc recording. Older collections may still contain 78-rpm recordings, which are no longer produced. The sound quality of 78-rpm records can be considered adequate at best. The newer and more prevalent $33\frac{1}{3}$- and 45-rpm disc records use a much smaller record groove (0.001 inches [0.025 mm] for $33\frac{1}{3}$- and 45-rpm records versus 0.003 inches [0.076 mm] for 78-rpm records) and reproduce sound of much higher fidelity. A further advantage of $33\frac{1}{3}$- and 45-rpm disc records is their availability in monaural (one-track), stereophonic (two-track) or quadraphonic (four-track) sound, all of which can reproduce a sound that closely simulates the original live performance.

When selecting disc recordings, it is essential to make sure that they are compatible with the equipment on which they will be used. It makes little sense to acquire stereophonic recordings if the equipment is only capable of playing monaural recordings. Most libraries, because they have maintained pace with technological developments in audio recordings, will in all probability have a variety of equipment capable of handling all available recording formats. At present, the 33⅓-rpm stereo disc recording (10 or 12 inches [25.4 or 30.5 cm] in diameter) is the most popular with record libraries. It is a longplaying record and often contains a musical composition of lasting value. The smaller 45-rpm disc recording (7 inches [17.8 cm] in diameter) plays only for approximately 3–5 minutes and usually contains popular music of a more temporary value.

Although most people think of disc recording only in terms of musical compositions, there is a wide range of spoken records available as well. The librarian should become familiar with the audio selection aids cited at the end of this chapter, which list a wealth of available audio recordings. Primarily, when selecting a spoken (i.e., nonmusical) recording, it is essential to consider the performing artist. A recording of Robert Frost actually reading his poems is a treasure that will grow in value over the years. Hearing two professional performers engage in the Lincoln–Douglas debates engenders a feeling in the listener of actually being there and reliving a historical event. Both of these examples are situations where the audio channel is really the one that was originally intended for communicating the message. The audio recording gives the message the full impact and delivery it rightfully deserves. In the first example, the actual poet is orally reading his own works in the way he intended them to be read. In the second example, professional performers give the debate a richness and quality that make it more meaningful.

A disadvantage of audio disc recordings is their susceptibility to scratching and surface damage. Although not fragile, they can nevertheless be damaged by worn-out recording styluses; and, even worse, easily scratched by abusive handling. Because many patrons have their own record players, disc recordings can be taken out of the library and used on the patrons' personal equipment; but patrons should be encouraged to use disc recordings under the best conditions possible (i.e., with a good stylus and by avoiding scratching, handling the record by its edge, and keeping it as clean and dust free as possible).

Audio disc recordings contain information in a convenient format that is readily accessible to patrons because the equipment needed to use them is so readily available. When compared to audiovisual forms (motion picture, videotape), they are much less expensive and have a wider range of selections. Because of the availability of such a wide range of recordings, the librarian can build a narrow, specific collection (e.g., major emphasis on classical music) or one that encompasses a wide range of audio forms (e.g., various types of music, famous speeches by the original presenter, reenactments of famous events, discussions of a plethora of topics). Audio recordings have their own unique characteristics and can be the best means of acquiring information that is intended to be heard. The disc recording amply satisfies these requirements.

Differences in Disc Recording Formats

The piece of audiovisual equipment that most people are familiar with is the record player. At present, libraries lend more disc records than all other nonprint media combined. Still, there are some additional fine points worth knowing about disc recordings that will help to preserve their physical quality.

Disc recordings are available in three playing speeds, $33\frac{1}{3}$, 45, and 78 rpm (revolutions per minute). A speed of $16\frac{2}{3}$ rpm, called a transcription, is also available, but these records are not generally found in libraries. The 78-rpm recording is no longer being commercially produced, but many libraries still have extensive collections. Today, $33\frac{1}{3}$ and 45 rpm are the only speeds of disc recordings acquired by libraries.

Figure 8.1 charts the differences among records made at the three different speeds. Most of the data on the chart are just informational, but the data on the stylus (phonograph needle) are of particular importance. You will note that the stylus used to play a 78-rpm record is 0.003 inches (0.076 mm) in diameter to fit a 0.003 inch record groove, whereas the stylus used to play a $33\frac{1}{3}$- or 45-rpm record is 0.001 inches (0.025 mm) in diameter to fit a 0.001-inch record groove. This means that when playing a disc recording, the proper size needle must be used; practically all record players are equipped with both 0.001-inch and 0.003-inch styluses. In many cases, this can be unfortunate, because some people never have occasion to play 78-rpm records, and when their 0.001-inch styluses wear out, they use the 0.003-inch styluses. This is false economy! The $33\frac{1}{3}$- and 45-rpm records will play, but the stylus is three times thicker than the groove, and it tends to gouge the groove. After a few playings, a record can be ruined—it would have been far less expensive to buy a new stylus for the $33\frac{1}{3}$- and 45-rpm records.

The following practical points are also worthy of consideration:

1. It is not recommended that stereophonic records be played on a monaural record player, even though some of the newer monaural record players claim that no ill effect will result.

2. The record grooves should not be touched with fingers.

3. If a record needs cleaning, the record grooves should be gently wiped with a soft cloth that has been dipped in cool water and wrung dry. (Record stores sell special cloths and brushes for this purpose).

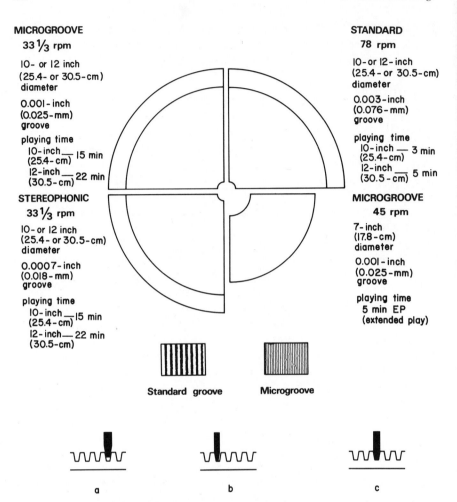

MICROGROOVE

33 1/3 rpm

10- or 12 inch
(25.4- or 30.5-cm)
diameter

0.001- inch
(0.025-mm)
groove

playing time
10-inch — 15 min
(25.4- cm)
12-inch — 22 min
(30.5- cm)

STEREOPHONIC

33 1/3 rpm

10- or 12 inch
(25.4- or 30.5-cm)
diameter

0.0007- inch
(0.018- mm)
groove

playing time
10-inch — 15 min
(25.4- cm)
12-inch — 22 min
(30.5-cm)

STANDARD

78 rpm

10- or 12-inch
(25.4- or 30.5-cm)
diameter

0.003-inch
(0.076-mm)
groove

playing time
10-inch — 3 min
(25.4-cm)
12-inch — 5 min
(30.5- cm)

MICROGROOVE

45 rpm

7- inch
(17.8-cm)
diameter

0.001- inch
(0.025-mm)
groove

playing time
5 min EP
(extended play)

Standard groove   Microgroove

a   b   c

Figure 8.1 Disc recording formats: microgroove 33⅓ rpm, standard 78 rpm (no longer produced), stereophonic 33⅓ rpm, and microgroove 45 rpm. As can be seen from the stylus-groove illustrations (a–c), if the stylus is not the same size as the record groove, damage to both the stylus and the record will result. In a, the stylus is too large, and in b, it is too small; in c, however, the stylus is the proper size.

4.   A stylus should never be allowed to sweep across the face of a record.

5.   The tone arm or stylus should never be pushed down into a record groove.

6.   The stylus should be replaced when its recommended playing life time has expired, regardless of how good records sound when played.

7. Records should be stored on edge, in dust jackets, and away from sunlight or direct heat.

Audiotapes

Another audio information form is the magnetic audiotape. It has the same capability of storing and playing back as the disc recording, but it has several unique advantages. Listening to an audiotape does not require the use of a stylus; hence, there is no physical wearing of the tape. Audiotape can store a far greater amount of information in considerably less space. Because of this compactness, the equipment needed to listen to an audiotape can be much smaller than an audio disc record player, and many tape recorders are portable, battery-operated models.

Although the range of titles available on audiotape is not as large as that available on audio disc recordings, it is still quite extensive and growing daily. Musical recordings are still more prevalent on audio discs than audio tapes, but the opposite is true for nonmusical recordings. Whereas a $33\frac{1}{3}$-rpm audio disc can play for approximately 22 minutes, an audiotape can play without interruption for 1 or more hours, depending on the length of the tape and the speed at which it is played. When selecting audio tape, concern must be given to the formats available: open reel, cassette, and cartridge. The open reel was the first format available, but it is gradually being replaced by the cassette and cartridge, which eliminate the need for physical handling of the tape, and, being automatic, do not have to be manually threaded onto a tape deck. Like audio discs, audiotapes are available in various playing speeds and recording formats (monaural, stereophonic, and quadraphonic) as well as various tracking configurations. The librarian selecting audio tapes needs to pay particular attention to these factors in order to insure that the audio tape selected is compatible with the equipment used in the library or by the patron at home. A certain amount of knowledge about audio tape characteristics is also beneficial.

Differences in Audiotape Formats

Tapes are made of plastic and coated with a layer of iron oxide or chromium oxide. The plastic is either an acetate or a polyester. Some people prefer acetate tape because it does not stretch, which causes sound distortion; others prefer polyester tape because acetate tape breaks too easily, and the tensile strength of polyester tape makes it very difficult to break. The likelihood that the tape will stretch is minimal, because a tape recorder usually does not have enough power to stretch a tape seriously, even when it is malfunctioning. In addition, polyester tape can be made thinner than acetate tape, which means a reel can hold more. The standard thicknesses of tapes are 1.5 mil, 1 mil, and 0.5 mil (1 mil = one thousandth of an inch [.025 mm]), 1.5-mil tape usually being acetate, and 1- and 0.5-mil tape being polyester. A 7-inch (17.8-cm) reel will hold 1200 feet (365.8 m) of 1.5-mil tape, 1800 feet (548.6 m) of 1-mil tape, and 2400 feet (731.5 m) of .5-mil tape. (Bear in mind that the thinner the tape, the more easily it will stretch).

Tape reels are available in the following popular sizes: 3, 4, 5, and 7 inches (7.62, 10.16, 12.7, and 17.8 cm) in diameter; each subsequent size is capable of holding twice as much tape (i.e., a 3-inch [7.62-cm] reel will hold 150 feet [45.7 m] of 1.5-mil tape, a 4-inch [10.16-cm] reel 300 feet [91.4 m], a 5-inch [12.7-cm] reel 600 feet [182.9 m] and a 7-inch [17.8-cm] reel 1200 feet [365.8 m]). All reels accommodate a tape that is $\frac{1}{4}$ inch (0.63 cm) wide. Playing times these sizes are listed in Table 8.1.

Cassettes are of two basic types: reel-to-reel cassettes and loop cassettes (usually called cartridges). Both cassettes and cartridges are designed to eliminate the need for threading. They are simply inserted into the tape recorder, and are ready to be played. The cassette tape is approximately $\frac{5}{32}$ inch (0.39 cm) wide, whereas the cartridge tape is $\frac{1}{4}$ inch (0.63 cm) wide. The cassette is reel to reel in design, which permits tape to be advanced or rewound at high speed, whereas the cartridge, being a loop, operates only in one direction and at one speed. Cartridge tapes generally travel at a speed of $3\frac{3}{4}$ inches per second (ips) (9.52 cm/sec) whereas cassette speed has been standardized to $1\frac{7}{8}$ ips (4.76 cm/sec).

Cassettes are labeled with a capital letter C followed by a number (e.g., C15, C30, C45, C60, C90, C120). This indicates total playing time (i.e., a C90 cassette will hold a maximum of 90 minutes of playing time).

Table 8.1 Playing Times of Audio Tapes (Single Track)

Reel diameter (inch/cm)	Tape length (feet/m)	Tape speed		
		$1\frac{7}{8}$ ips (4.76 cm/sec)	$3\frac{3}{4}$ ips (9.52 cm/sec)	$7\frac{1}{2}$ ips (18.55 cm/sec)
3/7.62	150/45.7	15 min	$7\frac{1}{2}$ min	$3\frac{3}{4}$ min
4/10.16	300/91.4	30 min	15 min	$7\frac{1}{2}$ min
5/12.70	600/182.9	1 hr	30 min	15 min
7/17.80	1200/365.8	2 hr	1 hr	30 min

Even though cassettes vary in playing time, they are all housed in the same size cassette. This is achieved by using thinner tape on the longer playing cassettes. As a note of caution, it is generally wise not to use a C90 or C120 cassette unless it is absolutely necessary because the thinner tape has a greater tendency to jam in the cassette; and once this occurs, it is difficult, if not impossible, to rectify.

All the preceding variables are important when selecting or producing tapes. The librarian must decide what length of tape, what size reel or cassette (and if cassette, which type), and what thickness of tape to purchase. It must be borne in mind that the tape chosen must be compatible with the equipment on which it will be used.

Electromechanical Characteristics
of Tape Recorders

The types of tape recorders discussed in this section are those available to the general public. Although there may be a tape recorder with features other than those described here, this would be an exception rather than the rule.

Reel-to-reel tape recorders operate placing the tape on the left spindle, threading it through the record and playback mechanism, and winding it onto a take-up reel, both reels rotating in a counterclockwise direction. As the tape is played, it first passes an erase head, then a record and playback head. When the tape is played for listening, the erase head is inactive. When information is being recorded on a tape, the erase head is activated and erases any existing information from the tape; then, when the tape passes the record head, new information is put on to the tape. In this way, a tape can be used time and time again. When information is no longer needed, it can be erased and new information recorded.

Tape recorders vary in their tracking abilities. (See Figure 8.2.) A full-track tape recorder records and plays back information on the full width of the tape; a half-track tape recorder uses only one-half the width of the tape. Then, when the tape is completely played through and wound on the take-up reel, the reel is flipped over and placed on the feed spindle. The tape is then threaded through the recorder and the other half is recorded on or listened to. If a tape recorded on a full-track tape recorder will play for 1 hour, a similar tape recorded on a half-track recorder will play for 2 hours. There is also a quarter-track tape recorder with which, by manipulating a switch, information can be recorded on four separate tracks.

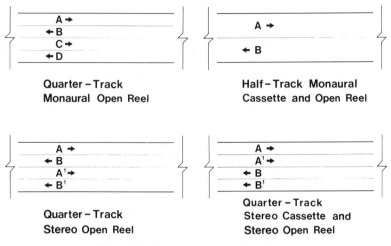

Figure 8.2   Tape recorder track patterns.

It is important to know tracking when purchasing commercially produced tapes. The format (i.e., tracking) with which the tape was recorded must be identical to that of the machine on which it is played. For example, if a full-track recording is played on a half-track machine, it will sound shallow and the fidelity will be poor because the half-track recorder is picking up information from only one half the width of the tape. Conversely, if a half-track recording is played on a full-track recorder, you will hear both tracks simultaneously, one played forward and the other backward, which results in a garbled sound. It must be borne in mind that the variable is not in the tape, but in the machine: the tape is the same; it is the machine that makes the difference.

Another variable in equipment is whether it is monaural or stereophonic. During recording, a monaural tape records information using one microphone; a stereo tape requires two microphones. This means that a stereo tape recorder records information on two tracks at the same time, one track for each microphone. (See Figure 8.2.) If it was recorded using two microphones, a stereo tape must be played back on a stereo tape recorder with two speakers, one for each track. A stereophonic tape can be played on a monaural tape recorder, but the separation of sound that is uniquely stereo is lost.

Still another variable is playing speed. The popular speeds are $1\frac{7}{8}$, $3\frac{3}{4}$, and $7\frac{1}{2}$ ips (4.76, 9.52, and 18.55 cm). A tape must be played at the speed at which it was recorded. If you purchase a tape recorded at $1\frac{7}{8}$ ips and your equipment plays at $3\frac{3}{4}$ ips, the tape will be played at twice the speed at which it was recorded, and the voices will sound like a high-pitched, fast-talking Donald Duck. Conversely, $3\frac{3}{4}$-ips tape played at $1\frac{7}{8}$ ips will sound base, extremely slow, and slurred.

Cassette recorders are usually available in either half-track monaural or quarter-track stereo format. Both monaural and stereo cassette recorders will record on one half the width of the tape; the cassette can then be flipped over and recorded on the other half of the tape. A C60 cassette records 30 minutes on one half-track in monaural or on two quarter-tracks in stereo; the cassette can then be flipped over and record an additional 30 minutes of monaural or stereo information for a total of 60 minutes.

Cartridge recorders are mostly of the 8-track stereo type. Remember that stereo requires two tracks to record information, so in fact an 8-track stereo has four channels of information, and the tape (being a continuous loop) will automatically advance to the succeeding three channels when the tape has played through the entire loop. The machine is also equipped with a channel selector allowing manual change to any of the four channels.

Selecting and Evaluating a Tape Recorder

"You only get what you pay for." If ever this adage were true, it is true of purchasing a tape recorder. Therefore, when selecting and evaluating a tape recorder, the two main considerations are cost and how it is to be used.

If the recorder is to be used by an individual to listen to speaking voices, a 3-watt amplifier will be more than adequate. On the other hand, if the recorder is to be used in a large room, an amplifier in excess of 25 watts and at least a 10-inch speaker are necessary. Again, the best criterion in selecting a tape recorder is actually to try it out under the conditions under which it will be used in order to make sure it has adequate power and tone quality.

A present trend in selecting tape recorders favors cassette units. They tend to be more compact, they are definitely easier to operate, and commercially prepared tapes are becoming more and more available in the cassette format.

If portability is a concern, you may want to consider a battery-operated tape recorder. If this is the case, it would be best to select a unit that also operates on AC or DC electrical current (i.e., can be either plugged into an electrical wall receptacle or operated by batteries. The transformer that allows the unit to use AC should be built into the unit;

when designed as a separate unit, it is just one more thing to misplace. As a note of caution, if a battery-driven unit is not going to be used for long periods of time, it is strongly recommended that the batteries be removed; even the best batteries are subject to corrosion, which can ruin the electrical terminals of a tape recorder.

If the tape recorder is to be used for listening to music it will be necessary to have a stereo tape recorder in order to realize the full potential of the tape because most musical recordings are produced in stereo. On the other hand, if the library's tapes are primarily recordings of speaking voices, a monaural tape recorder is more than adequate. Besides deciding whether the unit is to be monaural or stereo, a decision must also be made about tracking when selecting a reel-to-reel tape recorder. Half-track monaural and quarter-track stereo units are the most prevalent, but when deciding whether to acquire a full-track, half-track, or quarter-track unit, it is also important to investigate the software catalogs of the producers with whom the library does business to see what formats they provide.

Many institutions acquire tape recorders when, in reality, they never actually record any tapes, and use their equipment solely to listen to tapes. In such cases, only a playback unit is needed. When a tape recorder is purchased, it includes a microphone (two microphones if it is a stereo unit), as well as the erase–record electronics, all of which obviously increase the cost of the unit. If they are never to be used, a playback-only unit should be purchased at a lower cost. An added advantage is that with a playback-only unit—because it does not have erase–record capability—it is impossible for a user to accidentally erase information from a tape.

Although it has nothing to do with selecting a tape recorder per se, listening to many tape recorders in designated areas of a library requires the use of a headset. If this is the case, headsets must also be evaluated, for they become part of the unit. Headsets should be light, durable, adjustable, comfortable, and above all, capable of reproducing quality sound. An added consideration is hygiene; it is not recommended that headsets that are inserted into the ears be used unless provisions are made for sterilizing them after each use. Ideally, headsets with a large plastic-covered cushion pads are best; they do not have to be inserted into the ear, are easy to keep clean, are comfortable, and tend to block out room noise that could disturb a person listening to a tape.

All these criteria are basic. Obviously, there are other criteria that are unique to particular institutions. For example, if an institution has many patrons listening to the same tape at the same time, it may need a single playback unit with many headsets; if a patron needs to have information but cannot conveniently get to the library, a dial access system is needed; a patron learning a foreign language may need a tape recorder with which he or she can listen to a native voice, record his or her own voice, and then play the tape back to hear both the native voice and his or her own for comparison. In any case, the state of the art of tape recorders is such that with judicious evaluation, the librarian can select the right kinds of tape recorders for the particular ways in which they will be used.

Making a Tape Recording

Audiotape recorders allow libraries to produce their own audiotapes. There is always the possibility that a particular library might need something in audio form that is not commercially available. If this situation arises, a tape can be produced locally.

Attempts to record musical compositions will result in audiotapes that are, at best, only adequate in quality. Properly recording music requires a proper acoustical environment and a professional audio engineer. However, if the information recorded consists of spoken voices, audiotapes of respectable quality can be produced.

One of the more frequent situations in which libraries produce audiotape recordings is the making of talking books for patrons with visual handicaps or other reading problems.

In making a talking book or any audiotape, a professionally trained voice will lend polish to the recording, but it is not essential. A person with a pleasant-sounding voice, who can read in a natural way with natural expression is all the talent that is needed. A word-by-word reader or a voice with artificial expression is deadly. The voice does not have to be perfect, however; an occasional stammer or speech mistake is human; and, if it does not detract from the material being read, it could perhaps be beneficial, for it tells the listener that the speaker is human. Of course, speech impediments or unusual accents should be avoided.

While making the tape, the performers should be made as comfortable as possible in pleasant surroundings, in a room that is not acoustically dead (i.e., one in which the voice loses its vibrance and resonance), but that does not produce echoes or unwanted overtones.

The microphone should be placed approximately 15.2–20.3 cm (6–8 inches) away from the speaker's mouth, but not in a direct line with the speaker's breathing. This placement prevents the sound of breathing from being recorded, but puts the microphone close enough to the sound source to keep it from picking up ambient or extraneous sound (e.g., the hum of an air conditioner). On the tape recorder, there is some type of level device (a flashing light or a gauge) that indicates the best volume range for recording. If the voice stays within this range, the recording should be technically perfect, within the limits of the tape recorder. If a mistake or an undesirable sound is recorded, all that has to be done is to stop the tape recorder, rewind it, and re-record the correct information. It is advisable, when re-recording, to commence after a logical speech pause, like the end of a sentence or paragraph. A long recording that cannot be completed comfortably in one session should be terminated in a logical place, preferably the end of a chapter or at the end of the reel of tape. It is amazing how a voice can subtly change from one day to the next, and the difference can be distinguished when listening to a tape.

Making a copy of an existing tape is an occasion when the library would produce an audiotape locally. The best way to duplicate a tape is to use a patch (connecting) cord directly from the tape recorder, which will play the original tape to the recorder that will duplicate it. A patch cord (usually provided with the recorder when it is purchased) is an insulated wire connecting the output of the master recorder directly to the input of the duplicating recorder. When a tape is duplicated by this method, there is no concern for room noise because there is no microphone to pick up extraneous sounds. A patch cord also ensures that the duplicate tape will sound as close to the original as is electronically possible.

A consideration of which the librarian must be well aware when producing audiotapes is copyright infringement. If the information on the tape is created by the library, copyright violation is not a concern. However, recording a book on audiotape could be in violation of copyright, and the librarian should check the book to determine whether it contains any statement that expressly forbids duplication. More often than not, there is no objection to transferring information to another medium (i.e., print to audio). On the other hand, when making copies of existing audio recordings, the librarian must ascertain whether the material is copyrighted. If it is copyrighted, permission must be obtained from the owner before duplicating the tape. Failure to obtain permission would be a flagrant violation of copyright.

Speech Compression

Talking books provide a valuable service to patrons with reading handicaps, but listening to a talking book introduces the problem of comprehension speed. Normal speech is delivered at about 120 words per minute, and a maximum speed of about 170 words per minute is possible. Speaking faster results in poor enunciation and pronunciation. However, psychologists have reason to believe that the brain can comfortably think at 400 words per minute. Actually, the human voice, because of its slow speed, is an inefficient way to communicate.

A speech compressor is an electronic device that literally compresses information on an audiotape. Using such a device, one can play an audiotape much faster than it was recorded. It is no longer necessary for a person to plod along, listening to a tape at normal speaking speed, when by adjusting the speed, the reader can listen as fast as he or she can assimilate. This is a boon for people with visual handicaps who must use their ears to "read." The compression of sound is achieved without any loss of tonal quality. Although it is not advised that audio compression be used to listen to music or poetry, in which timing is essential for meaning and appreciation, it is of great help if the listener only wants to acquire information as efficiently as possible.

As an added option, some electronic speech compressors are also capable of expanding speech. This is especially useful with mentally handicapped people who have difficulty in comprehending a voice at normal speaking speed.

Selecting Professionally Prepared Audio Recordings

Before selecting any audio recording, the librarian must first formulate a policy about the type of audio service the library will provide. Decisions must be made regarding how and where recordings will be used, what types of collections will be acquired, and what services will be provided.

Deciding how and where recordings are to be used will determine what equipment is needed. If the bulk of the collection is to be used by patrons at home, disc recordings are the best selection, because more homes have record players than have tape recorders. However, the library may have a large collection of speeches available primarily on audiotape cassettes, in which case an inexpensive lightweight playback unit can be checked out by the patrons. Of course, any recording selected must be compatible with the equipment in your library.

Type of collection is predicated on the needs of the library's patrons. Special collections serve unique needs. If the special collection is educational, there are further areas of specialization within this category, each of which must serve unique needs. A collection of foreign-language recordings, for example, should use native speakers; make provision for the learner to make overt responses; and be organized so that the skill level progresses with each successive tape, therein permitting the user to select a recording comparable to his or her entry level skill and to acquire more skill with the completion of each succeeding recording. A history collection, should whenever possible, record the actual speaker or event and should provide a perspective that is unattainable from the printed word.

Music collections, which are the most popular audio holdings in most librarys can, and perhaps should, be educational as well as entertaining. The librarian selecting musical recordings, should be especially aware not only of the kind of music to acquire, but also of the best performing artists. It is even feasible to have the same music recorded by several different artists.

Ideally, in considering types of collections, it is best to make selections that serve a multiplicity of needs. The following questions are worthy of consideration:

1. What range of patrons will the collection serve (e.g., age, interest, ability, needs)?

2. What percentage of the collection should be devoted to each topic?

3. Does the collection have cross-applicability (i.e., is it educational, entertaining, multidisciplinary)?

4. Is it the type of collection that has high audio primacy (i.e., is an audio recording the best format in which to have this information)?

5. Are supplementary materials essential to the collection (e.g., musical scores, guidebooks, printed scripts)?

6. Should the collection, or particular recordings, be monaural, stereophonic, or quadraphonic?

Selecting audio recordings is an important library function. Too often, it is slighted because many people feel that in our current television era, people are no longer interested in audio-only information. It must be kept in mind, as indicated earlier in this chapter, that there have been and continue to be tremendous technological strides in the development of the audio-only media form. Commensurate with them is the growth in material available. There are recording companies whose sole purpose is to commit great books, plays, poems, and other printed works to an audio form. The quality of many of these recordings is truly remarkable. Through the use of professionally trained talent, the audio recording brings a living quality to the printed word. There is a slight problem, however, in acquiring materials from recording companies in that they are usually reluctant to provide material for preview. The reasons for this are quite obvious: The unethical librarian can easily copy the material; even more important, when previewed material is returned, there is no way for the record company to know its physical condition, and it may not be reusable. The librarian dealing with a recording company for the first time should request a "sampler" audio recording indicative of the company's product. Many companies produce samplers containing representative excerpts of their audio line, for promotional purposes and welcome requests for them. In this way, the librarian can assess a particular recording company's product and have some assurance that any recordings selected will be of comparable quality. If neither preview recordings nor samplers are available, the librarian will have to gamble on the company's reputation. But because audio recordings are not expensive when compared to other media forms, such a gamble will not be too risky, and the majority of companies have respectable products.

Still another consideration in selecting recordings is their relation to the services provided by the library. Recordings for handicapped people should attend to their handicaps. A recording for the blind should be made at a speed (assuming you do not have a speech compressor) that is efficient for a blind person; on the other hand, elderly people may need information recorded at a slower speed. If the library has story hours, recordings should be selected that require a minimum of introductory material but offer a great deal of opportunity for follow-up discussion. Although this is not part of the actual recording, if a library provides promotional programs as a service, a recording is more appealing when it is packaged in an attractive dust jacket containing well-written information.

Audio Recording Selection Aids

Audio recording selection cannot be accomplished by one universal selection aid. Therefore, a variety of selection aids should be available to the librarian selecting audio recordings.

Selection aids should provide basic bibliographic information (title, artist, producer, playing time, format, date, cost, annotation). In addition, selection aids that provide the following information should be available:

1. current listings and recent releases
2. listings of producers and distributors as well as the types of recordings they sell

3. listings of recordings by discrete categories (e.g., American opera, political speeches, shorthand dictation)
4. recordings made in foreign countries
5. recording evaluations and reviews
6. trends in library collections and programs
7. listings by title that include all the renditions of a particular recording by various artists and groups
8. listings by artists and groups, specifying the recordings they have produced
9. new technology that may affect the format of the recording selected
10. sources of free or inexpensive recordings
11. library's proprietary rights on recordings in its collection (i.e., duplicating, cost of multiple or replacement copies, broadcast, editing)

Obviously, several different kinds of selection aids are required to provide the essential information needed when acquiring recordings. Along with standard indexes, the librarian should subscribe to periodicals and be on the mailing lists of recording companies. Invariably, it is in the recording company catalogs (distributors' catalogs) that the most detailed information will be found. Obviously, these catalogs promote only one company's collection, but this should not be a problem. As indicated earlier, practically all recording companies have high standards of quality. The differences to look for among recording companies are the particular genre of recordings they distribute and the writers and performing artists they have under contract. By having a variety of producers' catalogs and cataloging them with regard to types of recordings, the librarian will have access to perhaps more audio recording selection aid material than could possibly be needed. In fact, because audio recordings are relatively inexpensive, and the general public spends hundreds of millions of dollars purchasing them; it is not uncommon for libraries to make their collections of audio recording selection aids available to patrons for perusal, and, in so doing, provide still another service to their patrons.

Using Audio Recordings

Listening to audio recordings is usually an individual, or, at most, a small-group experience. The impact of the informational message of an audio recording is considerably decreased when used by a group of 10 or more people. It is similar to reading a book. Reading is an individ-ualized experience, which if done in a group, is obviously for the pur-pose of later discussion or reaction to what was read. If the group is larger than 10 people, either not everyone participates in the discussion, or it takes too long for everyone to be able to express their views. Also when participants listen to audio recordings in a group, they must be well motivated toward acquiring the information to which they are listening, or, at least, favorably oriented toward the audio medium.

Usually, in a library, it is best to have a listening or learning center. A learning center is an area where the patron, either individually or in a small group, can comfortably listen to audio recordings. Wherever the listening is to occur, it should be away from library traffic and any disturbing ambient noise. The environment must be conducive to lis-tening with pleasant, nondistracting surroundings. If the recorded in-formation is to be studied intensely, it is advisable to have listening carrels for privacy and note taking. If the information being heard is solely for entertaining or appreciation, then it is perhaps a good idea to have comfortable lounge chairs for relaxed listening.

If a group of patrons is going to be listening to the same recording, then an appropriate size listening room will have to be provided. In some situations, it may be advantageous to have a listening center that employs headsets for group use that can all be plugged into a common junction box. Some libraries use a wireless listening system in which each listener wears a wireless headset and sits in an area where a wire loop is invisibly installed. Sitting within the range of the loop, the listener can receive the information through the headset. More elaborate wireless systems allow the listener to select one of several channels of information that are transmitted via the same loop.

If recordings are stereo, the listener must be provided with a stero headset (which, incidentally, is the best way to get true separation of stereo information). If the listener will be listening to stereo through regular speakers (i.e., without a headset), the placement of speakers becomes critical. The rule of the stereo "T" must be considered. Stereo speakers in a listening room should be placed far enough apart that the listener is no farther than two speaker-widths from them; for example, if the stereo speakers are 1.5 m (5 feet) apart, the listener should be no farther than 3 m (10 feet) away from them (Figure 8.3).

A rather unique phenomenon that is not as prevalent with other in-formation media forms seems to occur frequently when a person listens to an audio recording. It appears that with audio recordings, the interest span cannot be continuously maintained for more than about 30 min-utes. After listening for 30 minutes, the user feels compelled to take a

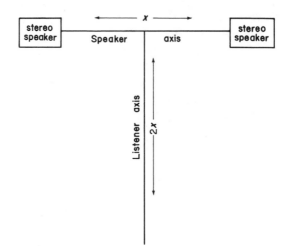

Figure 8.3   Stereo "T"—Placement of stereo speakers and location of listeners for obtaining the best stereo effect (x = distance.)

rest, even if only for a few moments. Although there are cassette tapes that can play continuously for 60 minutes, and reel-to-reel tapes that contain several hours of continuous information, the user has to make a sustained effort to maintain attention after 30 minutes. A possible explanation for this rather limited attention span could be hypothesized as being attributed to the information modality. As indicated earlier in this chapter, the brain can function much faster than the speaking voice can deliver information. This lag in delivery can cause the listener's attention to drift away from what is being said unless he or she makes a concerted effort to pay attention. Either way, the lag results in fatigue—hence the need for a respite. The librarian should take heed of how the patron behaves while listening to audio recordings, and should respond accordingly by selecting recordings that do not exceed 30 minutes in length. Alternatively, the librarian can encourage the patron to take a break after every 30 minutes of listening. Even more importantly, when locally producing audio recordings (e.g., book reviews, book talks), the librarian should strive to stay within a 30-minute time limit.

The librarian may also want to investigate the feasibility of using speech compression; the listener may be able to listen for longer periods of time if the speed of the information being presented more closely approximates the listener's comprehension speed. Even if the listener does need a break after 30 minutes as hypothesized, the speech compressor still has the distinct advantage of presenting much more information in the same 30-minute time period.

The time attention problem is not nearly as important with disc recordings because the playing time of the amount of information that can be put on one side of a disc is considerably less than 30 minutes. Furthermore, disc recordings mostly contain music, and the time tolerance can be somewhat extended because listening to music does not require the concentrated effort that is needed to listen to a speaking voice. Given this 30-minute rule of thumb for patron utilization of audio recordings, unless there is a particular need for continuous music, the library would not have to purchase record players with automatic change features; for as the patron manually changes the record or tape, he or she receives the mental break he or she naturally needs to listen efficiently.

Although the average person in our modern society spends as much as 45% of his or her waking day listening to information from the world about them, they still may need some basic training on how to listen well. This does not imply that the librarian must be a listening instructor, but rather that he or she should be consciously aware of some good basic listening habits and should pass these on to patrons who use the record collection. This might result in the audio-recording collection receiving more and better use. One way to expose patrons to good listening habits is to prepare and conspicuously display some simple charts and handouts.

The following is information that could be of value to the librarian and would also be beneficial to the user of the record collection. We respond to sound on three levels: (*a*) *hearing*, which is nothing more than sound waves striking the ear; (*b*) *listening*, which occurs when a sound that is heard is recognized and identified; and (*c*) *auding*, which is the mental indexing of a sound, that is, listening to a sound and responding to it mentally, (auding also subsumes communication and the acquisition of knowledge). For an audio recording to be meaningful, the listener must function on the third, or auding, level. This tends to further substantiate the facts that listening requires conscious effort and that concentrated listening can be tiring. Further compounding the problem is the fact that the listener is fortunate to remember 50% of what is heard. Research studies indicate that the listener forgets one third to one half of what was heard within eight hours, and, after two months, will remember only 25% of what was heard.[1] However, a lot of

---

[1] E. J. J. Kramer and Thomas R. Lewis, "Comparison of Visual and Nonvisual Listening," *Journal of Communication* 1(November 1951):16.

what is heard is obviously not worth retaining. The odds on achieving a meaningful audio-recording listening experience are greatly improved by the listener considering the following rules of good listening while listening to an audio recording:

1. Gather as much information as possible about the recording before listening to it.
2. Listen for the main and supporting points of what is being said. (Anecdotal information supports or illustrates points, but usually does not contain new information.)
3. Ignore distracting features of the presentation (e.g., accents or emotions of the speaker).
4. Strive to get the ideas being communicated, rather than the facts. (Understanding the ideas will make the facts more meaningful, as well as easier to remember.)
5. Do not try to memorize.
6. Try to anticipate what the speaker is leading up to, and, if possible, draw some conclusions.
7. Weigh the evidence the speaker uses to support his or her points.
8. Search for a more subtle or implied meaning in what the speaker is saying.
9. Summarize what was said and take time to put it into terms that are meaningful.
10. Periodically stop the recording, (at least after 30 minutes) to assess what has been said.

The librarian should follow these foregoing procedures when reviewing audio recordings for selection, as well as informing the patron of them. Their use will certainly result in a better record collection, and the patron will benefit by making better use of audio recordings.

Selected Bibliography

Burstein, Herman. *Questions and Answers about Audio Tape Recordings.* Blue Ridge Summit, Pennsylvania: Tab Books, 1974.
Cabeceiras, James. *Auto-Tutorial Audio Unit.* San Diego: Technological Applications Projects, 1974.
Crowhurst, Norman H. *ABC's of Tape Recording.* New York: Bobbs-Merrill, 1972.
Foster, Edward J. "How To Judge Record Playing Equipment." *High Fidelity* 27, 4(April 1977):60–63.
Foster, Edward J. "Which Tape Format Is for You?" *High Fidelity* 28, 8:(August 1977):50–51.
Hanna, Edna Frances. First Steps toward a Record Collection. In *Readings in Non-Book Librarianship,* ed. Jean Spealman, pp. 44–65. Metuchen, New Jersey: Scarecrow Press, 1968.

Hellyer, Henry William. *How to Choose and Use the Tape Recorder*. New York: International Publications Service, 1970.

Jorgensen, Finn. *Handbook of Magnetic Recording*. Blue Ridge Summit, Pennsylvania: Tab Books, 1970.

Understanding High Fidelity. Tokyo: Pioneer Electric, 1972.

Selection Aids

American Record Guide, Melville, New York: A.R.G. Publishers, 1934–.

Armitage, Andrew D., and Tudor, Dean. *Annual Index to Popular Music Record Reviews*. Metuchen, New Jersey: Scarecrow Press, 1975–.

Audio. Philadelphia: North American Publishing, 1947–.

Crawdaddy. New York: Crawdaddy Publishing, 1966–.

Directory of Spoken-Voice Audio Cassettes. Los Angeles: Cassette Information Services, 1972–.

Gibson, Gerald D., and Gray, Michael H. *A Bibliography of Discographies. Volume I: Classical Music 1925–1975*. New York: R. R. Bowker, 1977.

High Fidelity/Musical America. New York: Leisure Magazines, 1965–.

Index to Record and Tape Reviews: A Classic Music Buying Guide. San Anselmo, California: Chulainn Press, 1976–.

Library of Congress Catalogs: Music, Books on Music, and Sound Recordings. Washington, D.C.: Library of Congress, 1954–.

Music Index. Detroit: Information Coordinators, 1949–.

NICEM Index to Educational Audio Tapes, 5th ed. Los Angeles: University of Southern California, 1979.

NICEM Index to Educational Records, fifth edition. Los Angeles: University of Southern California, 1979.

Records and Tape Reviews Index. Metuchen, New Jersey: Scarecrow Press, 1971–.

Records In Review. Great Barrington, Massachusetts: Wyeth Press, 1955–.

Rolling Stone. New York: Straight Arrow Publishers, 1967–.

Russcol, Herbert. *Guide to Low Priced Classical Records*. New York: Hart Publishing, 1979.

Schwann Record and Tape Guide. Boston: Schwann Publications, 1949–.

Stereo Review. New York: Ziff-Davis Publishing, 1958–.

Tudor, Dean, and Tudor, Nancy. *Contemporary Popular Music*. Littleton, Colorado: Libraries Unlimited, 1979.

9

Television

Overview

Television as a means of communication is undoubtedly having a greater impact on the library than any other medium. For many people it is the dominant, if not the only, means of receiving entertainment and information about the world around them. As a result, the library has lost a great many potential patrons to the television medium and should therefore seek a means of encouraging these individuals to seek, need, and utilize library services. The librarian should not adopt an antagonistic position toward television, considering it as a foe that has drawn the public away from the library. Rather, the librarian should examine the contributions television makes in providing information services and determine how the library can in turn provide services that either complement those provided by television or that are unique because that they cannot be obtained from television.

Many libraries are realizing the value of television as a communications medium in which they should become involved and are building collections of videotapes to be used in the library or charged out to patrons. Some libraries are in the vanguard of using broadcast television for providing library services. These libraries are using local television stations and cable distribution systems for transmitting their messages to the public. It is quite conceivable that in the coming years, television systems coupled to microcomputers will be the means by which the bulk of the information contained in the library will be disseminated.

Impact of the Television Medium

When one stops to reflect that there are more television sets than bathtubs in the United States, one realizes this does not imply that we are becoming a less clean society but that we spend much more time watching television than we do bathing. In fact, the average American, between the second and sixty-fifth year, spends approximately 3000 entire days (almost 9 years of life) watching television. The growth of television has been phenomenal: In 1946, there were only 6 television stations and 8000 receivers (television sets) in the United States; just 20 years later, in 1966, the number had grown to 699 stations and over 70 million receivers. Presently, over 96% of the total United States population have television in their homes (60 million of these sets are color receivers).

A startling illustration of the impact of television can be found in an examination of the viewing habits of the 6- to 11-year-old age group, which amounts to over 24 million people. This group spends an average of 3 hours a day watching television. Considering that each child is awake about 15 hours a day, this means that television is consuming one fifth of his or her waking time. These data are quite astonishing, especially considering that by the time they reach the age of 14, these children will have seen some 18,000 murders on television, and by the time they reach 17, viewed over 350,000 commercials. The viewing habits of the overall population lean overwhelmingly toward commercial television in preference to educational television, or what should more properly be called the Public Broadcast System (PBS). Regardless of a person's socioeconomic status, after a busy day he or she seeks the entertainment offered by commercial television. A PBS television program is considered an astounding success when it captures 12% of the viewing audience. A program with such a rating would never survive on prime time commercial television. However, Wilbur Schramm *et al.*, in their 1961 study, *Television in the Lives of Our Children,* did find that families with highly educated parents watch television less than families in which the parents have more modest educations, and that families that believe in the middleclass social norm of work and self-betterment watch less television than families that do not subscribe to the middleclass norm.[1] Schramm *et al.* also found that when children with average or above average intelligence reach the 10–13 age range, they have a shift in viewing habits and begin to watch less television and do more reading.

[1] Wilbur R. Schramm, Jack Lyle, and Edwin B. Parker, *Television in the Lives of Our Children,* Stanford, California, Stanford University Press, 1961.

The preceding information is presented to give a brief idea of how television affects the public. The library cannot be considered a sacred tabernacle of information that the public must, or wants, to visit. Rather, the librarian should be aware of the impact of the television medium, as it too is a dispenser of information, and should work with it by providing needed information services not obtainable from television.

Bearing in mind that television is a visual medium, perhaps the librarian should consider having more visual material to assist the television-oriented patron in making the transition from television to print media. The library's film collection should contain films of a genre not available on television. A good film program is an excellent lure to get the patron from the television set to the library. Books that complement television offerings should be considered. The mid-1970s was the era of the detective and policeman on television; books on these topics also tended to be popular. When Alex Haley's "Roots", which traced his ancestry back to Africa in the seventeenth century, appeared on television, libraries suddenly received a plethora of requests from people who were eager to do a search of their genealogies.

Books that can fill a need not met by television should also be considered; the patron may want to escape from television to something more stimulating. But having films and books that complement television, as well as offering material that allows an escape from the medium, will have little impact on an unaware public. The library must advertise. It should have a daily or weekly review presented in the local newspapers, on radio, and yes, even on television, informing the public of what is happening at the library. Maybe a criterion in selecting material should be, "How would it appeal to the television-viewing patron?" The library provides an important function; it is not a sanctuary for people escaping television, rather it can serve the unique, varied, and *individual* needs of a society that is affected by the mass communication medium of television. The library can be human and personal, which is something quite difficult for television genuinely to achieve.

Trends in Library Television Utilization

In a few short years, television has had a pervasive effect on our society; to say it will not be an integral part of a library's program is a ludicrous denial of reality. Rather, the issue is when to incorporate television into the program (in many libraries this has already occurred), to what degree, and what services to provide. This is quite a challenge, and librarians will have to become more knowledgeable about the medium and its scope, limitations, and alternatives.

The library can be both a producer and a distributor of televised information. A library desiring to produce television information is taking a giant step that should be attempted only with considerable consultation with television production experts, and, maybe ultimately, with the addition of television producers and technicians to the staff. Too often, an institution proceeds on the premise that all that is needed to produce television is the necessary equipment, and the end result is usually that thousands of dollars worth of equipment receives little or no use. The library should know why it wants to produce its own televised information, what and how much it wants to produce, and finally, what staff and equipment is needed to achieve the objective. Once the decision has been made to produce television information, each program should have a uniqueness that precludes the far less expensive option of obtaining a comparable program from a commercial source.

When producing television programs, it is necessary to avoid the pitfall of thinking that they require little more than having the proper equipment and simply pointing a television camera at whatever is happening. Television production is both an art and a science. It is a task that can drain an individual mentally and physically, and the net yield is not that considerable in terms of the number of programs produced. As a rule of thumb, it usually takes at least 1 hour of production time to achieve 1 minute of finished product; and this does not include the time involved in scripting, rehearsing, setting up and striking equipment, and editing the final product. These requirements of both skill and time can be considered as being minimal demands on the library's resources, that is if the library intends to be involved in anything that resembles respectable quality. And, indeed, the quality must be there; for the producer must realize that the viewer is an experienced, sophisticated consumer of the medium who watches many hours of expensive network productions and will not be tolerant of the shoddy, amateur efforts of a library that is sincere in producing television but lacks resources and expertise.

The library that produces its own television information can provide a tremendous service to the community, but only if the information it produces is unavailable from any other source and reflects what the community wants or needs. Examples of televised information that the library might produce itself are interviews with authors or interesting community people, book talks and reviews, story hours for children, puppet shows, discussion groups, community events (e.g., social events, community government meetings), dramatic performances, art shows, programs on hobbies and vocational skills, and continuing education. The productions could be televised live or recorded for future use. Again, the librarian must determine the degree to which the library wants to, or can, get involved with local television production.

If a library decides that its role is limited to that of distributor of televised information, it can still provide a tremendous service. It can build a video-recorded collection of significant historical events; serve as a depositry for locally videotaped events and productions; and acquire commercially produced programs. It is predicted that video formats will eventually replace 16-mm films in libraries because videotape is cheaper and does not require a projector to be viewed. As mentioned already, over 96% of the population have television receivers; eventually, these sets will be either replaced or adapted with the necessary electronics to view recorded, nonbroadcast programs. The patron will obtain the video-recorded program from the library and play it back at home through his or her own television set. Although this is currently a projected trend, it is predicted that within 10 or 15 years, there will be millions of home television receivers with this capability. The wise librarian must know the technological trends in television and be ready to provide the type of library service that will be demanded by patrons.

Legal Implications of Making Video Recordings

A library can install television receivers for patron use, but once it records a program for future use, it could become involved in an infringement of copyright. For over a decade, the federal government has been wrestling with the copyright issue, realizing that modern technology can locally and relatively inexpensively copy or reproduce virtually any format of information. However, there is a fair use clause which, though still nebulous, can be interpreted to mean that a commercial television program can be recorded and played back at a future time only once, assuming that the time at which the program was originally broadcast was not convenient for viewing. Schools may record an evening television program to play back once during school hours, the premise being that it was not convenient to schedule a class during the evening broadcast time.

Actually, the 1909 law governing the copying from copyrighted works (e.g., books, periodicals, recordings) left the "fair use" clause to the courts for interpretation, which meant that any librarian copying copyrighted material was risking a lawsuit. Fortunately, the United States Congress, late in 1976, passed the much needed Copyright Revision Law, and the law is now more applicable to the technology of the 1980s that makes copying information such an easy process.

The guidelines of the Copyright Revision Law give a minimum, not a maximum, standard—which means that any type of copying not covered by the new law may still be permitted under the old law's "fair use" clause. It is now legal to copy (*a*) a chapter from a book, (*b*) an article from a periodical or newspaper, (*c*) a short story, short essay, or short poem, whether or not from a collective work, and (*d*) a chart, graph, diagram, drawing, cartoon, or picture from a book, periodical, or newspaper. It is assumed that these criteria can be applied to the television medium as well. Also in the new law is a provision for brevity and spontaneity. The *brevity* stipulation allows the copying of a part of an entire work. With printed material, this means that, depending on the size of the work, up to 10% of it can be duplicated. *Spontaneity* refers to the need for use arising so quickly that it would be unreasonable to expect a reply to a request for permission in time for it to be useful. The intention of the new copyright law is to prevent the copying of information in lieu of purchasing it, for the replacement or production of complete multiple copies, or for the sale of the copies for profit. The new law is a major improvement with regard to what the librarian can legally copy.

However, the issue of copyright remains very tenuous. It would be best for a library to obtain written permission from the producer, if a copied broadcast television program is to receive extensive use.

As regards videotaping of a library's own produced programs, the library should develop an explicit policy with the help of legal counsel. Any performer appearing before the camera, as well as producers, directors, and script writers should be informed of library policy; any necessary clearances should be signed prior to production. It is only fair that everyone involved know their rights and be properly protected.

Because copyright laws are still in flux and generating a great deal of controversy as regards rights to information in any format, it would be extremely wise for the librarian who is duplicating information continually to keep abreast of federal copyright legislation. (For a more definitive explanation of copyright laws and their implications, refer to Chapter 15.)

Video Recording Formats

When a library begins to build a video recording collection, it faces the dilemma of deciding which recording format to acquire. Perhaps there may be a need to select video recordings in more than one format. The library that restricts the use of video recordings to in-library use

only can perhaps settle on one format, but the library that will be circulating video recordings outside the library will have to survey the
library community to determine what kinds of playback equipment are
owned by the patrons.

The main considerations in selecting video recordings for in-library
use are (*a*) availability of commercial offerings in particular formats; (*b*)
complexity of use (if a video recording is to be set up by a staff person,
complexity is no problem, but if the patron must operate the equipment, simplicity is essential); (*c*) whether locally produced video recordings, which currently require open reel videotapes or videocassettes,
will be used; (*d*) quality of sound and visual image; (*e*) cost and durability of both video recording and playback equipment. An additional
consideration for circulating video recordings outside the library would
be the selection of video recording formats that are compatible with the
playback equipment owned by patrons. The trend in the domestic, or
home, market in videotape recorders at present appears to be divided
between the Sony Beta videocassette system and the JVC-VHS (video
home system) videocassette system. Both of these systems employ a
$\frac{1}{2}$-inch (1.27-cm) videocassette, which (unfortunately for the library) are
different in construction and therefore not compatible with each other.
This means that if the library is to loan out videocassettes, it may be
required to have the same information available on both the Beta and
VHS formats. Their popularity with and overwhelming acceptance by
the public have allowed these two formats to all but capture the home
market, which has resulted in a tremendous volume of videocassette
recorder sales. The Beta (Betamax) system developed by Sony is licensed
for sale by Sanyo, Sears, Sony, Toshiba, and Zenith; while the VHS
developed by JVC is licensed to Akai, Curtis Mathes, JVC, Hitachi,
Mitsubishi, MGA, Panasonic, and Sylvania. The marketing of these two
systems by such a range of large companies is perhaps an indication
that these two formats will be the standard for several years to come
and, therefore, perhaps also the standard by which the library should
determine which formats to include in its collection.

The librarian should bear in mind that any decisions made regarding
video recordings should not be final. New technology is continually
being invented, and, in all probability, decisions on video recordings
made today will have to be modified with the advent of new technology; conversely, the library that decides to wait for the final technological development so as to avoid obsolescence will indeed be obsoles-
cent itself in that it does not have a video recording collection. It is
strongly advisable to seek technical assistance regarding the projected
state of the video recording art, and then to make a selection decision

that can serve the patrons' needs for several years, regardless of techno-logical developments. What is needed is a 5-year program for selecting videotapes, after which an update assessment is made of the state of television trends and technology, and another 5-year program insti-tuted. A look at the current state of video recording formats will give a perspective on the magnitude of this problem and provide an idea of what the librarian should be considering for his or her particular library.

Open Reel Videotape

Videotapes are available in ¼-, ½-, 1-, and 2-inch (0.63-, 11.27-, 2.54-, 5.08-cm) widths. (See Figure 9.1.) Two-inch videotape is used for broadcasting, and there is little likelihood that libraries would be in-volved with this size. One-inch videotape is used mostly for studio production. Half-inch videotape is presently the most popular open reel format for localized viewing (*localized viewing* means that the image is viewed on a monitor to which the recording is directly hooked or via closed circuit television [CCTV]). Quarter-inch tape is presently in an early stage of development; as a result, its quality is being stringently

Figure 9.1 Prevalent videotape formats: (front row) ½-inch (1.27-cm) open reel videotape, 1-inch (2.5-cm) open reel videotape, and 2-inch (5.08-cm) open reel videotape; and (back row) ½-inch (1.27-cm) beta format videocassette, ½-inch (1.27-cm) VHS format videocas-sette, ¾-inch (1.90-cm) U-Matic videocassette, Capacitance videodisc, and laser videodisc.

compared with that of ½-inch videotape. If the quality of quarter-inch tape is acceptable, it would be the better buy, because its cost is obviously lower than that of ½-inch videotape and it can contain a comparable amount of information. Presently, most professional studios record on 1- or 2-inch formats and duplicate onto ½- and ¾-inch (1.90-cm) formats for marketing.

The use of open reel videotapes should be considered only if the type of equipment owned by the library is the open reel format. Otherwise, the ½-inch (1.27-cm) videocassette is strongly recommended for the following reasons: it is rapidly becoming the standard of the domestic market; unlike the videocassette, open reel videotape requires manual threading, which, to an inexperienced person, can be a complex task, and if the video tape is improperly threaded, it can be damaged; and furthermore, most television studios that produce video programs for library acquisition are presently using the ½-inch videocassette as their marketing format.

Videocassette

Videocassettes containing ½- and ¾-inch (1.27- and 1.90-cm) videotape are presently realizing tremendous growth (see Figure 9.1). It requires no special skill to operate videocassette playback equipment, which means the patron will have little or no difficulty using it. (See Figure 9.2.) However, the threading mechanism of a videocassette playback unit is extremely complicated, and it is advisable to be quite careful when moving the equipment.

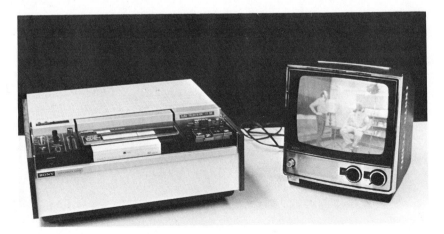

Figure 9.2 Videocassette playback unit.

The ¾-inch (1.90-cm) U-Matic was the first videocassette format designed and was intended primarily for industrial and educational use. It had the distinct advantage of being compatible with all ¾-inch videocassette recorders, regardless of manufacturer because it complied with the EIAJ (Electronics Industry Association of Japan) standard. (The EIAJ has determined the standards for the ¾-inch videocassette system, and all ¾-inch equipment manufacturers subscribe to these standards). The ½-inch (1.27-cm) videocassette systems were designed and intended for home use; however, the quality of the equipment and the good resolution of the televised image is such that it is making them a growing favorite of industry and education as well. The number of ½-inch videocassette units being sold indicates that they may eventually become the only formats with which the library will have to contend. The only apparent disadvantage of the ½-inch videocassette system is that it is available in two popular but noncompatible formats—the Beta and the VHS. As indicated earlier in this chapter, the library could, without any difficulty, acquire tapes in only one of the ½-inch videocassette formats, if the videocassettes were to be used only on library equipment. If the library intends to make videocassettes available for home use, it may very well have to acquire information in both the Beta and VHS formats.

Videodisc

In all probability, it will ultimately be the videodisc that libraries will use as a standard for acquiring commercially prepared materials. At present, videodisc systems are being sold in rather limited numbers; but it is anticipated that within a few short years, they will be in millions of homes and be as commonplace as audio record players. Of all the video recorded formats, the videodisc appears to be most economical in terms of both equipment and the cost of recordings. Several companies have developed videodiscs, and each company is trying to get its videodisc format accepted as the standard for the industry. At this time, RCA, Teldec, and MCA/Philips are the strongest competitors in the videodisc market. It must be borne in mind that these competitors are developing products that are incompatible with each other's systems. The possibility exists that all three formats could receive wide domestic use, and the librarian will then have to know what kind of system patrons are buying, in order to select videodiscs in the proper format. In some instances, libraries may have to purchase all formats; only time will tell.

Videodiscs have a promising future for commercial video recording. They can be duplicated faster than videotapes; the manufacturing materials are cheaper than those of videocassettes; the equipment is easier to operate, less sophisticated, and less expensive than videocassette equipment; and videodiscs will be able to store as much information as any videotape format.

The videodisc is similar to an audiodisc in that it is the same size and shape, and it has grooves. An audiodisc is generally black, whereas a videodisc is metallic and has an aluminized appearance. The Philips system rotates at a relatively high speed (1800 rpm) and employs laser electronics that do not require any stylus or sensing mechanism to come in physical contact with the videodisc. This means that there is absolutely no wear on the videodisc, and, therefore theoretically, it could last indefinitely; and that the videodisc can present a single frame of information on the television monitor for extended periods of time without any resultant wear on the videodisc.

The ability to present a single frame of information considerably expands the potential use of videodiscs. A single videodisc contains 108,000 grooves or frames (54,000 on each side) and thus has the capability of storing 108,000 pages of printed or "still" information. When a videodisc is used on a videodisc player with an electronic accessioning function, any particular frame can be retrieved and viewed in less than 3.5 seconds.

The RCA videodisc rotates at a fraction of the speed (450 rpm) of the Philips system. Moreover, the RCA system employs a sled, or stylus, that comes in contact with the videodisc, resulting in wear on the record and, hence, making it infeasible to produce a still visual because the sled will wear out the videodisc at that particular point in a few minutes time.

At present, videodiscs are limited to commercial production only; any local production must still rely on videotape, videocassettes, or Super 8-mm film. A library could conceivably utilize two basic formats, videodisc for commercially produced materials, and videotape for locally produced materials.

Selecting Video Equipment

There are many video formats and systems from which the librarian must choose. The problem is analogous to the Gordian Knot, but by relying on qualified technical consultants, keeping abreast of technological developments in the television industry, and assessing the needs of the patrons the library serves, the librarian can embark on a program that will keep pace with developments in television and be a valuable asset to the library.

In selecting video equipment, the librarian must think in terms of systems. There are various video formats available, and each format has its own unique characteristics, advantages, and disadvantages. Even more important is the fact that no two video formats are compatible with each other. All the video equipment selected must complement the format(s) chosen. Decisions must be made regarding the degree to which the library wants to be involved with the television medium, the size of the budget allocation for television, the kinds of information to be acquired (or produced), and how to distribute information in this format. If the library is to be involved in television production, it must set minimum standards of acceptable quality and provide for the necessary staff, equipment, and facilities that will be needed to achieve this aim. The library must contend with the basic decision of whether it wants solely to distribute information in a television format or to produce television programs as well. Therefore, video equipment can generally be categorized as either production or distribution equipment.

Production equipment requires space for producing videotapes and can even include a studio for recording elaborate productions. The most basic setup would be a single videotape recorder to record programs from broadcast television (of course the librarian must be careful of copyright violations). The next elaboration would be a portable single-camera videotape recording unit for televising and recording live productions. An expansion of the single-camera unit would include the use of two videotape recorders with editing capabilities, which makes a tremendous improvement in the quality of the finished videotape. Finally would come the multiple-camera studio which would, depending on the extent of commitment, include two, three, or even four video cameras, control equipment (switchers, special effect generators, audio mixers, lighting control), and equipment for editing and duplicating videotapes. Regardless of the degree of television production involvement, whenever television cameras are used, attention must be given to lighting, editing, audio control, and special effects.

Distribution equipment would include video playback units and television monitors and receivers. There is a difference between a receiver and a monitor; technically, the terms are not synonomous. A television receiver, which is what we are most familiar with and which is found in homes, works on a RF (radio frequency) signal. The RF signal transmits both the audio and video signals through the air. A monitor receives the audio and video signals separately by wire or cable. Some playback units do not transmit a RF signal, and a monitor is therefore required for viewing. There are television sets that are made that are both monitors and receivers, which obviously cost more than those that are just monitors or just receivers.

The following criteria give an idea of the scope of the problems that must be considered in order to select video equipment intelligently. The criteria do not explore minute areas, but rather highlight main concerns that must be considered in determining to what degree a library will be involved with the television medium.

Compatibility

Consider television as an electronic system. Each component must be perfectly compatible with every other component or the system will not function properly. If the videotapes produced are 2-inch (5.08-cm) and the playback equipment is in $\frac{1}{2}$-inch (1.27-cm) format, there is a compatibility problem that must be resolved by a recorder that can make $\frac{1}{2}$-inch copies from a 2-inch tape. If the library community will be charging out videotapes, the tapes produced or acquired by the library must be compatible with the patrons' equipment (or vice versa).

Black and White versus Color

The library will have to make a decision on whether to use black and white or color television. Again, considering the compatibility of the system, if the library has a black-and-white production facility, there is no need to purchase color television monitors. If color is not essential, the librarian should not even consider color equipment because it is considerably more expensive than black and white. The trend, however, is definitely toward using color equipment.

Portability

Studio production console equipment need not be portable. Playback equipment and receiver–monitors can be portable. Stationary built-in equipment is much more attractive and would be nice if the library can afford it, but if the library is going to produce on-location videotapes, or if it will be necessary to move the equipment around the library or even charged it out, it would be necessary to acquire portable, battery-operated video recording equipment.

Wiring

Adequate AC electrical wiring must be accessible. If a large quantity of equipment will be used simultaneously, it is essential to be careful that the equipment will not blow fuses or cut out circuit breakers. Along with wiring, battery-operated equipment should be considered; although the batteries must be charged, this type of equipment allows the most portability possible, for it can be operated away from an AC electrical source. Equipment layouts must be planned for, along with electrical wiring; television wiring (coaxial cable, audio patch cords, etc.) has to be used to connect cameras to recorders and recorders and cameras to monitor–receivers. All electrical wiring should include a ground wire (i.e., contain a three-prong polarized plug) to eliminate the possibility of electrical shocks.

Service

When television equipment is acquired, the warranty should be read carefully. The quality of maintenance and repair service should also be investigated. Equipment is of little use if it takes weeks to have a unit repaired when it malfunctions. Television equipment is extremely complicated and often quite delicate; therefore, equipment that has a reputation for being sturdy and backed by reliable service should be selected.

Monitors and Receivers

Determine whether the library needs monitors or receivers, and whether they should be black and white or color. It is necessary to know how large a group will be viewing a monitor or receiver at any given time. Ideal viewing requirements are as follows: the viewer should not be seated any nearer the set than 5 times the picture width, nor farther away than 15 times the picture width (although children at home usually view at a distance of 3.75 times the picture width).

Expansion

A basic video system may be all the library needs; expansion would only involve acquiring a second basic system, and so on. However, the librarian should also consider the possibility of acquiring a system that is large enough initially but that can be expanded later. For example, it may be practical to start with one video camera with the anticipation of adding a second camera later. If so, the original camera should be of a type that can be synchronized with multiple cameras. With regards to viewing monitors, if more than one will be used from the same video recorder, it should have what is called a looping feature (i.e., the capability to connect a series of monitors); it is also necessary to determine how many loops or monitors a $\frac{1}{2}$-inch (1.27-cm) video recorder can drive (some manufacturers state that their equipment is limited to handling a maximum of four monitors).

Purpose

It is necessary to know exactly the purpose or intended use of a particular piece of equipment before a decision is made on selecting it. To purchase a video camera with just one normal lens could be a waste of money if what is really needed is a zoom lens. In the same way, libraries purchase videotape recorders when all they actually need is a video playback unit because they have no intention of ever using the unit to record video information. Likewise, why should a library acquire battery equipment if the equipment will always be used in relatively close access to AC electricity?

All of the preceding criteria can be used as guidelines by the librarian who is considering the selection of television equipment, and again, it is always advisable to seek the assistance of an expert consultant when making this type of acquisition decision.

Impact of Cable Television on the Library

Cable television, also known as Community Antenna Television (CATV), is a service, usually privately owned, that sets up a master antenna and from it distributes television signals by means of a wire (coaxial cable) to subscribers in a licensed geographical area. Although the subscriber must pay for cable television service, it is no longer necessary to erect an antenna on the roof of his or her home in order to receive a high-quality signal from both local and distant sources and to have access to a greater number of television channels. Some televised information is available only via cable television. It is in this restricted access area that the library may become involved.

The librarian should become familiar with cable television policy as prescribed by law. The potential impact of cable television on the library is tremendous: It could provide a whole new concept in information dissemination. Being a community service, the library is entitled by law to transmit information via cable television. Libraries that are acquiring television equipment should consider how it complies with their current or projected cable television utilization plans. As an example, 2-inch (5.08-cm) videotape is the accepted standard for open broadcast television, whereas cable television usually distributes information recorded on ¾-inch (1.90-cm) videocassette and may even accept ½-inch (1.27-cm) videocassette. Being aware of this condition might eliminate plans a library might have for acquiring 2-inch videotape equipment. (Note: Cable operators require that any videotape be first run through a time base corrector (TBC) to insure that the video signal has broadcast quality stability.) Another example involves studio production. The cable television operator often maintains a minimal production facility and makes it available at a reasonable charge. This means that a library planning to produce television programs can do so without having to construct its own studio; because television studios must receive considerable use to justify their existence, the use of a cable television studio facility could result in great savings for libraries involved in limited television production.

Video recordings that patrons visit the library to view or charge out for use on their home video playback units can also be transmitted via cable television. The library could eventually develop a full program that would utilize cable television for several hours a day. It could present library reports to the community, motion pictures, story hours for children, live puppet shows, and book talks, and conduct discussions, inservice education, art and crafts programs, etc. Actually, the library, via cable television, could fill a huge void that presently exists in television as regards a community's cultural and educational needs. If enough people want to take a college course offered at a distant campus, they might arrange for the library to obtain video recordings of the course to be transmitted via cable. The library could also provide the necessary reference and resource materials (books, periodicals, etc.) so that patrons would be able to take the course as efficiently as if they had actually taken it at the distant college campus.

To project into the more distant future, the library will eventually provide individualized home library service through cable television. The technology currently being developed is exciting in regard to how it can affect the library. For example, a patron who wants to read a particular book will be able to call the library and have an ultrafiche microform of the book projected on his or her home receiver. The microform can then be transferred to the patron's own piece of photographic microform, to be read at leisure on his or her own microform reader. All this would take place without the patron ever having to leave home. Such capability is not destined for the distant future either; on the contrary, there are companies that are experimenting with the transmission of information for individual use via television right now.

Cable television is going to continue to grow in the number of subscribers it will serve, as well as in the types of services it will provide. It is the wise librarian who keeps abreast of cable television progress and uses it to provide more and better library services.

Selecting and Evaluating
Commercially Produced Video Recordings

In many ways, television is similar to motion pictures, and many of the criteria used for evaluating motion pictures are applicable to television (see Chapter 6). However, television does differ from motion pictures in that it is usually viewed at home on a small screen. Granted, much of current television presents movies produced for theater use, but it is exactly in this area that a distinction must be made in evaluating commercially produced videotapes. For example, a scene in the film *War and Peace* depicts armies preparing for battle, and thousands of movie extras are staged on a large field. The tremendous impact of viewing this many people on a large theater screen is keenly felt by the viewer in a movie theater, but when the same scene is projected on a 21-inch (53.34-cm) television tube, it loses most of its impact. Along with the criteria used to evaluate films, it is necessary to distinguish those criteria that are unique to television. An added selection consideration would be the acquisition of videotapes that are not available to the patron from other sources. The following are the qualities that make television unique in its ability to communicate effectively.

Close-Up Shots

Television makes extensive use of close-up shots of people. Tight, full-length shots or medium close-up shots are quite effective in that the viewer becomes more emotionally involved than he or she would with a wide-angle shot showing a panorama of scenery. But, close-ups do require careful transition from scene to scene in order to eliminate a jumpy production.

One-to-One Shots

Whereas the close-up shot evokes emotional involvement in the viewer, the one-to-one shot stimulates personal involvement. Television has been called a one-to-one medium: When the performer looks directly into the television camera, the home viewer gets the feeling that the performer is looking him or her directly in the eye and talking to him or her personally, on a one-to-one basis. Videotapes that use this one-to-one technique will have great viewer impact. The librarian should be aware of this technique and be able to evaluate how well it achieves its intended purpose. A variation of the one-to-one technique occurs when the performer looks slightly off camera, as if talking to another person in the studio. This makes the viewer feel involved in the conversation even though the performer is not speaking directly to him or her.

Lighted Room

Television is viewed in a lighted room and not in a darkened theater. In addition to a small screen, there are many things in the room competing for the viewer's attention. The videotape should be effective enough to command the viewer's attention. If a scene does not have enough motion or is held too long, the viewer's attention is likely to drift away from the television receiver, as he or she becomes more interested in the other features of the lighted room. Videotapes that make extensive use of a close-up of a person lecturing are deadly. Television requires continual motion, freshness, and a pace of action that holds the viewer's attention.

Special Effects

The electronics of television, by use of a special effects generator (SEG), can create a wide variety of visual effects. Information from a second video camera can appear on the monitor as a wipe from left to right or as a small square of information which can be expanded or contracted on different parts of the viewing surface. Information can appear in various shapes (diamond, rectangle, circle, etc.), images can be multiplied, and many other special effects can be generated. It is important to be aware of these special effects, for if they heighten the interest of the information presented, they are well used; but if their only purpose is to show trick camera work, and they cause the viewer to be distracted, confused, or annoyed, they have hindered rather than added to the effect of the videotape as a whole.

The preceding four qualities are uniquely relevant to television; when they are combined with selected criteria used for evaluating motion picture films, the result is a complete, intensive evaluation of videotapes. Other factors that can be considered when evaluating and selecting commercially produced videotapes are certain technological capabilities that are unique to television. Television (as well as radio), has the highest *multiplication factor* of any audiovisual communication medium (i.e., it is possible for millions of people to receive the same information at the same time). (Radio, of course, has the same capacity, though as a solely audio medium.) Television can also be a *live* medium in that what is being televised is actually occurring as it is broadcast and can be viewed many thousands of miles away. Another feature of live television is the capability for instant replay, which again is unique to television. These additional traits, although not necessarily germane to selecting videotapes, do, however, illustrate the uniqueness of the television medium; clearly, the librarian must be aware of the full potential of this medium.

Using Television

The patron who comes to the library to view television is a highly experienced viewer and obviously will not require any instruction in how to view video information. The librarian must take this fact into serious consideration. First of all, why should anyone want to go to the library to view television if indeed the same type of information is available at home? Hence, the first criterion for using television in the library should be that the information being presented is available only from the library and that the patron has a need for it. The surroundings for viewing television should be comfortable and relaxing, especially if the reason for viewing the information is entertainment. Entertainment viewing can be accomplished either individually or in small or even large groups. Again, if the viewing group is large, no viewer should be sitting more than 15 screen widths away from the television receiver. This may necessitate the use of several television receivers strategically placed around the room or in several rooms. A large screen television projector may be considered for group viewing; however at present, the resolution qualities of video projectors still leave much to be desired. If the video information is instructional, learning carrels housing a videocassette or videodisc player should be considered. In a carrel, the viewer can take notes and control the pace of the program by using the stop pause, fast forward, and reverse features. If there is a possibility that several video units, each with different programs, will be used simultaneously, it will be necessary to employ headsets for private listening.

If an informational video program is well prepared, it will in all probability include viewer involvement. It is important for the librarian to bear in mind that the patron is going to the library to view video information that is unavailable at home and, therefore, is information that is wanted and needed by the patron. It must be a rewarding experience. Libraries that presently have successful motion picture film collections in terms of patron utilization should seriously consider the possibility of how similar information in a video format will be received and used by their patrons. This is not to imply that television is replacing motion picture films, but rather that some types of information can be more effectively and efficiently presented on television. Current predictions indicate that within a very few years, millions of homes will be equipped with some type of video recorder, which will certainly result in an insatiable demand for video information. Much of this information will be consumed on a one-time basis; hence, the viewer may not be able to economically justify the expense of personally purchasing all the video information desired. The result will be that patrons will want to borrow video information from the library just as they currently borrow books from the library. Libraries that are cognitive of this trend and start preparing now for the eventual boom in television information needs will be able to meet the demand for video services. Ultimately, the television medium, which took many people away from the library, will inevitably return them to it.

Selected Bibliography

Adler, Richard, and Cater, Douglass, eds. *Television as a Cultural Force.* New York: Praeger Publishing, 1976.

Baggaley, Jon, and Duck, Steve. *The Dynamics of Television.* Lexington, Massachusetts: Lexington Books, 1977.

Barnouw, Erik. *Tube of Plenty: The Evolution of American Television.* Fairlawn, New Jersey: Oxford University Press, 1977.

Cable Libraries. Ridgefield, Connecticut: C. S. Tepfer Publishing, 1973–.

Ciccolella, Cathy. *A Buyer's Guide To Videocassette Recorders.* New York: Drake Publishers, 1978.

Educational and Industrial Television. Ridgefield, Connecticut: C. S. Tepfer Publishing, 1968–.

Feedback. Long Beach, California: California State University Long Beach, 1965–.

Gibson, George H. *Public Broadcasting: The Role of the Federal Government 1912–1976.* New York: Praeger Publishing, 1977.

Inside TV. New York: Macfadden-Bartell Corp., 1968–.

Kahn, Frank J., ed. *Documents of American Broadcasting,* third edition. Englewood Cliffs, New Jersey: Prentice-Hall, Inc., 1978.

Knecht, Kenneth. *Designing and Maintaining the CATV and Small TV Studio,* second edition. Blue Ridge Summit, Pennsylvania: TAB Books, 1976.

Liebert, Robert M., Neale, John M., and Davidson, Emily S. *The Early Window: Effects of Television on Children and Youth.* Elmsford, New York: Pergammon Press, 1973.

Look–Listen Opinion Poll. Madison, Wisconsin: American Council for Better Broadcasts, 1954–.

Public Telecommunications Review. Washington, D.C.: National Association of Educational Broadcasters, 1973–.

Videography. New York: United Business Publishers, 1976–.

Williams, Raymond. *Television: Technology and Cultural Form.* New York: Schocken Books, 1975.

Zettl, Herbert. *Sight, Sound, Motion: Applied Media Aesthetics.* Belmont, California: Wadsworth Publishing, 1973.

Selection Aids

Home Video. New York: United Business Publications, 1979–.

International Television Almanac. New York: Quigley, 1955–.

Limbacher, James L., ed. *Feature Films on 8 mm, 16 mm, and Videotape: A Directory of Feature Films Available for Rental, Sale, and Lease in the United States and Canada: With a Serial Section and a Director Index,* sixth edition New York: R. R. Bowker, 1979.

NICEM Index To Educational Video Tapes, fifth edition. Los Angeles: University of Southern California, 1979.

Television Index. New York: Television Index, 1949–.

Televisions. Washington, D.C.: Community Video Center, 1975–.

Video Programs Index, fourth edition. Syosset, New York: The National Video Clearinghouse, 1979.

The Video Source Book. Syosset, New York: The National Video Clearinghouse, 1980.

Weber, Olga S., comp. *North American Film and Video Directory: A Guide to Media Collections and Services.* New York: R. R. Bowker, 1976.

10

Programmed Instruction

Overview

As the emphasis on providing for individual differences in learning and the number of people involved in learning as a lifelong process grows, educators are continually researching methods for the improvement of instruction. One of the methods that has met with considerable success is programmed instruction. By using a well-designed program, a learner can acquire knowledge or a skill at his or her own pace, quite possibly without the intervention of an instructor. It is for these reasons that the library should strongly consider acquiring instructional materials in a programmed-instruction format. A learner (especially one not enrolled in formal education) can go to the library, and, using programmed instruction, can, in a sense become self-educated.

The librarian needs to become familiar with the basic principles involved in programmed instruction, the types of programs available and the hardware necessary to use the programs properly. It is not necessary for the librarian to assume a teaching role, but rather, to provide, on request from a patron, the types of programs that the patron can then proceed to use as an independent learner.

Programmed Instruction: A Definition

Programmed instruction is called a process, and before a definition can be constructed it is necessary to define process. As it relates to programmed instruction, a *process* is a controlled sequence of events leading to a desired outcome. If a sequence of events is controlled, there is more certainty that the goal will be achieved. As a brief example, if you wanted to change a tire on your automobile, you would first read the handbook on tire changing for your car, after which you would change the tire. It is hoped that you would succeed. But if the instructions for changing a tire were in a controlled sequence, you would receive a bit of information, perform the necessary act that follows from that information, then on successful completion of that act, receive another segment of instruction and carry out that ensuing act. The probability of success when information is presented in a controlled sequence is much greater than if it is presented in a handbook format.

By definition, *programmed instruction* is a process that involves a sequence of events leading to the acquisition of a set of desired learning objectives. The learner is given some information, then challenged on how well he or she knows the information by being required to make a response to a statement or question. On completion of the response, the learner is provided with a correct response so he or she knows immediately whether or not the response is correct.

Psychological Principle of Programmed Instruction

In preparing programmed instruction, knowledge of the learner's behavior is essential. Programmed instruction subscribes to the principles of behavioral psychology, specifically, stimulus, response, and reinforcement, or what is called the *S–R–R theory*. The procedure is quite simple. (See Figure 10.1.) The learner is given some information, the *stimulus*, is required to provide an answer, the *response,* and is given the correct answer immediately, the *reinforcement*. All these elements—stimulus, response, and reinforcement—are essential; and to assure any degree of success, the reinforcement should occur immediately after the student's response. Any lag in time between response and reinforcement destroys the purpose of programmed instruction; because, in essence, the reinforcement is a reward, and if it occurs immediately, the probability that learning is taking place greatly increases.

Figure 10.1 Psychological principle of programmed instruction.

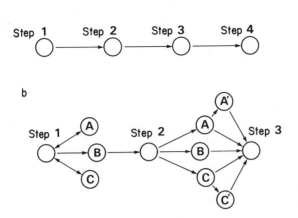

Figure 10.2   Schematics of (a) linear and (b) branching programs.

Linear and Branching Programs

Information in programmed instruction is usually presented in one of two formats, linear or branching. In Figure 10.2a, a linear program is diagramed (proceeding from left to right): At step 1, a learner is given some information; he or she responds to this information, and the response is immediately reinforced. The learner then proceeds to step 2, where he or she receives more information, responds to that information, is again immediately reinforced, and moves on to step 3. As the program continues, the learner schematically proceeds along a straight line or linear path, determining his or her own speed. Because a more intelligent learner can proceed through the program at a faster pace than a slower or less intelligent learner can, linear programs provide for individual differences in learning rates.

Figure 10.2b is a schematic of a branching program: The learner is again given some information (the stimulus), but is given a choice of alternative responses. Let's call these alternatives A, B, and C, with B being the proper response. If the learner chooses B, he or she proceeds to step 2 for more information. If the learner chooses A, which is incorrect, he or she is branched off to receive information as to why this response is incorrect and additional information that will assist him or her in making the correct response; he or she is then returned to the original piece of information (step 1) and given another opportunity to respond. The same procedure would follow if the learner answered C. The difference between A and C is that in both cases, the learner is given remedial information, but because A and C are not identical, the learner must be given different types of remedial information for each particular response.

A variation of the branching program is illustrated in step 2 of Figure 10.2b: Here, if a student chooses the incorrect response, for example A, he or she is branched to A given remedial information, and challenged. If the student answers correctly, he or she is directed to new information at step 3 and is back into the mainstream of the program. If the student answers incorrectly, he or she is given further remedial information at point A'; when the student finally answers correctly, he or she returns to the mainstream of the program, step 3. This type of procedure is usually found in programs utilizing a computer.

Major Developments

An understanding of the development of programmed instruction is beneficial to the librarian in selecting materials. The origin and copyright date of the material gives information regarding the type of program, its applicability to different types of learning, and perhaps even its level of sophistication.

Although many people have been involved in the programmed instruction movement, the names of Pressey, Skinner, and Crowder are associated with the major developments.

In 1926, Sydney Pressey developed one of the first examples of what is now called a teaching machine. Using the behavioral principle of stimulus, response, and reinforcement (S–R–R), Pressey's machine gave the learner a bit of information to which he was required to respond. The response was in the form of multiple choices. If the student made the correct response by pressing the proper switch, the machine would advance and present new information. An incorrect response was not rewarded; the machine would not advance to new information. This basic machine principle is still in use today. Because Pressey gave the learner an opportunity to make a choice, one of which was the correct answer, his program is called the recognition type—the learner recognizes the correct answer from multiple choices. Pressey's programs use the linear format for presenting information.

Pressey's teaching machine did not gain very wide acceptance, and it was not until the launching of Sputnik by the Soviet Union in 1957 that we find any substantial development in programmed instruction. After Sputnik, American education immediately initiated a crash program, especially in the sciences, in an effort to improve the rate of learning. Terms such as information explosion, knowledge explosion, independent studies, and individualized learning came into vogue. About this time, the name of B. F. Skinner came to the fore of programmed instruction. Skinner had been conducting extensive research on animal behavior involving the study of the S–R–R theory. The programmed instruction Skinner developed was essentially a linear type similar to that developed by Pressey, but instead of recognizing the correct response among several choices, the learner is required to construct an answer by filling in a blank with the correct response. Filling in the blank is a recall type of learning because the learner has to recall the answer rather than (as in the Pressey method) recognize it. After filling in the blank, the learner compares his or her answer with the correct response.

Norman Crowder is noted for developing the branching type of program, which utilizes corrective assignments for incorrect answers. Of the three types of programs, Crowder's is considered by many to be best because it provides for individual differences by giving the student, when needed, a corrective assignment. However, advocates of the Pressey and Skinner linear formats claim their programs also provide for individual differences by allowing the student to progress at his or her own pace.

Programmed instruction with the use of computers, computer based instruction (CBI) or computer assisted instruction (CAI), is the most recent development in this area. (The emerging role of the computer in programmed instruction is discussed in detail later in this chapter.)

This brief history of programmed instruction is important for the librarian responsible for selecting programmed instructional materials. The crash program that followed Sputnik resulted in a proliferation of programmed instruction that glutted the educational market. Much of it was produced by people with little or no knowledge of the principles of programmed instruction and was of questionable value because learners, for a multitude of reasons, did not learn. Today, we find programs being developed by teams of highly trained specialists. A team may consist of a psychologist with a knowledge of learning theory, an educational researcher, a curriculum specialist, computer programmer, and several teachers. Programs are extensively developed and field-tested before they are made available for purchase. It is essential to use caution in selecting any program produced prior to 1968; and for any program selected, the validation statement should be examined to ascertain how it was field-tested, by whom, and with what results. In this way, the librarian can be reasonably certain that the program selected is best for his or her patrons.

Textbooks versus Linear and Branching
Programmed Instruction Books

A *textbook* is defined as a book that gives instructions on the principles of a subject of study, or as any book that is used as the basis or partial basis for a course of study. A major difference between a nonprogrammed text and a programmed text is that the author of a nonprogrammed text is concerned with the presentation of content. He or she wants to be certain that the learner is provided with enough information to acquire knowledge of the topic being studied. Stated in a different way, the author provides the necessary information; all the student has to do is read and study the information.

On the other hand, the author of a programmed instruction text is primarily concerned with learner behavior; therefore, he or she must ask a very different set of questions: "How can I best present the information for the student to learn it? Does the program motivate the student? Does it challenge the student? Is the student successful with the program? What is the terminal behavior of the student?

When one examines formats of programmed instruction books, several factors become evident. Linear programmed instruction textbooks usually have smaller frames than branching textbooks. (A *frame* is a unit containing a presentation of information [stimulus], a provision for an answer [response], and the correct answer [reinforcement]). Because the frames are smaller, in linear programmed textbooks there can be several frames per page, and the answers are close to the response space (printed either on the page margin or on the following page). In a branching programmed instruction textbook, the frames tend to be larger—a single frame might cover several pages. When asked to make a response, the learner is referred to a page that discusses the correctness of the response. If the response is correct, the learner proceeds with the program. If the response is incorrect, the learner is given remedial information and then returned to the page containing the original set of responses, where he or she is given another opportunity to respond. By design, answers are located on various pages and not in any prescribed order. Actually, the arrangement of pages is somewhat scrambled, and such books are known by many as scrambled textbooks.

To summarize, the author of a nonprogrammed textbook is concerned with "what," whereas the author of a programmed instruction textbook is concerned with "how." Linear programmed instruction texts have smaller frames in sequence, whereas branching programmed instruction textbooks tend to have larger frames with a scrambled reading arrangement.

The Emerging Role of the Computer

The continuing refinement and sophistication of programmed instruction have inevitably led to the use of the computer. As indicated in the preceding section, programmed instruction authors are concerned with learner behavior. Actually, each individual approaches a learning situation with a unique set of learning behaviors; and providing for these individual differences can become quite a complex task, even with the use of a branching programmed instruction textbook. Hence, a computer with an infinite number of branching capabilities can branch the learner to the exact bit (frame) of information he or she needs.

Other advantages are possible with the computer. It can keep track of learner progress, reenter him or her into the program at the exact point where he or she left it, and keep him or her challenged at an optimum level of performance. If the learner makes a certain number of successive incorrect answers, the computer can detect a lack of readiness for the program and inform him or her to exit from, or leave, the program and engage in some other type of activity. A computer can give the learner a printed progress report; it can even report the overall effectiveness of the program, as well as information on any phase of the program in need of revision (e.g., a common rule of thumb is that if 90% of the learners are not correctly responding to 90% of the frames, the program is either in need of revision or not suited to the learners who are using it).

Computers can handle programs with verbal or visual information; the learner can respond on a typewriter keyboard or use a light probe and point to the response on an illuminated screen. With this level of sophistication, the computer can now challenge authors to make programs of infinite variety, with primary emphasis on the basic premise of programmed instruction, that is, learner behavior.

Programmed instruction utilizing the computer is generally identified as falling into two broad categories—computer based instruction (CBI) and computer assisted instruction (CAI). Computer based instruction involves a program in which the computer is the base, or prime contact, for learning; if necessary, an instructor can provide assistance. In computer assisted instruction, the learner gets basic instruction from a teacher and uses the computer to facilitate learning. There can be an overlap of function, and a program could be used for both computer based and computer assisted instruction.

Before a computer can be used for programmed instruction, a program must be produced, which can be extremely expensive and time consuming. But once a program is produced and properly field-tested, they offer the learner the opportunity to go to a library and, possibly without human intervention (i.e., a teacher), acquire knowledge that is now available only in a formal classroom environment.

Selecting Software and Compatible Hardware

Often, in selecting programmed instruction packages, librarians have a desire to use programs that include hardware (equipment). Some hardware appears to be quite exotic, making a programmed instruction text appear by comparison a dull enterprise for the learner. It is essential not to fall into this trap, but to adhere to the architect's dictum, "form follows function." The librarian must ask, "What is it that the hardware can do?" or better still, "What is it that I want the hardware to do?"

Many kinds of hardware are nothing more than "electronic page turners" with some kind of cheatproof device that will not allow the learner to see the answer until a response has been made. If this is the sole concern, there is quite a bit of inexpensive hardware that can meet this requirement. On the other hand, a thorough analysis of hardware capabilities will provide the direction necessary to selecting exactly the right piece of hardware, if needed, for a particular type of learner.

Hardware has a wide range of capability. It can perform the following functions:

1. present information in a linear format
2. present information in a branching format
3. present information in both linear and branching formats
4. provide for write-in answers
5. provide for multiple-choice answers
6. advance the program electrically or mechanically
7. make the program cheatproof
8. provide record of learner performance
9. accomodate several learners on same program at same time
10. provide audio information
11. project films, slides, filmstrips, or videotapes
12. automatically stop and start
13. use information in page, paper roll, or microform formats
14. use consumable or nonconsumable programs
15. accept locally produced programs

With this wide range of capabilities available, it becomes necessary for the librarian to determine which combination is best suited for the patrons' needs. Obviously, the more elaborate the hardware, the higher the cost. Prices range from less than a dollar for a scroll device to hun-

Figure 10.3 Programmed instruction hardware (Teaching machines): (a) (left to right) cardboard scroll box—linear program; electromechanical machine, which projects film on a rear projection screen—branching program; plastic hand-operated machine—linear program; and (b) computer terminal—branching program.

dreds of thousands of dollars for a highly sophisticated computerized system. (See Figure 10.3) Much of the hardware being purchased is generally in the $25–$1500 range.

Once a decision is made as to the type of hardware needed, a checklist (Figure 10.4) can assist in evaluating it. The checklist in no way implies that there is a best combination of features; for a machine that satisfies all of the library's unique needs may not exist presently. Rather, it is an aid to guide the librarian in selecting the best machine with regard to cost, maintenance, durability, effectiveness, versatility, and ease of operation.

Criteria can also be developed to analyze software (programs), which is perhaps more essential than the analysis of hardware; because it is the software that contains the actual information to be learned, and thus, its analysis could tend to be more subjective and personal. With the criteria in Figure 10.5, an assessment can be made of a program's value to the library as well as to the patron.

A final step in analyzing the merits of hardware and software, of course, is to find out which institutions are using it. A reputable manufacturer will have no reservations about providing such information. A discreet inquiry to an institution currently using the program could provide invaluable information in reaching a decision.

Using Programmed Instruction

When used in a school library, programmed instruction is usually a teacher-prescribed activity that is an integral part of the curriculum. As such, the student entering the school library knows specifically what type of program is needed. It is the responsibility of the classroom teacher to monitor the student's progress. In a public library situation, although the librarian is not accountable for the patron's learning efficiency, it is still a good procedure to solicit feedback as to how well the program achieved its intended objectives. A simple response form (Figure 10.6) can provide the librarian with the information needed to make an assessment of the program's effectiveness and is also useful for future reference in selecting other programs and in making recommendations to other patrons who may have similar learning needs.

Programmed instruction can be dispensed in anything from a basic programmed instruction textbook to a sophisticated computer program. Depending on the packaging, the program can be either used in the library or charged out for home use. In the case of a consumable program (one where the user writes a response right on the program), it is

Name of Machine_____ Manufacturer_____

Cost _____

Directions: Respond by checking the appropriate boxes and providing any additional information that is pertinent.

1. Construction of machine ☐cardboard ☐wood ☐plastic ☐metal   comments:
2. Method of operation ☐manual ☐mechanical ☐electric ☐electromechanical   comments:
3. Ease of operation ☐simple ☐easy ☐complex ☐difficult   comments:
4. Type of format used ☐linear ☐branching ☐linear–branching   comments:
5. Available programs ☐none ☐one ☐several ☐special or general   comments:
6. Physical characteristics of program ☐printed page ☐roll of paper ☐slide or filmstrip ☐sound–motion–color   comments:
7. Learner response ☐written ☐keyboard ☐button or lever ☐light probe   comments:
8. Intended type of learner ☐elementary ☐junior high ☐senior high ☐college–adult   comments:
9. Provision for correct response ☐manual ☐automatic   comments:
10. Compares learner response with correct response ☐yes ☐no   comments:
11. Tamperproof feature (e.g., can the learner change an answer or see the correct answer before responding) ☐yes ☐no   comments:
12. Feedback to librarian ☐tally counter ☐punch card ☐answers on separate paper ☐electronic printout ☐none   comments:
13. Consumable materials ☐yes ☐no   comments:
14. Group use ☐yes ☐no   comments:
15. Approximate weight   comments:
16. Approximate dimensions   comments:
17. Length of warranty   comments:
18. Cost of maintenance service contract   comments:
19. Location of nearest dealer or service office   comments:
20. Overall rating ☐excellent ☐good ☐fair ☐poor   comments:

Figure 10.4 Programmed instruction hardware evaluation checklist.

Name of program_____ Producer_____

Copyright date_____ Cost_____

Directions: Respond by checking the appropriate boxes and providing any additional information that is pertinent.

1. Authority (credentials of program designers and areas of expertise)   comments:
2. Validation studies (who were subjects? where? when? results?)   comments:
3. Completeness ☐each program an entity ☐series comments:
4. Adjunct materials (require use of materials outside of program) ☐yes ☐no comments:
5. Availability of other nonrelated programs that can be used on the hardware ☐yes ☐no comments:
6. Communication orientation ☐print ☐visual ☐motion ☐sound comments:
7. Availability of pretest–posttest materials ☐yes ☐no comments:
8. Program length (approximate time, number of frames, number of pages, etc.) comments:
9. Objectives (specifically what is being presented, and how successful is the presentation)

Figure 10.5   Criteria for in selecting programmed instruction software. This form should be used in conjunction with the programmed instruction hardware evaluation checklist (Figure 10.4).

Programmed Instruction Response Form

To help us assess the programmed instruction package you have just used, we would appreciate your response to the following statements. Please either check the appropriate boxes or fill in the blanks. Any additional comments you would like to make would also be appreciated.

1. Program title _____
2. Approximately what percentage of the responses did you answer correctly? _____ %
3. Did you complete the entire program?
   ☐yes Approximately how long did it take? _____
   ☐no What percentage of the program did you complete? _____
4. Did the program fulfill its objectives (i.e., did you learn what you expected to learn? ☐yes ☐no
5. Do you think programmed instruction is an efficient way for you to learn this information? ☐yes ☐no
6. Overall assessment
   ☐good I enjoyed it and would not hesitate to try more programmed instruction.
   ☐fair it was okay, but other methods (e.g., a textbook) would work as well.
   ☐poor I did not like it and would not use it again.
Comments:

Figure 10.6 Response form to be filled out by user on returning program instruction materials.

recommended that program cost be reduced by providing blank sheets of paper, paper rolls, or inexpensive forms for learner responses in lieu of the learner writing on the program itself. If a device or machine is to be used, the specific advantages of the machine or device should be assessed to determine whether it is worthwhile for the library to acquire it. As indicated earlier, many machines are nothing more than electromechanical page turners with some sort of cheatproof device that will not reveal an answer until the user has made a response. In a public library situation, cheating is not a concern of the librarian; furthermore, the patron has a desire to learn or he or she would not request the program in the first place, and cheating would only decrease the possibility of a successful learning experience.

A major factor in the user's success with programmed instruction is motivation. If the user has a sincere desire to learn, the program, with its skillful arrangement of information and concern for learner behavior, will contribute greatly to the success of the learning. The new user should be informed that the program does require the learner to be motivated to learn the material. The user should also be informed that if he or she is not responding to the questions with at least a 90% efficiency rate, then perhaps he or she should not continue with it because it could become frustrating, and the possibility of achieving the program's objectives would be severely diminished.

Some programs may require the manipulation, synthesis, repair, or construction of a device. If this is the case, the device needs to be available when the program is actually being used. Not having the necessary supplementary materials available defeats the intended purpose of the program; for it is in the transfer of the information learned from the text of the program to the actual manipulation of materials that is an intrinsic part of achieving such a program's objectives. The librarian must therefore consider whether the supplementary materials can be used in the library; and, if so, whether the library will have to provide them. If the materials cannot be provided by the library, the program must be of a type that can be used by the patron wherever the materials are located (e.g., in the case of a program on auto repair, the patron must be able to use the program where the auto is parked).

Programmed instruction packages, because they are designed for individualized, independent study, lend themselves very well to use in learning carrels. In the carrel, the user has the space and privacy necessary to learn the information efficiently. The librarian can further assist the patron, by giving him or her an indication of how many frames the program contains, any prerequisite skill or knowledge required, the approximate time needed to complete the program (this would obviously vary depending on the ability of the user), and any supplementary materials required. Adjunct materials that go beyond the scope of the program but may still be of value or interest to the user could also be recommended.

More often than not, the patron who uses programmed instruction will do so to learn only a specific body of information and will not want to know background, perspectives, theory and other information about the program, which although enriching to the value of the learning experience is not necessary to achieve program objectives. Programmed instruction is precise and to the point; the learner is told the objective and proceeds to be given information for accomplshing that objective. Many people do not like to use programmed instruction for this reason; it seems too didactic. However, for the person who is motivated to acquire some specific information, it is an ideal way to learn. The person who is not so inclined, will prefer to use a nonprogrammed textbook, which develops content more fully, but less scientifically. Usually, after progressing through a few frames of programmed instruction, the user will know if it is suited to his or her learning style with respect to level of difficulty and method of presentation. It would be somewhat absurd to use a program that is difficult and unappealing. Programmed instruction is intended to provide an experience that is effective and efficient and that rewards (reinforces) learner behavior. The librarian should recommend programmed instruction and explain its purpose and use; but it is the patron who must decide whether this method of learning is best for his or her particular needs, and who, after using the program, can best inform the librarian of the program's effectiveness and worth.

Selected Bibliography

Bullock, Donald H: *Programmed Instruction.* Englewood Cliffs, New Jersey: Educational Technology Publications, 1978.

Journal of Programmed Instruction. West Nyack, New York: Journal of Programmed Instruction, 1962–.

Programmed Learning and Educational Technology. London, England: Kogan Page, 1964–.

Unwin, Derick, and McAleese, Ray, eds. *The Encyclopedia of Educational Media Communications and Technology.* Westwood, Connecticut: Greenwood Press, 1978.

Selection Aids

Bibliography of Programmed Instruction, Vols. 1–10. New York: International Publications Service, 1974.

Hendershot, Carl H. *Programmed Learning: A Bibliography of Programs and Presentation Devices,* fourth edition. Bay City, Michigan: Hendershot Programmed Learning Consultants, 1971.

Hendershot, Carl H., comp. *Programmed Learning And Individually Paced Instruction: Bibliography,* fifth edition. Bay City, Michigan: Hendershot Programmed Learning Consultants, 1978.

Hoye, Robert E., and Wang, Anastasia C., eds. *Index to Computer Based Learning,* fourth edition. Englewood Cliffs, New Jersey: Educational Technology Publications, 1973.

International Directory of Programmed Instruction. New York: Unipub, 1973.

Razik, Taber A., ed. *Bibliography of Programmed Instruction and Computer Assisted Instruction.* Englewood Cliffs, New Jersey: Educational Technology Publications, 1971.

11

Maps

Overview

Maps, because of the way they present information and their physical characteristics, must be categorized as a type of media. Generally, maps depict a geographic area, over which is superimposed a mathematical grid of lines of longitude (meridians) and latitude (parallels). Information is presented in a graphic or pictorial form; maps can therefore be broadly categorized as nonprint media. The content of maps can range anywhere from single-community maps to celestial maps. The data they present may include, for example, spatial relationships, physical features, political boundaries, geography, demography, and natural resources. A map's physical characteristics can assume a wide variety of sizes and shapes, from a three-dimensional globe or relief model to a two-dimensional piece of paper or plastic. Because maps do have various physical forms, they require special storage spaces that can properly accommodate them. Maps are indeed a unique media form, and it is not uncommon for a library to assign to specific personnel the task of maintaining the map collection.

Properties and Characteristics of Maps

By definition, *globes* and *maps* are symbolic replicas of the earth's features or characteristics. The librarian should have a basic knowledge of globe and map properties and characteristics in order to select from the various types available those that best serve the needs of the library. Globes and maps vary in the amount of detail they contain and in the accuracy with which they are intended to represent a portion of the earth. When they are intended for the novice or young person, globes and maps may limit the amount of information they contain, whereas when made for the expert, they may contain highly specialized information in great detail. But whether the globe or map is intended for novice or expert, it is important that it be accurate in presenting the information it was designed to show.

The earth, being a sphere, is best represented by a sphere, or globe. The globe is an accurate replica of the earth, in miniaturized detail. For ease in translating, both the earth and globe replicas are measured in like units, which are then expressed as a ratio. The earth has been found to have a diameter at the equator of approximately 500 million inches (1.27 billion cm), therefore, a globe 50 inches (127 cm) in diameter will have a ratio of 50 to 500 million. This ratio, reduced to 1: 10 million would be printed somewhere on the globe as a fractional scale, or representative fraction (RF), (e.g., 1/10,000,000 or 1:10,000,000 means that 1 inch [2.54 cm] on a 50-inch [127-cm] globe is the same distance as 10 million inches [254 thousand m] on earth). Once one has determined the representative fraction, scales in other units can easily be transposed (e.g., miles, kilometers). A 50-inch (127-cm) globe tends to be rather large for the library. The prevalent diameters of commercially produced globes range from 8 to 24 inches (20.32 to 6.96 cm), 12- to 16-inch (30.48- to 40.64-cm) globes being the most popular. Regardless of size, it is important that the librarian examine the accuracy of detail and legibility of information.

A globe has a unique advantage over maps in that it can be used to measure true distances in any direction using only one scale. However, globes have several inherent disadvantages: (*a*) no more than one half of a globe can be seen at any time, (*b*) globes tend to be bulky and unwieldy and occupy valuable space, (*c*) they are difficult to store, (*d*) it is difficult to make measurements on a curved surface, (*e*) globes are expensive to reproduce because the materials required are expensive when compared to those required to reproduce flat maps, (*f*) a globe contains the whole earth, and in most cases a patron is interested in examining only a portion of it. Unless globes are needed for particular courses of study, libraries tend to have very few of them in their collections. Usually, one large earth globe suffices as an accurate replica of the earth that can be used as an orienting referent whenever a patron wants a precise representation of the earth unavailable from any map. The librarian may also consider having globes of the universe, of the planets of the solar system, and of the moon. These globes would also be used in conjunction with their map counterparts.

Because the earth is a globe, it is impossible to represent it accurately in its entirety on a flat surface. Therefore, cartographers, in their efforts to represent the earth as accurately as possible, have to make some sacrifices in distance, shape, or form. Most of the properties of map projections are the result of scale relationships that are either maintained or altered in the process of transforming spherical data to a flat surface. Map projections of extremely large areas are limited in their kinds of accuracy. They may (*a*) accurately represent true angles around any point of the map, (*b*) show direction correctly, (*c*) show distances between points correctly, or (*d*) replicate shapes or sizes of areas precisely enough that all parts of the map are in proper relation to each other. A map, or flat projection, can achieve any of the four preceding characteristics either singly or in combination, but it cannot achieve all four at the same time. Usually, maps that attempt to achieve accuracy on all four characteristics are difficult for the novice to read and comprehend. The Mercator map projection is especially popular with novices, and although it distorts areas and distances, it is true along parallels and represents shapes quite well within restricted limits anywhere on the map. Bear in mind that although the problems of maintaining the accuracy of the four preceding characteristics are evident when large areas of the earth are mapped, they virtually disappear when small geographic areas are mapped.

When selecting a map, there are basically four fundamental considerations that are applicable to all maps: (*a*) map scale, or the size of the map area represented compared with that part of the earth it represents, (*b*) type of projection used, (*c*) types of information represented on the map and the various methods or symbols used to illustrate them, and (*d*) quantity and quality of detail.

Map Scale

Map scale is determined by the same method used for globe scale, that is, as a ratio of the distance on the map to the actual distance it represents on earth. The size of the area being mapped and the actual physical size of the map will determine the scale to be used. Obviously, the smaller the ratio, or representative factor, the more detail can be included (e.g., a map of a city can include more detail than a map of a state). It is recommended that the map scale be in a ratio that is amenable to easy application and measurement. With certain types of map projections, several scales may be required on different areas of the map. Usually, maps requiring several scales are not intended to be used for measuring distances; and when distances are needed, a key or table is usually provided indicating distances between major points.

Map Projection

A map projection involves a grid of intersecting lines (longitudes and latitudes) on which the earth or a portion of it is plotted. As stated earlier, it is impossible for a map projection to be accurate in all aspects (distance, shape, area, and direction). The cartographer selects the projection that best depicts a partial feature or aspect of the earth. This also means that map projections are truer in some areas of the grid than in other areas. The librarian must select the map projection that provides the best and truest means of displaying information for a particular need. If accuracy of polar areas is important, a map projection that is best and truest for these areas will probably achieve its purpose at the expense of distorting equatorial areas. Compromises are unavoidable in map projections. In order to maintain accuracy in some aspects, the accuracy of other aspects must be sacrificed. It is also important for the librarian to bear in mind that a map with the most accurate replication of a particular aspect may indeed be undesirable if it is in a type of projection difficult for the user to comprehend, especially if the user is a novice. It is important to have a variety of map projections of varying degrees of complexity in the collection. A good map collection ranges from maps that are used to learn how to read maps to maps that are read to learn. Figure 11.1 illustrates the more popular types of map projections and their respective properties, uses, and limitations.

Information Represented

Maps illustrate the areal distribution of many things that are on the face of the earth. This information is represented by the use of a vast array of symbols, codes, and colors that attempt to communicate such features as shape, size, outline, pattern arrangements, land relief or elevation, and the distribution of actual or relative statistical values. When these are presented effectively, the map provides a graphic means through which the user can easily and efficiently recognize, compare, and examine patterns, relationships, surface features, locational data, scientific data, places, ocean currents, geologic formations, climate, weather, demographic distributions, political boundaries, economic data, agricultural capabilities, industrial production, military disbursement, etc.

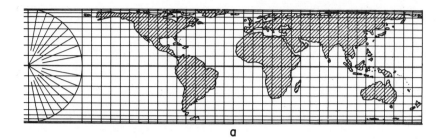

a

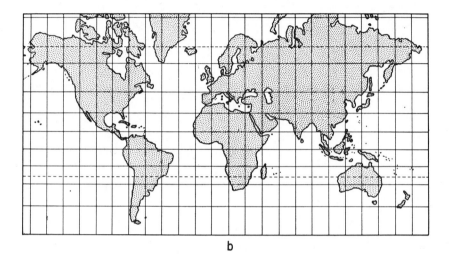

b

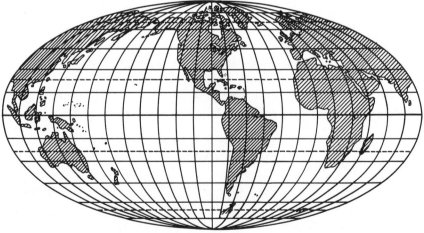

c

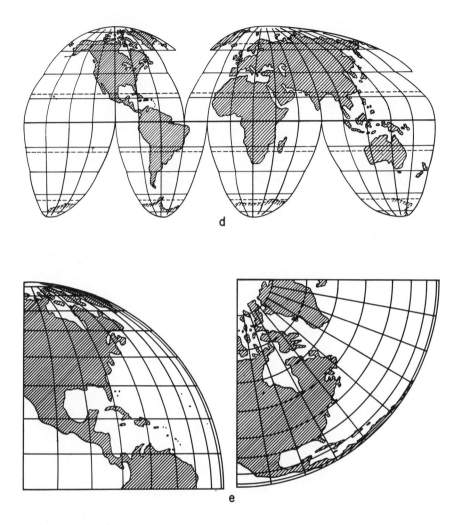

Figure 11.1 Map projections: (a) Cylindrical Equal Area Projection, use—illustrates the problems of projecting a globe onto a flat surface—and properties—higher latitudes are stretched out; (b) Mercator Projection, use—navigation and compass location— and properties—land distortion in the higher latitudes; (c) Mollweide (oval) Projection, use—equal areas—and properties—depiction of the central middle latitudes is best and the polar axis is one half the length of the equatorial axis; (d) Goode's Homosoline Projection (interrupted), use—fairly accurate in shape and area—and properties—inter- ruption in overall continuity; and (e) orthographic projections (left, centered on the equator, and right, centered on the North Pole), use—give a rounded, three-dimensional perspective—and properties—cannot project the entire globe and distortion increases from the center.

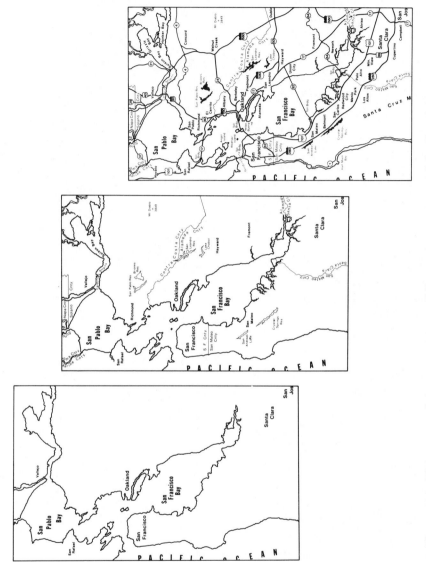

Figure 11.2 Three maps of the same area, providing various amounts of detail and information.

The symbols and codes should be easy to understand and to interpret and should appear in the legend. The legend is the key to the map, and it should clearly and succinctly define the codes and symbols used. Color greatly enhances a map. It is used for identifying such features as land, water, political units, elevation, rainfall, and vegetation. Various shades of blue usually indicate water areas and their respective depths; white is used for polar regions, green for lowlands; and yellow, red, orange, and brown for progressively higher elevations or lower rainfall. The important criterion when examining the use of color in maps is that its symbolic meaning be easily and readily understood.

Quantity and Quality of Detail

Again, it is important for the librarian to be aware that one map cannot accurately provide all kinds of information. If a map becomes too cluttered with information, it does so by obscuring other equally important details; even worse, it deters the reader from using it. It is far better to have several maps of a particular area, each of which reveals a particular characteristic, than to have one map that does it all. This is clearly illustrated in Figure 11.2. With regard to quality of detail, it must be realized that distortions are often necessary for the sake of conveying information. An example of this might be an exaggeration of the size of the Nile River Delta in an attempt to portray its shape and meanderings; however, if this is properly done, the reader will readily understand the distortions as a means of representing particular aspects of the Nile River Delta.

Perhaps the most accurate maps available are those made by aerial photography. Libraries can now acquire maps based on photographs taken from airplanes and manmade satellites. Many aerial maps are reproduced at a scale of 3 inches to the mile (7.62 cm to 1.609 km), or a ratio of 1:20,000. Cartographers in the United States use aerial photography as an aid in making accurate maps. The standard United States topographic maps made by the United States Geological Survey, containing a quadrangle of 0°15′ latitude and longitude, are available in ratios of 1:60,000 (1 inch = 1 mile [2.54 cm = 1.609 km]) or 1:24,000 (2.5 inches = 1 mile [6.35 cm = 1.609 km]).

Knowledge of the essentials involved in map making is important in selecting the right maps for the library collection. It is equally important for the librarian to know something of the material characteristics of various maps, as well as some of their advantages. Consider the following:

1. *Atlas*   Atlases are books of maps that are available in many dimensions and are intended for individual use.

2. *Wall maps*   Wall maps are considered as entities, that is, they are unbound. They are usually 40–65 inches (101.60–165.10 cm) wide. It is important to know the map scale because it will determine how far away from the map a person can stand and still be able to read it. Wall maps are intended for display and group use. They can be folded, mounted on spring rollers, or attached to dowels for hand rolling.

3. *Bound wall maps*   Bound wall maps are designed to be attached to a tripod or stand, which permits them to be flipped over.

4. *Overhead transparencies*   Maps on overhead transparencies are designed to be used expressly on an overhead projector. Information can be added by the use of overlays or can be written directly on transparencies with water-soluble ink (which can be erased).

5. *Slides and filmstrips*   Maps photographed on slides and filmstrips are intended to be projected on a screen in a darkened room.

6. *Relief maps*   Relief maps provide a three-dimensional perspective of the earth's surface. The relief, to be at all effective, must be grossly exaggerated in some of its proportions. For example, if a relief map of the world 72 inches square (182.88 cm^2) were to depict Mount Everest accurately (5+ miles [8.05 + km] high) in relief, it would be less than $\frac{1}{60}$ inch (0.42 mm) high.

A final consideration is the physical durability of the map. Folded maps usually wear out at the folds or creases. Maps with cloth backing, printed on heavy durable paper stock will last longest. Add to this a plastic lamination on the front surface, and the map can be written on with washable inks and crayons and protected from dust, dirt, and tearing. The librarian must determine before selecting maps how they will be used, under what conditions, and for what purposes.

Selecting Maps

Once acquainted with the various kinds of information maps can contain, the cartographers methods of plotting information on a map, and the types of physical characteristics of maps, the librarian should be able to acquire maps for the library collection. Depending on the size of the library, there should be at least one large globe of the Earth on perpetual display—preferably in the area where the maps are located. Smaller globes can be made available for extensive individual study. A series of large maps of the Earth in various projections should be acquired for comparing and analyzing the advantages, as well as the disadvantages, of each type of projection. The library will need maps of major world areas (e.g., continents and oceans), of countries (political maps), and the fifty states of the United States. Often, the best political maps of a particular country are printed in the language of that country and can present a problem in the translation of verbal information on the maps. This is a small inconvenience, however, if the map is the most accurate representation available in both detail and other information.

The librarian should define the local or regional area for which the library will provide maps and the kinds of maps it will acquire. It may well need local maps of many characteristics: geography, agriculture, soils, minerals, water distribution, topography, history, commerce, industry, demographic distribution by various factors (e.g., census, resident age, economic, educational), political boundaries (e.g., wards, precincts, voting characteristics), and distribution of public agencies (e.g., schools and fire and police departments). Quite often it is the local library that acquires the most complete and extensive maps of a local area by developing an archive collection of maps. Maps have an historical value in that they depict how a community has developed and changed over extended periods of time, the location of its former landmarks and property that no longer exists, and changes that have occurred in the layout of highways and streets. The archive value of such a collection cannot be underestimated; it could well be that these maps are the only ones in existence, and as such are invaluable for historical research or even the settling of boundary disputes.

If the collection of local maps becomes too extensive and cumbersome to maintain, rather than weeding out old maps, it may be advisable to consider committing them to microform. As a matter of fact, though the large paper map is still the prevalent form, there is a growing trend toward acquiring cartographic material that is recorded on microfilm because of the cost and required storage space of paper maps.

Using Maps

The basic criteria for providing maps for patron use are (*a*) the type of information needed and (*b*) how it is to be used. It is possible that because of limited demand, some cartographic information is only available in a particular format. Therefore, if the only available format is an atlas, it could be used, at most, by only two or three people at one time; whereas a large map, on the other hand, can be used profitably by a group of people. More likely than not, requests for special types of maps do not involve large groups of people. If a request should arise wherein a relatively small map must be used by a large group, the map can easily be enlarged and projected onto a screen with an opaque projector.

Conversely, when a large map is to be used by an individual, it may be advisable to have large map tables with tilted surfaces for comfortable viewing and examination. As an added service, it is convenient to have basic map accessories available (e.g., magnifying glasses, compass roses, parallel rulers, dividers). If a patron is going to make extensive measurements on the map, he or she should be cautioned not to make any marks on the map that cannot be completely removed. The library may consider laminating the maps or providing clear plastic sheets to cover the maps; the patron can then use a water-soluble marker that can easily be erased after each use, which allows complete flexibility of use without any damage to the map. Finally, the patron must be encouraged to return the maps in the same condition in which they were received. This is especially true of accordion folded maps, which if haphazardly folded, are difficult to store and easily worn or damaged.

Selected Bibliography

Crone, Gerard R. *Maps and Their Makers: An Introduction to the History of Cartography*, fifth edition Hamden, Connecticut: Archon Books, 1978.

Dickinson, Gordon C. *Maps and Air Photographs: Images of Earth*, second edition New York, Halsted Press, 1979.

Drazniowsky, Roman. *Map Librarianship: Readings*. Metuchen, New Jersey: Scarecrow Press, 1975.

Larsgaard, Mary. *Map Librarianship: An Introduction*. Littleton, Colorado: Libraries Unlimited, 1978.

Low, Janet Grant-McKay. *The Acquisition of Maps and Charts Published by the United States Government*. Occasional Papers No. 125. Urbana: University of Illinois, 1976.

Nichols, Harold. *Map Librarianship*. Hamden, Connecticut: Linnet Books, 1976.

Special Libraries Association, Geography and Map Division. Bulletin. Bethesda, Maryland: Special Libraries Association, 1947–.

Stevenson, Edward L. *Terrestrial and Celestial Globes: Their History and Construction, Including a Consideration of Their Value As Aids in the Study of Geography and Astronomy*, (2 vols.). New York: Johnson Reprint, 1921.

Thompson, Morris M. *Maps for America: Cartographic Products of the United States Geological Survey and Others*. Washington, D.C.: Superintendent of Documents, 1979.

Selection Aids

The Bibliography of Cartography, (5 vols.) Boston: G. K. Hall, 1973.

Carrington, David, and Stephensen, Richard, eds. *Map Collections in the U.S. and Canada: A Directory*, third rev. edition. New York: Special Libraries Association, 1978.

Index to Maps in Books and Periodicals. (10 vols.). Boston: G. K. Hall 1968, first supplement 1971. second supplement 1976.

Murphy, Mary. "Atlas of the Eastern Hemisphere." *Geographical Review* 64(Jan. 1974):111–134.

Stephenson, Richard W. "Atlases of the Western Hemisphere: A Summary Survey." *Geographical Review* 62(Jan. 1972):92–119.

Stephenson, Richard W. "Published Sources of Information about Maps and Atlases." *Special Libraries* 61(Feb. 1970):87–98, 110–112.

Types of Maps Published by Government Agencies. Reston, Virginia: U.S. Geological Survey, 1977.

Winch, Kenneth L., ed. *International Maps and Atlases in Print.* second edition New York: R. R. Bowker, 1976.

Wise, Donald A. "Cartographic Sources and Procurement Problems." *Special Libraries* 68(May–June 1977):198–205.

12

Models, Realia, and Games and Simulations

Overview

There are some media forms in the library that cannot be conveniently categorized as purely audio and/or visual. These media forms, because of their size, shape, and presentation of informational content, are intended to be manipulated, interacted with, or somehow kinesthetically used. Included in these forms are models, realia, and games and simulations.

Models tend to closely represent objects in the real world, and are acquired by libraries whenever it is not feasible to include the actual object in the library collection. The informational value of a model is that it can show with little or no verbal description what an object looks like or does.

Actual objects are categorized as realia, and these can be either natural or manufactured. When practical and feasible, the acquisition of realia should be strongly considered because they can provide the user with a direct, purposeful, and concrete experience. Anything less than realia is an abstraction, and thus requires some degree of communication skill to interpret its relation to the actual object. Often realia are selected because they provide an authentic kinesthetic experience that can be quite meaningful in and of itself.

Games and simulations can range in physical makeup anywhere from a set of printed directions to a complicated board game or computer activity that requires the manipulation of various pieces or components. In either case, games and simulations require active, rather than passive, participation; nothing will happen until the user reacts with or to them by making some kind of overt response that draws on the user's knowledge, skill, or luck.

The extent to which libraries are committed to these various manipulative media forms usually depends on how their value is perceived. If the librarian considers them to be expensive frills, their acquisition will obviously be a low priority if they are considered at all. However, if the librarian deems them essential for providing a particular type of information experience, their acquisition will be considered a high priority. In either case, the acquisition of realia should be given careful thought in terms of their cost, maintenance, ease of use, and contribution to the library's pool of information services.

Models

A *model* is a replica or representation of a real object. Often, when the real object is inconvenient to examine and observe, a model is used to facilitate its investigation. Although an abstraction of the real thing, a model provides a three-dimensional representation of the original and thereby permits a highly concrete learning experience. When the printed word or a visual cannot communicate the informational content of an object adequately, a model can perhaps successfully fill this gap. In the preceding chapter, globes, which are models of the earth, were discussed. Obviously, when globes are considered, it is impossible to observe the real object that a globe represents in its entirety, and printed words or visuals cannot communicate or describe the physical appearance of the earth as well as a globe.

As replicas of real things, models provide a means of close examination and investigation. Perhaps models are able to satisfy people's inquisitiveness about the world around them. Models on display in libraries always seem to draw attention, and patrons are not only fascinated by them, but find that they learn from them as well. The librarian should not overlook the fact that not only do models communicate extremely well by virtue of being replicas of real things, but also people are extremely familiar with them. Children grow up, mature, and learn by manipulating toys that are indeed models taken from real life (e.g., dolls, dollhouses, toy cars and trucks, stuffed animals), and the fascination with models does not end with childhood. Many adults become involved with the construction of model trains, boats, or automobiles.

Practically every home is beautified and decorated with a model of some type (e.g., ships, statuettes, miniatures). In essence, models do not require the use of special skills in order to be understood or appreciated. What may be difficult to comprehend in written form becomes immediately lucid in a model.

When selecting models, the librarian needs to be critically aware of their characteristics and attributes. The intended use of the model will determine the degree of accuracy required. To use the globe as an example, if some of the rivers that appear on the globe were accurately replicated as to size and shape, it would require a magnifying glass to see them. This is a case in which accuracy can be sacrificed for the sake of more essential information, such as location, direction, and general shape. It has been found that when people examine models, they are more concerned with the functionally significant parts. Both adults and children seem to prefer models that are less complex than the original things, in which the emphasis is on the major concept, function, or operation of the things represented. This fact further supports the idea that models do not have to be exact replicas in every detail. Again, the accuracy with which the model represents the original should depend on the intended use of the model. A transparent model of a human in which the internal organs and structure of the body can be observed, need not have a liquid representation of blood; this would only obscure the view of the internal organs and structure. Indeed, this is a case in which too much attention to detail would distract or confuse the viewer, who is primarily interested in significant organic structure.

Models are made because it is difficult or even impossible to view the real objects. Generally, models are reproduced in three relative sizes: the same size as the original, an enlarged or blown-up replica, or a reduced or miniaturized reproduction. Exact-size models are used chiefly as substitutes for an original that could be dangerous, expensive, rare, fragile, perishable, odoriferous, or difficult to maintain in a library. Enlarged models are extremely helpful in examining very small things; it would require an electron microscope to view the invisible molecular world, but a representative model of a molecule vividly portrays its structure in three dimensions. Conversely, a miniaturized model affords the opportunity to view the immensity of a large object in its entirety (e.g., a globe of the earth). Because of various size alterations in the relation of models to the things they represent, the model should always be labeled with regard to its scale. It is significant to know the extent to which the size of the model represents the real thing. This is especially important when models are close to the exact size of the original. The degree of scale exactness provides the information necessary to prevent misconceptions in learning. A replica of a cross section of a human torso that is slightly enlarged or reduced could result in a misconception about body parts that are unfamiliar to the user. However, the librarian should always consider the possibility that a slightly enlarged or reduced model of any object may be easier to view, handle, maintain, or store, and might even be less expensive to purchase. Regardless of the intent of acquisition, information concerning scale should be conveniently available to the user.

Various types of models are available, and the librarian should be familiar with such terms as exact model, simplified model, static model, working model, mock-up, cutaway, transparent model, cross section, and diorama. An *exact model* is one that except for enlargement or reduction is exact in *every* detail and can even be a working replica. A *simplified model* contains only those parts of the original that are necessary for study or observation, and even then, the parts are in simplified form. An example of an exact model is a model airplane in which each part, at exact scale, is included. When selecting models that work, it may be necessary, in a pure sense, to distinguish between a model and a miniature. If an item is made of the same material and can perform the same function as a larger version, it should be called a *miniature* rather than a model. As an example, it is possible to purchase an electric motor that can fit in the palm of the hand (e.g., the motor of an electric shaver); this then is not a model of a motor, rather it is a real, working motor. If the motor needs an outside mechanism in order to function (i.e., cannot operate in and of itself), it is a model. An exact model is essentially a replica of the original that is authentically enlarged or reduced for easier examination.

A *static model* is one that has no moving parts, even though it is quite possible that the original item it replicates does have moving parts. The purpose of a static model is basically to show what the original looks like, rather than what it does. A *working model* shows how the original operates and functions; and, unlike the static model, it does not necessarily have to show what the original looks like, but rather what it does. This leads to the next type of model, the mock-up. A *mockup* is a symbolic version of the actual object designed to show how the object works, even though the mock-up does not resemble the actual object in many aspects. Although it would be difficult and complex to show the operation of an actual hydraulic system, a mock-up can demonstrate the primary functions of the system's various components, and the use of liquid in the manipulation of the model illustrates how the system functions. A mock-up is used to illustrate the principles involved in the function or purpose of a real object.

The next type of model is a cutaway. A *cutaway*, as the term indicates, is a model with a surface that has been removed or cut away to reveal the inner working, function, or structure of the actual object. A cutaway can be extraordinarily revealing and informative in cases where the interior of the actual object cannot be seen. Models of the human torso are available in which the flesh and bone are cutaway to reveal the inner organs. Similar to cutaways are *transparent models* in which the outer surface is made of a clear plastic and the interior parts are clearly visible. Both the cutaway and the transparent model have distinct advantages. Although in the cutaway part of the exterior surface has been removed, the interior parts are physically accessible. With the transparent model, the color of the actual object is lost, and the interior is not physically accessible; but none of the exterior surface has been removed. These are the general characteristics of cutaways and transparent models; however there are commercially made models that combine the best attributes of both, having see-through capability and removable, or cutaway, surfaces.

Similar to a cutaway is a cross-sectional model. Rather than having a portion of the surface removed, a *cross-sectional model* is literally a slice of the model that reveals the interior arrangement, location, and function of the actual object. A cross section of a model automobile engine is an excellent device for showing how an automobile engine is constructed.

A *diorama* is a three-dimensional scene enclosed within a painted set. Objects are arranged to depict an actual scene; to add a greater sense of realism, the scene is set within an appropriate background. A homemade diorama constructed within a shoebox in which the inside areas are appropriately painted and decorated is easy to make and enjoyable to look at. Libraries make extensive use of dioramas by constructing them inside glass display cases. A diorama can contain real objects, like flora and fauna, and range in size from a small diorama using the inside of an eggshell for a scenic background to a large room-size display of the kind found in museums. Not as common as dioramas are *cycloramas,* which differ from dioramas in that instead of being viewed from the outside they are made to be viewed from within a large circular room. A planetarium is a form of cyclorama. Perhaps the most famous cyclorama is one that is housed in its own building near Atlanta. It depicts the Battle of Atlanta fought on July 22, 1864. It combines real objects, models, and a background painting 50 feet (15.24 m) high, 400 feet (121.92 m) in circumference, and weighing 9 tons (907.18 kg). It is considered to be the largest painting in the world.

Selection

The terms used to describe the various types of models indicate their predominant features. Many models combine several of the characteristic features of the various model types. For example it is possible to have a cutaway, cross-sectional, mock-up, simplified, working model of a real object. Again, it is the librarian who must in selecting a model determine which features are most desirable and effective in realizing the objectives for which the model is selected.

There must be a reason for selecting a model. It should contribute information on a subject that cannot be communicated by other media as well or as economically. It should replicate the original and provide better information than the original for the reasons cited earlier. Some models are intended to be handled, thereby providing a tactile experience. The following criteria should be used to evaluate a model being considered for selection:

1. Is it feasible to include the original item in the library collection?
2. Does the model provide a service that is better than or not provided by, other media?
3. Is the scale of the model properly represented, and are all related parts of the same scale?
4. Is the model accurate? If there is any simplification that decreases the degree of accuracy, is it wholly justifiable?
5. Could the model misinform a user who is not familiar with the actual object? If inaccuracies are evident, are they there for a purpose, and is it highly unlikely that they will confuse the user?
6. If the model is to be handled, is the construction durable?
7. Can the model be stored and/or displayed efficiently and effectively? (It should not occupy (consume) valuable library space in excess of its actual worth.)
8. Is cost of the model justified? (Because models tend to be relatively expensive, their purchase should be justified in terms of use, efficiency in providing information, and, perhaps, esthetic value.)

Utilization

Because models have the capacity to communicate without extensive periods of examination, they will most likely be used in the library, or in adjacent areas, for relatively short periods of time. The user, unless involved in making sketches or measurements, can complete an examination of a model in a few minutes. Even models that involve user manipulation can achieve their objectives quite rapidly, which demonstrates the value of a model. Exceptions occur when the model is used for an activity, such as a simulation, or when the model has to be constructed or disassembled. In many situations, all that is needed to use a model is a space large enough to accommodate it. Models that require little or no manipulation can quite often simply be left on display for casual perusal.

If the library has an extensive collection of models, it may be practical to store them on open shelves. In all probability, most of them could be examined without having to remove them from the shelf area. A few multipurpose tables or carrels near the model storage area may serve to facilitate a closer examination of models that require more detailed study.

If models are to be charged out of the library, they will probably be used for aesthetic purposes (e.g., as a display, a decoration, or an object that will motivate or inspire the observer), and should be properly packaged for safe transit. The patron needs to be informed of his or her responsibility for properly handling the model and liability if damage should occur. The library will need to formulate a special policy for loaning out models even to the extent that it may have to consider charging a use fee in order to cover the cost and maintenance of the items.

Realia

As described in the preceding section, a model is a representation of the actual object to be used when it is not feasible to house actual object in the library collection. However, there are a great many objects that the library can acquire in order to provide the patron with firsthand experiences. Real items, specimens, relics, and real materials are collectively classified as *realia*. It cannot be disputed that the more real the object being viewed, the more concrete and permanent the learning experience will be. Realia have a natural, built-in, intrinsic interest. After all, why should an individual view or learn about an object via a substitute communication means (e.g., models, films, books) when the actual object is available for examination? Realia are capable of providing substance to a study.

It is practically impossible, and certainly extremely dangerous, for a library patron to go off in search of a rattlesnake, but a stuffed rattlesnake can be conveniently and safely examined in the library. The library patron is practically afforded a firsthand sensory experience. The rattlesnake is not viewed in its natural habitat, but even that can be simulated by displaying the snake in a diorama.

Realia can be quite costly, and in order to justify their expense, it is recommended that their use be incorporated into a systematized approach. Too often, libraries regard the realia in their collections as nothing more than dust-collecting junk, when they can provide truly valuable information and enjoyment. Realia should be displayed or used with other materials. For example, a stuffed rattlesnake can be prominently displayed in a diorama, study prints can be put on a display board, and relevant motion picture films and books can be shown or made available. In this way, a total sensory approach is provided: The patron can see, and perhaps even handle, a real rattlesnake; study various pictures of it; view a film of it living and functioning in its natural habitat; and, finally, obtain further extensive and intensive reading material about it. The total systematized approach affords the library patron either the opportunity to examine a rattlesnake via a multitude of sensory and media channels or the option to select the media channel he or she deems most appropriate. But regardless of how the patron decides to investigate rattlesnakes, it is practically a foregone certainty that he or she will not bypass the opportunity to examine the real thing.

In utilizing realia through a systems approach, the librarian should strongly consider the acquisition or local fabrication of realia kits. A *realia kit* is a collection of real things, near-real things (models), and other supporting media (films, books, art prints, charts, audio tapes, etc.) that provides a saturated study of an actual object. A realia kit has three distinct advantages: (*a*) it contains the elements of a complete, multisensory, multimedia study of an actual object; (*b*) practically everything the patron needs is assembled in one package from which he or she can select whatever is wanted, thereby eliminating the need to search all over the library for individual materials; and (*c*) the realia kit contains all the materials for constructing a display or exhibit. Realia kits do have the disadvantage of tying up a lot of material; and when they are used or checked out by a patron, all the items in the kit are taken even if the patron intends to use only a portion of the items. Obviously, all the items cannot be used when charged to a single patron, simultaneously.

When dealing with realia, the librarian can also consider a realia exhibit, which is essentially a collection of related materials. The acquisition of realia to be used in exhibits can be justified in terms of having displays in the library that are both aesthetically pleasing and of educational value and interest. If the librarian wishes to have realia exhibits, it is important that they be displayed dynamically, with purpose and meaning. Too often, exhibits are static and uninspiring and are left on display well beyond their period of importance. Realia exhibits are not intended merely to take up space in the library; they are meant to entice the viewer to investigate, learn more about, and perhaps even develop an interest in the realia. If realia exhibits do not motivate patrons, they cannot be justified. An effective realia exhibit should communicate the purposes, functions, and structures of the realia, as well as the interrelationships of these, and the relationship of the realia itself to the viewer.

Another category of realia is that of the *specimen*, which is part of a real thing or one unit of a thing that is representative of a class, genus, or whole. As an example, a particular species of bird may be representative of a particular type of birds in a particular region. For example, if the librarian wished to provide information about birds that function as predators in a particular region, it would not be necessary to collect several species of predators; one bird that is representative of the group as a whole would be sufficient. When selecting a particular bird, it would be beneficial to include a specimen of its skeleton, which would provide information regarding its internal structure. The selection of specimens is a complicated process, and the librarian should consult a person with expertise in order to insure that the right specimen is selected and that it provides the best means of informing the patron.

Selection

When selecting realia, the librarian needs to consider whether or not they will be handled by patrons. If a particular specimen is particularly delicate, it may be best to put it in a display case. If it can be encased in clear plastic, it can be picked up and examined without damage. Ideally, patrons should be able to handle realia, because this affords a sensory awareness of the object unobtainable by other means. A final consideration when selecting fauna specimens is the possibility of displaying live animals. Many libraries have been extremely successful in providing patrons with live animals, which indeed provides about as real and concrete an experience as a patron can have. Of course, live animals create a host of unique problems (e.g., care, feeding, handling, the safety of the animal, and the safety of the patron). Many librarians feel that having real animals available is well beyond the scope of the library's mandate to serve the community, but libraries involved with live animals are gratified by the requests for them from patrons. It is up to each library to decide to what extent it is to be involved with realia, with regard to scope, specimens, kits, exhibits, handling, and whether living specimens are to be included in the library collection. The library could indeed justify a decision not to deal with realia per se, and provide a reference service instead. This can be achieved by simply referring realia requests to other agencies in the community (e.g., zoos, museums, and other similar places more knowledgeable and better equipped to display particular types of realia). The library might even go as far as to borrow realia from these agencies in order to make them available for a particular request or event.

When it comes to the actual selection of realia, the librarian will be amazed at all the various resources that are available. Certain companies (e.g., Ward's Scientific Co.) provide scientific realia to libraries and educational institutions. There is usually an abundant supply of realia available in the library's immediate community, which, if solicited, can be either loaned or donated to the library. The hobbyist, amateur, and professional are usually gratified to have the opportunity to display their collections in the library, and will often serve as resource persons as well.

To avoid a proliferation of realia beyond the needs of the library, the librarian should, first, classify areas of realia and, then, determine what types are essential to the library program. Once realia are classified, it becomes apparent which types from each classification would be beneficial to the library and should be considered as bona fide informational realia. General classifications include the following:

1. *Applied sciences and arts* realia related to industry, home, health and medicine, military science, and recreation
2. *Humanities and the arts* realia related to art, music, drama, and the humanities
3. *Science* realia related to biology, chemistry, geology, natural science, physics, meteorology, ecology, and environment
4. *Social sciences* realia related to anthropology, geography, ethnic studies, geography, history, psychology, and philosophy

Having set up a classification of realia, the librarian can determine the types of materials needed to enhance the library collection and decide whether such materials need to be purchased outright or can be obtained from the community on a loaned or donated basis. It is extremely gratifying to locate really fine realia in the community that can be made available to the library at no cost. It is a good idea to start a community realia resource file listing locations for obtaining stamp collections, rare and foreign coins, rock collections, flora and fauna (both live and preserved), artifacts or relics of significant social value, and mementos of important events. Such realia certainly enhance the library's collection and make it a more stimulating place to visit. It is even possible that a room or space in the library can be set aside as a museum area where library patrons have an opportunity of gaining a direct and purposeful experience by seeing and perhaps even handling realia. When obtaining realia from the community, via either solicitation or donation; it is important to develop a form to be signed by the contributor, stating explicitly the library's obligation in accepting any materials. The form should indicate specifically: (a) how the realia will be used, (b) who will be responsible for their maintenance, (c) who will assume the cost of replacing damaged or lost items, (d) what the dollar value of the item is, (e) whether it is permissable to modify the realia in any form, (f) if the realia are loaned, what is the time period during which they will be available to the library, (g) if they are donated, how should the library dispose of them when they are no longer needed, and (h) what acknowledgments should be accorded to the contributor. If a procedure is followed whereby both the contributor and the library sign a form stating the terms under which the library accepts the realia (or any other material, for that matter), there will be no ambiguity of proprietorship, and certainly no subsequent occasion for dispute if problems do indeed arise.

The capability of realia in enhancing the library's program should not be overlooked. They provide concrete, sensory learning experiences, and they are useful in clarifying principles, functions, and classifications. Realia can also provide an aesthetic experience by bringing the real world into the library. The library patron will gain and appreciate the powerful learning experience that results from the use of realia.

Utilization

The consideration for using realia are similar to those of using models. Both the librarian and the user need to be aware of the uniqueness of realia as an informational medium and respond accordingly. As with other media, the library will need to develop a policy specifically applicable to the acquisition and use of realia.

Games and Simulations

In an attempt to provide the patron with a wide variety of media alternatives from which to choose, the library can offer games and simulations as still another means for acquiring information. Games and simulations furnish an experience in which the patron is actively involved in the learning process, rather than playing a passive, observing role as in the case of viewing a film or reading a book. By being actively involved, the patron experiences a greater psychological impact than he or she could possibly gain by observing. Also, games and simulations produce an enjoyable experience that often involves group interaction, which is difficult to obtain from other types of media.

Games and simulations are structured activities with specific rules and parameters designed for the purpose of actively involving the participant(s) in exploring, investigating, or experiencing certain aspects of a contrived procedure, event, or situation, the control and outcome of which is affected, directly or indirectly, by the skill and behavior of the participant(s). When assessing and selecting games and simulations, it is important to bear in mind that the terms *game* and *simulation* are not dichotomous. For the purpose of identification, it would be best to decide where the activity should be positioned on a continuum, on which game is at one end and simulation is at the other. An activity that can be classified as a pure game or a pure simulation is very rare; each almost always contains elements of the other.

Actually, the term simulation, as used in this context, has its origins in World War II. It was adopted by the military to describe certain procedures for training pilots. As part of a pilot's training, he was required to fly blind and land aircraft in conditions of poor or zero visibility (e.g., bad weather or darkness). To practice flying under such adverse conditions is obviously extremely dangerous, with an inherent high risk of losing both the pilot and the aircraft. To eliminate this danger, the military used the Link trainer, which *simulated* most of the conditions and sensations of flying in situations of zero visibility without the student pilot ever having to leave the ground. The student pilot could make a "bad landing" without the resultant risk to himself or his aircraft. Hence, the Link trainer produced a simulation of a real activity in which the student pilot was actively involved with and in control of the eventual outcome. A similar type of simulator familiar to many high school students is a driving simulation trainer. Again, the student is actively involved in learning, is in control of the outcome, and experiences many of the sensations of driving an automobile without risk to the student or to a real automobile. Many other games and simulations are commercially available to the library, and the librarian should seriously consider their inclusion in the library program as a service to patrons.

Games and simulations are generally chosen to make available a structured activity in which knowledge, information, or learning experiences can be acquired. Although the entertainment aspect is often an inherent factor of games and simulations, it is not the primary reason for selecting them. Rather, they are selected as one means, perhaps even the best means, of achieving a learning experience. Therefore, it becomes critical for the librarian to know exactly what the stated objectives of the game or simulation being considered are and then to determine if it is the best means of achieving these objectives.

In order to assess games and simulations intelligently, it is necessary to understand their elementary characteristics and the functions they are intended to serve. Again, the best way to assess the characteristics of games and simulations, is to place game at one end of a continuum and simulation at the other, bearing in mind that although a characteristic is *usually* associated with either a game or simulation, it is not exclusive to it. The following discussion should prove helpful in identifying the characteristics of games and simulations.

Games The element of chance is usually involved in games. This is achieved through the use of dice, spinners, counters, cards, etc. The participant, regardless of skill, has no control over the chance element. If he or she is unlucky enough to have a poor roll of the dice, a bad spin, or to pick a poor card, it will affect his or her performance at that point in the game and very possibly the outcome of the game as well. Games usually involve a win–lose situation. The game reaches a climax and a conclusion when the winners and losers are identified. This also suggests that games have definite points of termination (i.e., when someone wins or loses). Games are usually used to *learn* subject matter, data, or concepts. The game, although a pleasurable activity, also provides the participant with a means to learn, develop, amd master skills.

Simulations Participant behavior is usually emphasized in simulations. The skill and ability the participant brings to the simulation will directly affect the progress of the simulation and influence the eventual outcome. This aspect of simulations should be carefully scrutinized because it pertains to the active involvement of the participant, which is one of the primary reasons for selecting a simulation. Moreover, a simulation is usually based on a real-life situation. Hence, it has no finite ending other than that imposed on it by the participants (i.e., the simulation lasts as long as the participants wish to participate). The simulation involves a "slice of life" whereby the participants act out an event. They are in control, and their behavior affects the outcome. The simulation can use such devices as scenarios, role playing, and recreated environments. It is quite common in a simulation for a participant to play the role of another person. In a play or drama, the role-player cannot affect the scripted outcome; but in a simulation, the outcome is predicated on the skill of the participant. The simulation focuses on individuals interacting either with other individuals by engaging in verbal discourse or with equipment by performing a task (e.g., flight training). Finally, simulations are usually used to *apply* skills. Once a skill is learned, the simulation provides the context in which the skill can be tried out, giving the participants an opportunity to experience an event within the partial framework of a real-life situation.

As a result of the foregoing characteristics, games and simulations can be used to achieve the following goals:

1. *To motivate and increase enthusiasm for learning* Because the participant is actively involved in the process and contributes to the outcome, he or she has a personal interest or stake in the activity. Also, most games and simulations incorporate an element of play that tends to make them enjoyable.

2. *To stimulate more sophisticated and relevant inquiry* The participant is not passively acquiring information, but is using personal skills to effect outcomes; therefore, knowledge is not only being acquired, but also applied. Because they allow participants to apply knowledge, games and simulations offer the added features of meaning and relevance.

3. *To improve decision-making, communicating, and learning skills* It is one thing to know something, but to apply knowledge requires a good deal more ability. Games and simulations afford participants an opportunity to exercise and apply learning in a controlled situation. Many simulations are designed to involve human interaction, one participant must communicate with other participants and persuade them to accept other viewpoints. The ability to persuade another person to accept a particular point of view involves a much higher order of skill than just holding and accepting that opinion oneself.

4. *To improve information interpretation skills* The participant must use newly acquired information and apply it in a real-life social context. The information now has much greater meaning, and the degree to which it is used in various simulated situations will enhance its applicability to a host of broader, real-life situations.

5. *To provide an opportunity to examine the rational and emotional components of a process* Because the participant is competing with or being influenced by other participants, personal outcomes of the game or simulation are always in doubt; joys as well as frustrations can be experienced. Because the participant is actively involved in the process, he or she cannot help but become aware of the rational and emotional components that would be involved in the real-life situation.

6. *To make learning real* Whether the subject is flying an aircraft in a Link trainer or buying Atlantic City real estate while playing Monopoly,

the experience provided by a game or simulation requires far more involvement than that provided by just reading about it or viewing a film on it. Perhaps, for a brief moment, the participant is able to escape from his or her own real world and to enter into the fantasy world of the game or simulation to learn, experience, feel, and apply, in a controlled situation, new knowledge unattainable by any other means.

Considering these goals, it becomes apparent that games and simulations can replicate certain aspects of the real world in an environment on which some controls can be exercised so that the participant will not be in any real danger or risk, but, at the same time, can become verbally, physically, and emotionally involved in a learning-by-experiencing situation.

Selection

The librarian's task selecting games and simulations involves several considerations.

Purpose   It must be ascertained whether the game or simulation is a discrete entity or is to be specifically incorporated for use with other types of informational media. Also to be considered is whether the game or simulation is designed for the purpose of introducing, exploring, or investigating information, and whether this is to be achieved in a cursory or in-depth fashion.

Objective   The goals and objectives of the game or simulation should be clearly and concisely stated. The expected behavior or knowledge to be acquired by the participant needs to be known. Although the game or simulation is not intended solely for the purpose of fun, it should nevertheless be an enjoyable and rewarding experience for the participants. In the case of pseudogames and pseudosimulations like Tinkertoys, the librarian will need to conceive activities and objectives for their use that are in keeping with the characteristics and goals stated previously in this discussion.

Patron   Certain facts need to be known about the patron who is expected to use the library's games and simulations. A supposedly wise selection is of no value if it is never used. The game of Monopoly is a good example of selecting games and simulations with the patron in mind. If most of the patrons in the community the library serves own their own Monopoly games, then they will obviously not be going to the library to request them. Nor will there be any requests for the game if the library's community has no need for or interest in it.

Type of Use Basically, there are two places where games and simulations will be used: in the library and outside the library. If games and simulations are to be used in the library, an activity area must be allocated for this purpose. Because games and simulations often involve verbal interaction, spaces used should have audio privacy so that participants neither disturb nor are disturbed by other patrons. When games and simulations are used outside the library, concern for their conscientious use by the patron becomes paramount because the patron is no longer under the control or supervision of the librarian. Because games and simulations are often boxed items containing many individual pieces, the patron needs to be encouraged to return them in a respectable condition so that they can be used by other patrons thereafter.

Management Because games and simulations contain many individual pieces, they can be difficult to manage. For example, it would be absurd for the librarian to have to check in each individual item included in a game of Monopoly. It would be equally foolish not to assume that at least some of the pieces will eventually become lost. All the parts of a game or simulation will be used and therefore can be expected to become worn. The librarian must project the life expectancy of a game or simulation, based on the expected number of uses. Again, using Monopoly as an example, if a librarian determines that after 25 uses, enough pieces will have been lost, destroyed, or received sufficient wear so as to impair the use of the game as a whole; the librarian should inform the administration that a replacement is justified after 25 uses. The actual figure for the number of uses will be based on experience, and eventually a revised number of uses will be more in line with the actual need for replacement. The point here is that unlike a book, which is far easier to control and does not receive the same kind of punishing wear, a game or simulation requires a use-based life expectancy rather than a time-based life expectancy.

Utilization

As indicated previously, games and simulations can be used in or out of the library. If used outside the library, it is advisable to strongly suggest that the patron be considerate of other patrons when using games and simulations by making a concerted effort to return items in approximately the same condition as when they were borrowed.

When used in the library, appropriate areas will have to be provided to allow for the interaction and activity necessary to achieve the objectives of games and simulations. It is quite conceivable, in the case of simulations, that the group involved might consist of both participants and observers. In all probability, this will require something in the form of a structured activity, which will require someone to be a monitor and, even more importantly, a facilitator during the debriefing. It will be necessary therefore to have a monitor who is skilled in using a particular simulation as well as experienced in guiding its progress. It is not necessarily the responsibility of the librarian to be the monitor, since considerable time could be required to supervise such an activity. (If the librarian is the monitor, the role should be so designated and adequately supported by the administration.) In making games and simulations available for patron use, it may be advisable to list each of their major characteristics (e.g., whether monitor is essential, whether debriefing will be required, the length of necessary time to complete the activity, the type of overt activity that will be performed). It would certainly be an invaluable service if the librarian could construct bibliographies of games and simulations in the library collection that would give those interested in using these materials important information as to what is available, where it can be used, for whom it is best suited, as well as some information about the objectives of each activity and how it attempts to accomplish these goals.

Introducing and encouraging the use of games and simulations in the library can be a welcome and valuable service. They are an interesting and exciting way to learn information and acquire new skills. They do have a place in the library, and their value as tools of communication and knowledge should not be underestimated. The bibliography at the end of this chapter contains valuable resources and references for the librarian who needs to know more about the use of games and simulations, as well as sources for obtaining them.

Selected Bibliography

Models

McLaughlin, Terrence. *Working Toys and Models*. New York: Larousse and Company, 1978.

Realia

Hektoen, Faith H., and Rinehart, Jeanne B., eds. *Toys to Go: A Guide to the Use of Realia in Public Libraries*. Chicago: American Library Association, 1976.
"Realia in the Library." *Booklist*, 73(Jan. 1977):671–674.

Games and Simulations

Gibbs, C. I., ed. *Handbook of Games and Simulation Exercises*. Beverly Hills: Sage Publications, 1974.

Megarry, Jacquetta, ed. *Aspects of Simulation and Gaming: An Anthology of Sagset Journal*. London, England: Kogan Page, 1977.

Sagset Journal. Leicestershire, England: Centre of Extension Studies, University of Technology Loughborough, 1971–.

Simulation and Games. Beverly Hills: Sage Publications, 1970–.

Sullivan, Dorothy D., Davey, Beth, and Dickinson, Dolores P. *Games as Learning Tools: A Guide for Effective Use*. New York: McGraw-Hill, 1978.

Selection Aids

Models

Wasserman, Paul and Herman, Esther, eds. *Catalog of Museum Publications and Media*, second edition Detroit: Gale Research, 1980.

Games and Simulations

Belch, Jean, comp. *Contemporary Games: A Directory and Bibliography*, (2 vols.). Detroit: Gale Research, 1974.

Horn, Robert E., ed. *The Guide to Simulation/Games for Education and Training*, third edition (2 vols.). Cranford, New Jersey: Didactic Systems, 1976.

13

Microforms

Overview

When categorizing information media forms, the microform can truly be considered a hybrid. It is the amalgamation of both print and non-print media in that it makes print information available on a film format. The most obvious advantage of the microform is that it can store vast amounts of information in a relatively small space. But a subtler and perhaps equally important advantage is that the library, through microform acquisitions, can obtain out-of-print works in their original manuscript form. For example, St. Louis University in Missouri has had ancient manuscripts from the Vatican microfilmed for the study of medieval history. In their original form, rare works would obviously be beyond the financial range of most libraries, but they become affordable when committed to microform. Also, when there is an option whether to acquire information in microform or paper print, the microform is usually less expensive.

Although the microform collection is presently almost solely limited to in-library use, there are companies that manufacture portable reading devices that are in an affordable price range. The serious patron may consider purchasing his or her own reader and, in turn, will want to borrow microformed materials from the library. The microform is neither a new nor a static media format. The Library of Congress started microfilming books as early as 1928, and today, just about every library in the country has a microform collection. Presently, it is the most efficient form for storing printed information because of tremendous savings in both space and material. It is a media form that will be present for years to come; and although it will eventually be replaced by digitalized information that can be stored in computers, the microform is presently a media format capable of providing certain information more effectively and efficiently than any other format. The librarian must be open to selecting information in this format and must create conditions conducive to its utilization.

Definition of Microform

Microform is a generic term that identifies visual information originally in paper form that has been photographically reduced. Examples include books, magazines, newspapers, maps, charts, and cancelled checks. The magnification needed to read microforms ranges anywhere from 10 times (10×) to 210 times (210×). The resultant savings in storage space is hard to conceive. For example, the 20,000 volumes of the *Library of American Civilization* in book form occupy 2000 feet (609.6 m) of shelf space, but on microform they can be stored in a single file drawer. Ten issues of the *New York Times* (approximately 830 pages of information) will easily fit on a 100-foot (30.48-m) reel of microfilm occupying a space of only $3\frac{3}{4} \times 3\frac{3}{4} \times 1\frac{5}{8}$ inches (9.53 × 9.53 × 4.13 cm). Microforms are indeed the miniaturization of the printed page.

The advantages of microforms are numerous: they are a way of preserving information contained in rare documents; they are easy to duplicate; they save space; they do not need to be bound, so binding problems are eliminated; they are less expensive than books; they are never out of print; and they are tough and durable.

But before committing the library to a microform system, the librarian should also consider the possible disadvantages of microforms: they require some type of machine or device to enlarge them to readable size; because of their small size, they can easily be misfiled; and because the viewing machinery is located in the library, outside use, if possible at all is very limited. Moreover, there is a whole array of microform standards, each involving its own system of equipment, storage, duplication and retrieval; therefore, the patron who is not familiar with microform tends initially to be a little reticent about using this medium, but this problem is usually temporary. This resistance to using microform could very well be attributed to a conditioning factor; that is, patrons are generally not accustomed to reading print information that requires a machine to make it readable. After a few uses, this objection tends to dissipate; eventually, microforms are even appreciated when patrons realize that

Figure 13.1   Assorted microforms: (a) 3- × 6-inch (7.62- × 15.24-cm) negative microfiche; (b) 3- × 5-inch (7.62- × 12.70-cm) positive microfiche; (c) 4- × 6-inch (10.16- × 15.24-cm) positive microfiche; (d) 1⅜- × 7-inch (3.49- × 17.78-cm) ultrafiche; (e) 3- × 5-inch (7.62- × 12.70-cm) negative microfiche; (f) 6- × 9-inch (15.24- × 22.86-cm) positive micro-opaque card; (g) 4- × 6-inch (10.16- × 15.24-cm) ultrafiche; (h) aperture card; (i) 16-mm microfilm cartridge; (j) 3- × 5-inch (7.62- × 12.70-cm) positive micro-opaque card; (k) 35-mm microfilm cartridge; (l) 16-mm open reel microfilm; and (m) 35-mm open reel microfilm.

microform is the only format in which much archival information is stored.

Physical Features of Microforms

Microforms come in four basic physical arrangements: (*a*) microfilm, (*b*) microfiche, (*c*) micro-opaque material, and (*d*) aperture card (see Figure 13.1).

Microfilm is a microform stored on a roll or reel of film. If the film base is made of acetate, a reel will hold 100 feet (30.48 m) of film; if it is made of polyester, the same reel will hold 200 feet (60.96 m) of film. Microfilm is available in both 35-mm and 16-mm formats, with or without sprocket holes, with or without self-threading cartridges, and in color or black and white.

Microfiche, commonly called fiche, (a French word meaning card) is a single piece of film about the size of a postcard. Microfiche is available in either color or black and white, the prevalent sizes are 3 × 5 inches (7.62 × 12.70 cm) and 4 × 6 inches (10.16 × 15.24 cm).

A micro-opaque card is similar to microfiche but the information is reproduced on a white opaque card rather than on film. Whereas fiche is similar to a film negative, the micro-opaque card is analogous to a photographic print. The sizes available are 3 × 5 inches (7.62 × 12.70 cm) 4 × 6 inches (10.16 × 15.24 cm) 5 × 8 inches (12.70 × 20.32 cm), and 6 × 8 inches (15.24 × 20.32 cm). Very little information is currently being made available on the micro-opaque cards, and they are becoming obsolete.

An aperture card, as the name indicates, is a card with an aperture or cut-out hole to which a piece of film is bonded. The aperture card is a standard electric accounting machine card, and can be stored and retrieved electronically. The aperture is usually the size of a single frame of 35-mm film. The application of the aperture card is generally limited to industry, where it is rapidly being replaced by computer stored information.

Image Magnification and Storage Capacity

Along with the wide array of physical features and formats available in microforms, consideration must be given to image magnification. In order to view microforms, a lens magnification system is necessary to enlarge the information to a readable size. Magnifications usually range from 10× to 40×, the most common being 19× and 21×. In the microfiche format, a still greater image reduction is possible on super or ultrafiche. Ultrafiche requires anywhere from 50× to 210× magnification and is generally available in 60×, 150×, and 210× magnification.

As an indication of how magnification affects the amount of material that can be stored on a 4- × 6-inch (10.16- × 15.24-cm) card, up to 98 pages of information can be stored on a single microfiche, whereas up to 3000 pages can be stored on an ultrafiche card.

Positive Microforms versus Negative Microforms

Microforms are available on either positive or negative film. When viewed on a reader, the information on a positive microform looks just like the original. Conversely, on a negative microform, the type is white, the background is black, and a photograph looks like a photographic negative (i.e., the black and white are reversed. Many government and academic institution microfiches are only available in negative film. Reading print from a negative image is not a problem; the information is clearly legible, and although an individual using a negative microform for the first time may find it odd to read white print on a black background, this should be viewed as a conditioning factor rather than an inconvenience. In fact, some users prefer negative microforms because they seem to reduce glare on the screen.

On occasion, the patron will need a hard (paper) copy of microform information, in order to satisfy this request, the library will need to acquire a reader–printer. A coin-operated reader–printer seems to be the most convenient type because all the patron has to do is select the information to be copied and insert a coin, and the machine automatically makes a copy. The present generation of reader–printers can be set up to make either positive or negative copies, depending on the type of chemical toner being used. A positive copy looks just like the original microform; a negative copy is the opposite of the original. Negative toner is recommended if most of the microform collection is also negative, because a negative of a negative yields a positive. The cost of reader–printers starts at about $2000; and it is highly recommended that the librarian seriously consider a service–maintenance contracts when selecting a reader–printer. These machines are highly sophisticated and will obviously require a program of regular maintenance if they receive considerable use. In fact, if a considerable amount of copying is anticipated, it may be advisable to acquire two reader–printers so that if one requires maintenance, the other can serve as a backup.

Selecting Microforms

The librarian must decide just what type or types of microform should be in the library collection. Of course, patron needs as well as the current state of the art should serve as guides in this decision. In some instances, however, there is no decision to make; the information is available only in one particular microform format, and the library will need to have the proper equipment to accommodate that format. The librarian should read the selection aids carefully in order to determine which of the various microform formats and magnifications available are compatible with the equipment the library has on hand.

Micro-opaque cards are inefficient, and as already mentioned, may soon be obsolete. The opaque cards are thicker than microfiche film and can be easily torn; more importantly the image produced on the viewer is generally not as brilliant as that produced by film. This is because projection light is reflected off the opaque card, whereas it passes through film, giving the latter a better image generally. A library would have occasion to acquire micro-opaque cards only if they were the sole microform format in which the information was available. Incidentally, there are still some periodicals, for example, some European scientific publications, that are available only on micro-opaque cards.

Periodicals, especially newspapers, are available on 35-mm microfilm. Microfilm is a convenient form for low-access information (i.e., information that does not require immediate or frequent access) because several months of this type of information can be stored on one reel of film.

Polyester film is preferable to acetate film solely because, as already mentioned, a reel can hold twice as much polyester film, but the librarian must be certain that the equipment in the library can accommodate polyester film. Since polyester film is also relatively new, the librarian must know to what extent information is available in this format.

In making a decision between 35-mm and 16-mm microfilm, the librarian should ascertain first of all if the 16-mm reel holds as much information as a comparable 35-mm reel. If this is true, then an examination must be made of the magnification differences—16-mm will require greater magnification to give the same size image as 35-mm film. The librarian should make a side-by-side viewing comparison of the two formats before making a decision.

Whether to use open reel or cartridge microfilm can best be decided by determining the extent of patron use. If patrons are occasional users, a cartridge is better because it requires very little, if any, operation instruction. If patrons are frequent users, an open reel may be the most satisfactory option because although an open reel is more difficult to thread, once a patron is given some initial instruction he or she will be able to thread the machine fairly easily. Another advantage of an open reel is that it does not require a self-threading device, which can break down, and because neither a cartridge nor a self-threading device is necessary, the cost of equipment acquisition and maintenance is lower. On the other hand, an advantage of the cartridge system is that the film in a cartridge is never handled.

A final consideration in favor of microfilm is that the reels are relatively large in comparison to other microforms, which permits an open shelf policy. This is not practical with other microforms because being so thin, they can easily be misfiled. Imagine what would happen if patrons were allowed to remove and return cards from the card catalog.

Microfiche is well suited for high-access information. Whereas a reel of microfilm can store issues from several months of a periodical, a fiche would more than likely store only a single issue; therefore, a patron would not tie up several months of periodicals while examining one issue. Fiche also has the advantage of rapid access to information, because the user can go directly to a particular page without winding through a reel. Actually, information can be located as quickly as it can in the original paper document. With microfiche, it is possible to purchase only the information that the library actually needs. For this reason, single manuscripts are best acquired in the fiche format. Documents reproduced on fiche are easily identified by labels provided on the fiche that can be read with the naked eye, a feature that greatly facilitates accessioning and storing.

Aperture cards require the use of a card sorter if they are to be utilized to their best advantage. Usually the information, because of the relatively small aperture, is limited to a few pages. The aperture card is well suited for applications that require access to complex cross-indexed information because patrons have computerized access to many combinations of aperture cards. Because of computer speed and accuracy, aperture cards can be refiled quickly and without possibility of human error.

The majority of information on microform is available in the $10\times-40\times$ range of magnification. Ultra magnification, the $60\times-210\times$ range, requires equipment in which alignment is extremely critical. A slight misalignment will render the machine unusable. Presently, ultra magnification is available only in some types of fiche and shortstrip, and only in black and white. But the reduction of space required for storing information is tremendous. For example, thirty 100-page periodicals could all be stored on approximately thirty standard magnification 4- × 6-inch (10.16- × 15.24-cm) fiches or on one 4- × 6-inch (10.16- × 15.24-cm) ultrafiche. Ultrafiche is obviously ideal for institutions requiring the storage of either tremendous amounts of information or extremely valuable low-access information that would be stored in a vault.

Normal $10\times-40\times$ range magnification is presently the standard for libraries serving the general public. The standard magnification of United States government documents is $24\times$, which is also the standard being adopted by many other government institutions that are just beginning to commit information to microform. The quality of magnified images is generally good, and equipment is relatively simple in design. An attractive feature for normal magnification is the availability of color on reels of microfilm. The film used is 35-mm sprocketed film. Results are excellent, and color film is ideal for magazines.

It is important to note here that some information currently being generated is availably only in microform, and if the library needs this material, there is no choice as to media format (e.g., parts of the periodicals of the Royal Astronomical Society, and of the Mathematics and Computation, and Geological Society of America are available only in microfiche). There is also a very good likelihood that even more information will be available only in microform because of the valuable savings in printing costs and storage space this medium can provide. There are printers of school textbooks who are making some of their works available in both hard copy and microfiche, and it has been found that children in the elementary grades respond well to the microform format. This acceptance can be attributed to the fact that children have not had the many years of conditioning that adults have had, and are therefore more receptive to any type of media format.

The type of film processing selected also has to be considered. There are three prevalent types: diazo, vesicular, and silver halide. Each of these processing types has its own inherent advantages and disadvantages. Diazo film processing provides a virtually grain-free image, but it is the most susceptible to fading, especially if it is left exposed to light for long periods of time. Vesicular film processing is quite durable and produces a good image, but quite often when the information is transferred to paper, the resultant image lacks good contrast. Silver halide film processing is the most durable but also the most expensive and can be easily scratched. Because all three types of films are chemically processed, it is recommended that they not be stored together in order to prevent the possibility of one film causing a latent chemical reaction in one of the other films. This is not a physically dangerous or volatile situation, but it could adversely affect the quality of the printed images. The current trend appears to be toward the vesicular process because it is more resistant to fading than the diazo, less expensive than the silver halide, and still produces an excellent, enlarged image. When selecting microforms for archival purposes, however, silver halide, because of its high quality, is the only process that can be considered.

With regard to price, information on microform is less expensive than on bound paper copy. This is especially true for books and research abstracts. However, periodicals are considerably more expensive in microform than in the original paper format, (e.g., a monthly subscription to the *New York Times* is $55 on vesicular film and $66 on silver halide film). This higher price is primarily attributable to the fact that much of the cost of producing a newspaper like the *New York Times* in paper form is absorbed by the advertisers. The advertisers cannot be assessed for the microform edition, however, because it is of no commercial value to them since the microform is received by the library at a much later date than the original newspaper is, and the advertisements are therefore out of date.

Trends in Microform Selection

One particularly irksome problem that confronts librarians with respect to microforms is the multitude of standards. Institutions that rush headlong toward every microform innovation usually end up with a crazy patchwork quilt of incompatible systems. Other institutions adopt a "wait-and-see" or "wait-until-it-is-perfected" attitude, and as a result, the microform world passes them by. Perhaps the best solution to this dilemma is to investigate alternative systems, near-future trends, and the particular needs of the institution; and then to commit the library to a system that can serve it at least 5 or 10 years. In this way, an amortization plan will evolve that can justify the microform system over a given period of time. It would also be a good idea to investigate other libraries to see what their microform equipment preferences are. Finally, Educational Products Information Exchange (EPIE),[1] an independent testing agency, publishes evaluative reports on various types of audiovisual equipment that are quite extensive and very informative. Another impartial resource is the Educational Research Information Center (ERIC),[2] which is a department of the United States Office of Education (USOE).

The present trend appears to be toward 35-mm open reel, positive black and white microfilm in the 10×–40× magnification range. A probable cause for this trend is that many newspapers and magazines are available in this format and will be for many years. This availability has also relieved librarians of a tremendous storage and retrieval problem. Still another reason is that the machinery used for viewing this type of microfilm is fairly simple to operate, low in maintenance, rugged and durable, and not too expensive.

Following closely behind 35-mm microfilm is the 4- × 6-inch positive microfiche in the same 10×–40× magnification range. There is also a preponderance of information available only on negative fiche. The popularity of microfiche is attributable to the demand for high-access materials stored on quick retrieval, single sheets of film; in addition,

---

[1] Inquiries may be addressed to Educational Products Information Exchange, P.O. Box 620, Stony Brook, NY 11790.

[2] Inquiries may be addressed to Educational Research Information Center, Washington, D.C. 20202.

many professional periodicals, books, and research papers are stored on this format.

Many institutions are committed to a combination of the 35-mm microfilm and 4- × 6-inch (10.6- × 15.24-cm) fiche system. This allows the institution the versatility of being able to store information on either high- or low-access modes, in a format for which the bulk of material that a library usually uses or wants on microform is commercially available.

Because most patrons view microforms in the library, the microfilm and fiche systems are the easiest to manage because fiche is a closed-shelf collection and microfilm can be an open-shelf collection. Currently, the theft of microforms is not much of a problem, but this is, at best, a temporary situation. Most patrons do not presently have a means of viewing microforms outside the library, but companies are now manufacturing home microform viewers and selling them at prices that reasonable enough for the serious user to consider buying one. A really good viewer, in an attaché case, sells for less than $200. One company sells, for $1.50, a home viewer that is nothing more than a magnifying glass attached to a microfiche holder. Although this viewer is neither very sophisticated nor overly convenient to use, it does magnify information to an easily readable size. With the expectation that patrons will want to use microform materials outside the library comes the problem of illegal removal of these materials from the library. As a means of preventing their illegal removal from the library, microform materials will have to be sensitized to respond to security alarm systems. Within the next few years, many patrons will own their own microform readers, and the trend will be toward 10×–40× magnification fiche readers. With the added feature of fiche reproduction, the patron will be able to pay a small fee to purchase a fiche and add it to his or her own collection.

Another change that can be expected in print information storage will be the use of the video disc, which has the capability of storing 54,000 pages of information on one side of a single disc. This is considerably more than can be stored on a comparable amount of microform. It is also expected that the video disc will be much cheaper to purchase than microforms. It is projected that within the next 10 years there will be 6–8 million video disc players in American homes, which means that many people will have the means to view printed information on their television sets.

The trends just discussed are *immediate future* trends, meaning that these trends are either actually happening now or will be prevalent within a few years. Well before 2000, microforms will be computer stored, which means that a patron sitting at home with a computer terminal, will be able to request the almost immediate appearance on his or her television of information from the library collection. He or she may also obtain a permanent paper or magnetic-tape printout. Such systems are already in prototype stages, and it will take only proper marketing to make them available in American homes. Therefore, the library that is moving in the direction of the microform trend will be ready for the technology that will be available to citizens in the near future. However, this does not mean that the librarian should stop acquiring information in the microform formats that are presently available, for they are still the best, and in most cases the only, format in which information is being miniaturized. Microforms are still needed and may very well coexist or even dovetail with the computer formats of the future.

Knowing which kinds of microforms are available, the librarian can now intelligently use the selection aids. It is essential to know if the particular microform being selected is in the format being used by the library. There are several selection aids particularly designed to assist the librarian in locating information on microforms. The information provided in some microform selection aids is often minimal; therefore, it is well to bear in mind that materials available in microform were formerly available in a printed format and that additional data can be obtained from selection aids prepared expressly for the printed versions.

Selecting Microform Viewers

In addition to keeping abreast of current trends in microform materials, the librarian must also be aware of developments in viewing and reproduction equipment. Every microform format requires viewing equipment that is compatible with it in order to read the material. Furthermore, as new format refinements and changes have occurred, a host of adapters have been designed for existing equipment; yet modifying existing equipment has created more problems than it has solved. The best equipment program is one that is tied into the library's 5- to 10-year commitment to a particular microform, so that the equipment as well as the microform is included in the amortization plan. In this way the librarian can periodically justify new equipment requests and does not have to jury-rig existing equipment.

If only one or at most two microform formats are to be used, it will be necessary to acquire only one or two types of viewing equipment. When selecting viewing equipment, the librarian will need to consider cost, warranty, ease of operation, ease of maintenance, versatility, quality of projected image, noise, cooling, lamp size and ease of replacement, and physical dimensions.

The following questions should be considered when selecting equipment:

1. Does the equipment require a darkened room for adequate viewing?
2. If the equipment is to be used for viewing microfilm, does it make considerable noise when winding or rewinding film?
3. Does the equipment require a fan to cool the lamp, and if so, is the fan quiet?
4. If the equipment is to be moved frequently, what is its means of portability?
5. What is the length of lamp life, and how expensive is a replacement lamp?
6. How much space does the equipment occupy, and can the library afford to set aside this amount of space?
7. Is the equipment currently being used elsewhere, and if so what are the opinions of those institutions regarding the equipment's effectiveness?
8. Is the equipment easy to focus, and is the image brilliant, crisp, and sharp?
9. Can the patron learn to operate the equipment without assistance from the librarian?
10. Can the equipment be serviced locally? How long will service take, and will loaners be available?
11. Does the equipment provide for a varied selection of lenses in the $10\times-40\times$ range?
12. Can the equipment be adjusted to store material on both a horizontal and vertical format?
13. If the unit is motorized, does it require a special electrical outlet?
14. Are the construction and alignment of parts sturdy and durable?
15. What safeguards does the machinery have for preventing damage to the film (e.g., tears, burns, scratches)?
16. Is the machinery equipped with or does it require a dust or storage cover?

Along with these questions, there may be concern for speed of operation. Some types of viewing equipment are motorized to give rapid access to information on microfilm. Motors can turn microfilm reels at much higher speeds than a manual crank can, and keyboard devices permit the user simply by pressing a few keys to display information automatically on the screen. If the patron's time is quite valuable, these motorized features should be considered.

If paper reproductions of information will be requested, the microfilm reader will have to have print capabilities. The librarian should be aware of the following considerations:

1. Does the printer require use of chemicals?
2. Does the printer make a wet or a dry copy?
3. Can the printer reproduce positive copy from negative film (or vice versa), or can it give positive copy from positive film?
4. If necessary, can an attachment be added to make the printer coin operated?
5. Can the patron operate the printer without assistance?
6. Can the printer accommodate various microform formats?

A major premise for using microforms is that they allow for a tremendous savings in space, and this rationale must extend to the equipment selected to store the microforms. Here is one instance where the standards are pervasive. Regardless of the particular microform used, there is one set of physical dimensions for that form. For example, all 35-mm reels, and of course all 4- × 6-inch (10.16- × 15.24-cm) fiche, are the same size. This means that storage equipment should be acquired that is exactly the same size as, and is designed for a particular microform. When selecting storage equipment for fiche, closed file drawers should be chosen as a means of reducing the accumulation of dust. If there is a possibility of water being splashed on floors when the library is cleaned, storage should be high enough from the floor to prevent water coming in contact with the microforms.

Basic Microform Selection Aids

There are several selection aids available to assist the librarian in locating information on microforms. The five aids described here are basic tools that tell whether certain information is available on microform. As already mentioned, however, further information about any particular selection can be obtained from aids that list, annotate, and review the item in its original paper format.

Books on Demand (3 vols.), published by University Microfilms International, Ann Arbor, Michigan.

1. *Scope* a comprehensive listing of domestic and foreign books that are out of print and available in microform

2. *Entries* entered by author, title, and publisher, and original date of publication is provided
3. *Special features* contains a section on Slavic language titles and a supplement, *The O-P Bookfinder,* which is free on request to librarians, is available bimonthly

Guide to Microforms in Print published by Microform Review, Westport, Connecticut.

1. *Scope* an annual cumulative guide in alphabetical order to books, journals, and other materials that are available on microfilm from United States publishers (theses and dissertations are not listed); prices of materials are also included.
2. *Entries* books are entered by author, and the entries include the title and date of publication of the work in its original form; newspapers are entered by state, city, and name; archival materials and manuscripts are entered as listed by the original publisher; projects (e.g., publishing all the works cited in a bibliography) are entered by the compiler and/or the subject.
3. *Special features* an alphabetical listing of publishers and a directory of publishers by alphabetical designation; also includes pertinent advertisements

Newspapers on Microfilms and Special Collections published by Micro Photo Division, Bell & Howell Company, Wooster, Ohio.

1. *Scope* an annual publication that lists over 5000 newspapers (domestic and foreign) and all periodicals available from Bell & Howell Company; also has a listing of special interest collections and special educational products and gives information on microform-related equipment
2. *Entries* newspapers are entered by state, city, name, and dates available; periodicals are entered by title, dates available, and price; special interest collections are listed by title and have a full-page description
3. *Special features* information on obtainable newspaper facsimiles and a section on special newspaper collections

Serials in Microform published by University Microfilms International, Ann Arbor, Michigan.

1. *Scope* lists the largest and most comprehensive selection of periodicals, documents, newspapers, and other serial literature available anywhere in microform; lists titles from 1669 to the present; includes nearly 7000 listings

2. *Entries*   ordered alphabetically by title in the main section but also includes a subject-category section; each entry includes an order number, title, city of publication, backfile listings, current volumes, and external and publisher indexes
3. *Special features*   backfile and current publications are listed in *Serials Bulletin,* which is available bimonthly and free on request

Subject Guide to Microforms in Print   published by Microform Review, Westport, Connecticut.

1. *Scope*   a biennial, comprehensive guide ordered by subject classification to materials that are available on microform from United States publishers (theses and dissertations are not listed)
2. *Entries*   books are entered by author, and the entries include the title and date of publication of the work in its original form; newspapers are entered by state, city, and name; archival materials and manuscripts are entered as listed by the original publisher; projects (e.g., publishing all the works cited in a bibliography) are entered by the compiler of the bibliography and/or the subject
3. *Special features*   an alphabetical listing of publishers and a directory of publishers by alphabetical designations; a list of subject classifications and index to subject classifications

A step beyond acquiring microforms from outside sources would be having some of the library's own material committed to microform. Many companies provide this service, and it is suggested that the librarian consult the publisher of the local newspaper for further information about this service. With the information in this chapter, the librarian can provide specifications to the microphotographer as to the exact kind of reproduction services desired.

Using Microforms

Microforms should ideally be contained in one area of the library and should be kept in properly designed storage compartments (e.g., drawers and shelves) that, as already mentioned, will capitalize on the space saving potential that is unique to this medium. Microform readers and reader–printers should be in close proximity to the storage area.

The prime consideration in managing the use of the microform collection is deciding on the conditions of patron access. The options are an open-shelf system, a closed-shelf system, or a system that combines both open- and closed-shelf collections. The major concern is to make certain that all material is returned to its proper place after it is used. Microfilm information is on reels, all of which are boxed and uniform in size. Therefore, when one reel is removed from its storage area, the resulting vacant space makes reshelving fairly easy and misshelving easy to discover.

In the case of microfiche or micro-opaque cards, storing is not as simple. Thousands of individual fiche or cards are filed in the same drawer; and if the person reshelving them is not extremely conscientious, material can easily be misfiled and therefore for all practical purposes, can be considered lost. For these reasons, microfilms can be open shelved; whereas microfiche and micro-opaque cards should be closed shelved. Some libraries allow the patron direct access to fiche and cards, but in such cases, it is extremely important to stipulate that the patron should not under any circumstance refile these microforms. This eliminates the possibility of an unskilled person misfiling the fiche or cards because all materials are refiled by competent library personnel. Some libraries allow certain patrons who make frequent use of the collection direct access to microforms, but this access is granted only after the patrons have been oriented on how to use the collection and made aware of how crucial it is that the materials be correctly refiled. It is also recommended, regardless of whether the collection is managed on an open- or closed-shelf system, that all materials be returned after use to a common depository area. In some libraries, the patron must sign out for all materials used and have the charge canceled on return.

The area in which the patrons will actually use the microforms should be comfortable and conducive to study. Too often librarians tend to make the reading area very dark, thus creating an environment that is almost ominous. Granted, there has to be concern for protecting the projection screens from ambient light; however, the newer reading machines have remarkably improved projection systems and are usually well-shielded from ambient light. If it is found that the area must be darkened to the point where less than 20 footcandles of light are available (i.e., too dark for writing) each machine should be equipped with a light for note-taking. Each microform utilization area should be large enough to accommodate the reading machine comfortably and should also allow sufficient space for the patron to take notes and use supplementary materials. Individual seating arrangements must be such that the patron is comfortable and in a position to read the projected microform easily. Too often, reading machines are placed without concern for this consideration; and, as a result, the patron has to twist and contort in order to read the microform.

The microform reader has to be equipped with lenses of proper magnification. There are some machines that are equipped with several different lenses to accommodate microforms of various magnifications. If the library is considering acquiring such a machine, it would be wise to test the functions of each lens before purchasing the machine because sometimes the magnification does not allow a whole page of information to be properly projected over the entire screen.

There must also be some provision for adequate electrical current since all machines utilize a projection lamp, and some are equipped with a cooling fan and/or a motor drive to wind microfilm. The machine should not be too noisy, because if several machines are used simultaneously, the noise could be distracting. The librarian should always be prepared to instruct a patron in the operation of a machine and should keep in mind that even a machine that is easy to use might confuse the infrequent user.

The librarian will need to have access to the proper indexes in order to locate information as well as to make any search conducted by a patron a fairly easy and worthwhile experience. When acquiring large quantities or blocks of microform information, indexes are essential; for without them, information retrieval is virtually impossible. There are many publications that do not have indexes and the librarian must be aware of this fact. If such materials are acquired, some means of indexing them will have to be devised. A good case in point is that a local newspaper may not have an index for its microform; but the *New York Times* is indexed, and can therefore serve as a pseudoindex for the local newspaper.

Microforms are a valuable information resource. Not only do they save a tremendous amount of space, but more importantly, they are virtually the only source for out-of-date (and out-of-print) information. A patron who wishes to obtain information from an old newspaper has practically no recourse but to seek the information from a library microform collection. The acquisition of microforms can only be justified if they receive proper use, but their use is increasing at an accelerating rate, and a strong possibility exists that sometime in the near future microforms will be the major format on which most information in the library is stored.

Selected Bibliography

Bahr, Alice A. *Microforms: The Librarian's View,* second edition. White Plains, New York: Knowledge Industries, 1978.

Introduction to Micrographics. Silver Spring, Maryland: National Micrographics Association, 1973.

The Journal of Micrographics. Silver Spring, Maryland: National Micrographics Association, 1967–.

Lee, Thomas G. *Microform Systems: A Handbook for Educators,* fifth edition. Silver Spring, Maryland: National Micrographic Association, 1971.

Microdoc. Surrey, England: Microfilm Association of Great Britain, 1962–.

Microform Review. Westport, Connecticut: Microform Review, 1971–.

Micrographics Equipment Review. Westport, Connecticut: Microform Review, 1976–.

Micrographics Today. Silver Spring, Maryland: National Micrographics Association, 1967–.

Saffady, William. *Micrographics.* Littleton, Colorado: Libraries Unlimited, 1978.

Selection Aids

Books on Demand, (3 vols.). Ann Arbor, Michigan: University Microfilms International, 1977.

Guide to Microforms in Print. Westport, Connecticut: Microform Review, 1961–.

Guide to Reprints, 1982, (2 vols.). Kent, Connecticut: Guide to Reprints, 1982.

International Microforms in Print. Westport, Connecticut: Microform Review, 1961–.

International Microforms in Print: A Guide to Microforms of Non-United States Micropublishers, 1974–1975. Westport, Connecticut: Microform Review, 1974.

Library of Congress Catalogs: National Register of Microfilm Masters, 1965–1979, (6 vols.). Washington, D.C.: Library of Congress, 1976–.

Library of Congress Catalogs: Newspapers in Microform, 1948–1972, Vol. 1: United States, Vol. 2: Foreign Countries. Washington, D.C.: Library of Congress, 1973.

Microform Review. Westport, Connecticut: Microform Review, 1971–.

Microform Review: Index, 1972–1976, (5 vols.). Westport, Connecticut: Microform Review, 1976.

Microform Source Book. New Rochelle: Microfilm Publishing, 1974–.

Microform Market Place: An International Directory of Micropublishing, revised edition. Westport, Connecticut: Microform Review, 1976–.

Microform Research Collections: A Guide. Westport, Connecticut: Microform Review, 1978.

Micropublishers' Trade List Annual, revised edition. Westport, Connecticut: Microform Review, 1976–.

National Register of Microform Masters. Washington, D.C.: Library of Congress, 1965–.

Newspapers in Microform and Special Collections. Wooster, Ohio: Micro Photo Division, Bell & Howell Company, n.d.

Serials in Microform. Ann Arbor, Michigan: University Microfilms International, n.d.

Subject Guide to Microforms in Print. Westport, Connecticut: Microform Review, 1976–.

Subject Guide to Reprints, 1980–1981, (2 vols.). Kent, Connecticut: Guide to Reprints, 1980.

14

Local Preparation of Information Materials

Overview

It is becoming increasingly more common for libraries to become involved in the local preparation of information materials. This preparation often goes well beyond simply copying or duplicating existing commercially produced materials. Certainly, many duplicating requests can often be accomplished directly by the patron using a coin-operated machine (e.g., photocopying machines and microform reader–printers). However, there could be a need for materials that are not available commercially, and these, if they have merit, can be produced locally either by or under the direction of library personnel.

The production of some information materials can be accomplished with nothing more than very basic skills and a few fairly simple devices or pieces of equipment (e.g., a ditto or a chart). Other materials, such as a polished television production, might require professional expertise and some rather sophisticated equipment. But even with television, a satisfactory simple one-camera production can be made by a person with only minimal skills in the medium. The point being made here is that information materials can be locally produced, but it is also important that such efforts coincide with the parameters of the library's policy for providing such services. To become involved in producing information materials is not a decision to be taken lightly. Invariably, locally produced information materials are more expensive than their commercially prepared counterparts, because they require personnel, equipment, and production space. On the other hand, if the requested information is not available elsewhere and the library has at its disposal the resources necessary to produce the information locally it may very well be justified in doing so.

Rationale

Occasionally, situations do arise that require locally produced materials. Perhaps there is a need for a bulletin board, a display, supplementary material not available from commercial sources, unique materials applicable to a particular locality, or embellishments or modification for a distinct patron need of existing materials. Given a situation in which materials are unavailable, the librarian has the alternatives of either informing the patron that the request cannot be satisfied or making the necessary material. If the latter alternative is chosen, a plan of execution must be instituted. For the school librarian, the problem is easily resolved: The request is communicated to the school's media specialist, who is equipped to handle such contingencies. In the case of libraries that do not employ a media specialist, the problem is not quite as easily resolved. The librarian must use his or her own resourcefulness to see that the materials are produced.

First, a determination must be made as to exactly what types of materials can or should be locally produced. This determination is predicated on the librarian's degree of skill in materials production, as well as the equipment necessary to do the job. There are some excellent materials preparation manuals available (see Selected Bibliography) that are designed for the nonprofessional in need of a particular skill or procedure, and with adequate practice, the end product can be of professional quality.

Bearing in mind that local materials preparation is an adjunct service, the librarian should not expect to become involved in sophisticated production activities, but rather to produce materials that help fill an information gap not filled by commercially prepared materials. Generally, the materials that can be produced by the librarian who does not have professional training in materials production include: dittos, models, transparencies for overhead projection, mounted and preserved materials for display, hand puppets for story-telling, prepared specimens, photographic slides, audiotapes, basic 8-mm sound or silent motion pictures, simple videotape or video cassette recordings, and traced enlargements of graphic materials using an opaque projector.

Before becoming involved in materials production, the librarian must make a priorities assessment. Time will have to be alloted for making materials, which in some circumstances can consume a considerable portion of the working day. Furthermore, making materials requires the procurement of production tools and equipment. A decision needs to be made as regards the extent to which the library should become involved in materials production. The library should examine its policy to determine whether its role is solely to acquire but not to produce information, or to provide information by whatever means possible. Circumstances, and even the philosophy of the library, may dictate whether materials can or should be locally produced. Locally produced materials can provide a service, but not without incurred costs. If the costs can be justified, a policy of local material production should be strongly considered.

Basic Production Equipment

In order to produce even the simplest types of informational materials, the library will need some basic kinds of equipment. The equipment is basic in that neither special skills nor training are required in order to operate it. Depending on the extent of involvement, the library engaged in the production of informational materials should consider the acquisition of the following equipment:

1. *Photocopier* to make copies of existing materials; most libraries acquire the coin-operated variety, which allows the patron to make his or her own copy; copyright infringement becomes an important concern
2. *Spirit duplicator* (*ditto*) requires the transfer of the information being copied to a ditto master which is good for a run of about 150 paper copies; multicolored copy (red, blue, green, purple, black) can also be made
3. *Mimeograph machine* requires the transfer of the information to a master; mimeograph master is more expensive than a ditto master, but results more closely approximate professional printing quality, and the master is good for at least 1000 copies
4. *Basic drafting equipment* compasses, T-square, triangles, guides, etc. to make charts, graphs, and diagrams
5. *Assortment of lettering guides* to produce professional quality printing (Unimark, Wrico, Dyno, Rapidograph, Leroy, and Kroy are examples of the types of mechanical lettering systems that are available)

6. *Primary typewriter* a typewriter with a large type font to be used for producing typed information that can be comfortably read at a distance of approximately 3.04 m (10 feet)

7. *Paper cutter, X-acto knives, and scissors* for cutting and trimming paper, cloth, and cardboard

8. *Thermal copier* to produce overhead transparencies directly from newsprint or any other black-and-white materials; requires the use of thermal transparency material, which is available in black, red, blue, green, and yellow; the copier can also be used for making thermal ditto masters or paper reproductions from black and white originals

9. *Diazo copier* to make colored overhead transparencies on low-photosensitive film; produces transparencies with vivid, brilliant colors

10. *Dry mount press* for affixing photographs and other visuals to cardboard for display purposes; can also be used for bonding reinforcing materials (cloth or cardboard) to the backs of large visuals and for laminating the front surface of visuals

11. *Camera and copystand* for making pictures and slides; the copystand aids in taking photographs of material in books and magazines; an array of cameras and copystands are available, and the local camera dealer can be consulted about the equipment that will be most compatible with the library's needs and the library staff's ability

12. *Audio tape recorder (reel-to-reel or cassette)* to record print information on an audio format for the visually handicapped or to duplicate existing audio tapes; again, local dealers can be consulted for assistance in selection

13. *Opaque projector* for tracing and enlarging materials—indispensable for libraries with limited budgets, time, and graphic skills; can also be used for projecting opaque materials directly onto a screen

14. *Miscellaneous materials and accessories* the local art supply or business office supply dealer can provide invaluable selection assistance

15. *Videotape recorder (reel-to-reel or cassette)* depending on the level of production, the system could range from a fairly simple portable unit with a couple of spotlights all the way to a multiple-camera facility capable of producing video programs of broadcast quality (even at the minimum level of production, a basic training and knowledge of the medium is strongly advised)

This equipment is the type prevalent in facilities involved in the nonprofessional production and duplication of informational materials. What is actually acquired will depend on the needs of the particular library. The equipment can range from inexpensive, easy-to-operate models to expensive, complex varieties. It is recommended that, prior to becoming involved in the production of information materials, the librarian employed by a city library should consult with the media director at a local school media center in order to obtain a better understanding of what is involved and practical for his or her particular situation.

Production Space

If the library is to be involved to any extent in producing information materials, it will be necessary to allocate space for this activity. There is no specific formula for space allocation, but some thought must be given to providing a comfortable environment in which materials can be efficiently produced. The equipment in the production area should not be crowded to the extent that it cannot be conveniently used. Some equipment, by its very nature, will not be used regularly and therefore can probably be stored when not in use. Ample room must also be provided for the manipulation of whatever is being produced.

If a graphics area is to be included in the facility, it should contain a graphics table that is large enough to allow the production of any size graphic that may be used by the library. The graphics area will also require additional glare-free lighting (approximately 150 footcandles on working surfaces).

If live audio recordings are to be produced, the construction of a sound booth with acoustically treated floor, walls, and ceiling for sound absorption may be required. The sound recording booth, depending on surrounding noise levels, may require some degree of soundproofing. Sound control can best be determined by experience. If a recording is made for which the quality could be enhanced by improving the environment, the necessary modifications should be made. It is important to note, however, that too much sound control and soundproofing can be detrimental in that it may yield an acoustically flat, or "dead," recording—the sounds recorded must have a *natural* timbre and resonance.

For photographic work, supplementary lighting will be needed, as well as enough space to place cameras at a proper distance from the work being photographed. More than likely, most photography will involve copying existing information and can be accommodated quite easily by a copy stand, which is a complete, self-contained unit that does not require much space.

If the library is to become involved in video taping or motion picture filming, the space requirements will be extensive because a basic studio set will be necessary. The set will have to be in a windowless area, with at least minimal acoustical treatment and, ideally, an overhead lighting grid. Space must be provided for easy movement of both cameras and talent.

Perhaps the best way to plan space requirements for a production facility is first to determine approximately how much space the library can allocate to such an activity. It is conceivable that little or no space can be allocated, which would in turn severely limit the amount and kinds of materials that can be produced. Concomitant with space requirements are personnel requirements: How much staff will have to be assigned to material production, and what kinds of skills will the staff have to possess? Having resolved space and personnel allocations, the next step is to diagram a floor plan and construct a cardboard model with a top view perspective of the facility. The latter will involve making scale representations of all the furniture and equipment to be installed in the facility. By manipulating and experimenting with various layouts, a projection can be made regarding the feasibility of creating an arrangement of furniture and equipment that will be conducive to an efficient production operation. If the facility is going to be complex, it would be advisable to retain the services of a qualified consultant and, most certainly, to obtain the input of the personnel who will actually be working in the facility.

Free and Inexpensive Materials

Being able to provide library patrons with locally prepared materials is indeed a worthwhile service, however this decision must be predicated on the fact that the materials to be produced locally are unavailable from commercial sources. This unavailability could be a result of the uniqueness, or special character of the item, its applicability to a very restricted group or locale, or an insufficient demand to make commercial production of it profitable. This does not preclude the possibility that some organizations might produce an item for precisely the same reasons a commercial organization would not produce it. Private organizations, both profit and nonprofit, produce and distribute materials either to promote a product or as a public service. Many of these materials are available to the general public at little or no cost. It could prove to be valuable for the librarian to investigate these resources prior to becoming involved in producing an item locally. A free or inexpensive item could cost much less than the time and materials it would take to produce it locally.

There are selection aids designed solely to provide information on sources, types, and availability of free and inexpensive materials (see Selection Aids). These selection aids are usually well indexed and contain information regarding types of material, areas of applicability, content, producer, datedness, and cost (if any). The materials covered in these aids include books, pamphlets, charts, realia, audio and video recordings, filmstrips, and motion picture films. Some requested items are given to the library, while others are available on a free loan basis. The selection aid provides information regarding copyright use, loan procedures, availability of multiple copies, and suggested lead time required to receive material.

Along with professional selection aids, the librarian should not overlook community resources. There are many excellent private and public organizations that will on request provide the library with materials. Community agencies, civic government, educational establishments, public utilities, and private businesses have a plethora of materials available, and welcome the opportunity for an institution such as a library to distribute these materials. An excellent local selection aid is the telephone directory. The yellow pages list practically every community resource that is likely to have materials available to the library.

As with many other selection aids, those that contain listings of free and inexpensive materials cannot provide complete content descriptions and do not evaluate each item. The librarian should scrupulously evaluate any free or inexpensive material prior to issuing it to a patron. Of course, all acquisitions should be evaluated, but this is crucial with free and inexpensive materials in order to ascertain the intended purpose of the material and ensure that their use does not violate library policy. Consideration must be given to whether the intent is propaganda, advertisement of the product or service, as well as to the material datedness, authenticity, truthfulness, bias, quality of content, and general value. Although most producers of free and inexpensive materials are sincerely trying to provide a public service, unfortunately, some may, on occasion, violate the public good and be more concerned with the achievement of profit motives. In summary, the selection aids tell what is available; it is the librarian's responsibility to determine what is selected.

Some librarians are reluctant to use free materials because they feel their ulterior purpose is to sell something. A closer examination of free materials will reveal that most of them do serve a purpose. They are prepared by people who, by virtue of their contact with a particular product, possess special knowledge. The materials are generally up to date and often are only readily available from these sources. Apart from objectively evaluating these materials for their presentation effectiveness, importance, and freedom from undesirable bias or advertising, the librarian should also be aware of how these materials can be used in the library. In the final analysis, perhaps the most important consideration when contemplating local material production is the determination, through a survey of the free and inexpensive material selection aids, of whether an outside source can provide the materials needed at a substantial savings of time, labor, and material.

Production Criteria

Assuming that you have the necessary production materials and resources and that the material to be produced is not available from any outside source, there are some basic production and design criteria that should be considered when planning to produce informational materials. The following are the essential questions the librarian must answer when analyzing requests for materials that will be produced locally:

1. What purpose is the material to serve?
   Will it satisfy a current request?
   Is it being prepared in anticipation of a future need?
   Will it provide supplementary or enrichment information?
   Will it serve a promotional function?
2. How is the material to be used?
   Will it be used by one patron, many individual patrons, or a group?
   What is the anticipated frequency of use? Will it receive only one use or many repeated uses?
   Will it be used only in the library, or outside the library as well?
   Will it be used as an adjunct to existing material or as a discrete entity?
3. What is the best format to use (e.g., ditto, photographic slide, overhead transparency, mounted visuals, poster, 8-mm film, model, audiotape)?
   Will it be manipulated and handled by an individual patron or used by a group?
   Should it be produced in print, illustration, or photographic form; and if the latter, should color, sound, and/or motion be incorporated?

How durable should it be?
Should a combination of formats be used?
Will there be any problem in storing the materials when they are not being used?
4. What is the complexity of producing the materials?
How much time will it take to produce the materials?
What tools and materials will be required for production?
How many pieces of material will be produced?
Are any special production skills or equipment required?

After considering these four basic production criteria, the librarian is in a better position to ascertain if local production of materials is warranted.

Design Criteria

If, after answering the questions in the preceding section, the decision is to proceed with production, the next step to consider is design factors. Granted, the format used will be a major factor in determining design, but some basic design details need to be appraised regardless of format.

The finished product should be neat, clean, and easy to use. In the case of visual materials, they should be comfortable to read and view. The information should be arranged in a design that has a smooth flow and continuity. The visual should contain only essential information. Remember, the purpose is to provide information that is not available elsewhere; the use of good texture, color, perspective, arrangement, and layout greatly enhance the quality of the material, but fancy artwork and superfluous detail are not only unnecessary, but also probably require more professional skill and time than the library can afford to allot to local production of materials.

Audio materials should be easy to hear and comprehend. They should not be too lengthy; and, when used with visual materials, they should collaborate, not compete, with the visuals. The librarian does not have to be an artist; making materials that are aesthetically pleasing does not require a special talent. However, taking a little extra concern and time for quality will be well worth the effort.

It is strongly advised that the librarian who is a novice in the production of materials read Morlan's *Preparation of Inexpensive Teaching Materials* in order to gain a better understanding of what is entailed and what can be accomplished.

Evaluation Standards

Evaluating locally produced informational materials can be summed up in one term—cost/effectiveness. Too often, materials are produced without regard for cost. Incidentally, the greatest cost, and that which is most often overlooked, is the amount of time and/or labor required to produce the material. If it takes 1 hour to produce an item, the realistic time cost is 1 hour of labor. A professional librarian should be critically aware of the time factor involved in producing materials; perhaps the task can be accomplished more economically by a staff paraprofessional. The librarian who claims that tasks such as producing materials can be accomplished in spare time without allowing for additional labor cost should closely examine the library's operations system, for obviously, an inefficient use of staff time exists.

In the term cost/effectiveness, effectiveness refers to the performance of the finished product. An assessment must be made regarding extent of use. As an example, if an item takes 3 hours to produce at a labor cost of $3 per hour and consumes $1 in materials, the item costs $10. If the item is to be used once, as supplemental information, by one patron, its effectiveness would be rather limited. It is doubtful that a librarian would purchase a $10 book if the anticipated use was this narrow. Simply stated, the effectiveness of an item must justify the cost.

The librarian should not regard cost/effectiveness solely as a criteria to be considered during the planning stage, but rather as a mathematical ratio. As illustrated in the preceding example, the cost half of the ratio is easily computed as a real dollar figure. Computing the effectiveness half of the ratio is not quite as clear cut; it must be constructed in terms of units. The librarian will have to formulate an effectiveness-value chart in which certain degrees of effectiveness are assigned a unit value. There is no set criterion as to what constitutes effectiveness or what unit of value should be assigned to it. Moreover, every library has a unique set of needs and scope of services; therefore, effectiveness value will vary among libraries. The librarian must develop criteria of anticipated effectiveness that apply to his or her particular library. Using patron use as an example of an effectiveness criteria, if a patron were to use a locally produced item one time as a primary source of information, it could be assigned a unit value of 1, and if 10 patrons were to use it, the item would have a unit value of 10.

The critical question the librarian must answer is what is the minimal acceptable ratio of dollar cost to unit effectiveness that will determine if an item is to be produced? Once this ratio is determined and a chart of effectiveness units is prepared, all future decisions regarding local production of materials become purely objective and justifiable. If a request for locally produced materials is below the minimum cost/effectiveness ratio, it is automatically rejected; conversely, if it is above the minimum ratio, the librarian can expect that the item will receive profitable use.

The following are some basic effectiveness criteria that the librarian might consider in developing criteria that are germane to his or her particular library situation.

1. *Patron usage*   What is the anticipated number of patrons who will use the material?

2. *Timeliness*   Does the material because of the nature of the information have an immediate time value and is it obtainable by any other means?

3. *Datedness*   Is there a specified period of time during which the material will be of value?

4. *Use*   Will the material be used as basic or original information, as supplementary information, or as promotional material (e.g., bulletin boards, displays)?

5. *Service*   Will the material serve a very specific use (e.g., for handicapped patrons) or a general broad use?

6. *Consumption*   Will the material be consumed, that is, either written on or permanently kept by the patron? (This applies to situations involving multiple copies, such as, dittos).

7. *Demand*   Was the material requested by a patron(s) or recommended by the library staff?

A certain amount of this information can be gleaned from the initial request form. Figure 14.1 is an example of a request form that can serve not only as a means of illiciting evaluative input from the patron, but also as a record of the evaluative process as a whole.

An item that has survived the scrutiny of the cost/effectiveness ratio must then be evaluated with regard to format, durability, and quantity of copies. Is the format requested the best choice considering the materials intended use and the library's staff and production facility capability? For example, if the information is for group use, perhaps an audiotape and slide series should be considered in preference to dittos with graphic data or illustrations. If the material is to receive considerable handling, it must be durable, for it has been shown that a positive correlation exists between extent of use and durability. Due to such factors as the material's limited durability or requests made by many patrons at one time, it may be necessary to produce multiple copies, and the librarian must assess this possibility during the evaluative process.

Finally, all requests must be analyzed within a space–facility–staff context. Space must be allocated for the production of the materials, the

Date of request:
Name:
Occupation:
Date needed:
Description and purpose of material needed:

How is material to be used:

☐Individual
☐Group
☐Display

Recommended format:

☐Ditto   ☐Photos
☐Audiotape   ☐Overhead transparency
☐Model   ☐Slides
☐Mimeo   ☐Poster
                ☐Other

Extent of use:

☐Once   ☐Repeated
☐Long time   ☐Heavy short time

Office Use Only

Availability of material for other sources:
 Commercial   ☐Yes   ☐No
 Free and Inexpensive   ☐Yes   ☐No

Cost of materials:
Time to produce:
Are materials and time available: ☐Yes   ☐No
Cost/effectiveness ratio:
Priority of request:
☐Immediate
☐Can be deferred
☐Explain:
Decision to produce: ☐Yes   ☐No

Figure 14.1 Sample request form for locally produced materials.

necessary equipment for production must be acquired, and skilled staff must be scheduled to devote the time that is necessary to produce the materials.

Local production of materials is not a perfunctory task that can be taken lightly. Locally produced materials can fill an information gap, but a specific, detailed policy to guide the librarian in deciding whether the library should undertake the local production of information materials is essential.

Using Locally Produced Materials

Legality is a primary concern in the use of locally produced materials in situations where original information is copied. If the material is copyrighted, then it is illegal to reproduce it if such reproduction is in violation of existing copyright laws (see Chapter 15). Conversely, some of the information materials produced by the library may be of value, and should therefore be protected by copyright. It is even possible that some locally produced materials may be marketable and yield a financial return to the library, which in turn can be used to absorb some of the cost of conducting the materials production operation.

Feedback as to the effectiveness of the material is especially beneficial in the case of locally produced materials. Once the material has been produced and put into circulation, inquiries could be made of users as to how well it fills the particular need for which it was intended, its professional quality, its ease of use, and its overall value. In this way the librarian can verify whether the item was worth the time, materials, and effort that went into producing it.

Locally produced materials should be used and managed in the same way as any other material in the library collection. Records should be kept regarding their frequency of use and the maintenance that is required to keep them in good repair. In the final analysis, locally produced materials should receive an amount of use that justifies the expense of producing them. If this is indeed the case, then their production will be valued and appreciated, in that they are providing a service that is unobtainable from any other source.

Selected Bibliography

Brown, James, and Lewis, Richard B., eds. *AV Instructional Technology Manual for Independent Study*, fifth edition. New York: McGraw-Hill, 1977.

Bullard, John R. and Mether, Calvin E. *Audiovisual Fundamentals: Basic Equipment Operation and Simple Materials Production.* Dubuque, Iowa: William C. Brown Co., 1974.

Hardestry, Larry L. *Use of Slide–Tape Presentations in Academic Libraries.* New York: W. W. Norton, 1978.

Hunter, Kathleen M. *Audio Visual Skills: A Laboratory Manual.* Portsmouth, New Hampshire: Entelek Inc., 1977.

Kemp, Jerrold E. *Planning and Producing Audiovisual Materials,* third edition. New York: Harper & Row, 1975.

Kinder, James S. *Using Instructional Media.* New York: D. Van Nostrand, 1973.

Making the Most of Charts: An ABC of Graphic Presentation. Washington, D.C.: United States Government Printing Office, 1970.

Minor, Edward O. *Handbook for Preparing Visual Instructional Materials,* second edition. New York: McGraw-Hill, 1978.

Morlan, John E. *Preparation of Inexpensive Teaching Materials,* second edition. San Francisco: Chandler Publishing, 1973.
Morlan, John E. and Espinosa, Leonard. *Electric Boards You Can Make.* San Jose: Personalized Learning Associates, 1974.
Nelson, Leslie W. *Instructional Aids,* second edition. Dubuque, Iowa: William C. Brown, 1970.
Romiszowski, A. J. *The Selection and Use of Instructional Media.* New York: Halsted Press, 1974.

Selection Aids

Aubrey, Ruth H. *Selected Free Materials for Classroom Teachers,* sixth edition. Belmont, California: Pitman Learning, 1978.
Educator's Guide to Free Guidance Materials. Randolph, Wisconsin: Educator's Progress Service, 1962–.
Educator's Guide to Free Health, Physical Education and Recreation Materials. Randolph, Wisconsin: Educator's Progress Service, 1968–.
Educator's Guide to Free Science Materials. Randolph, Wisconsin: Educator's Progress Service, 1960–.
Educator's Guide to Free Social Studies Materials. Randolph, Wisconsin: Educator's Progress Service, 1961–.
Free and Inexpensive Learning Materials, nineteenth edition. Nashville: Incentive Publications, 1979.
Index to Instructional Media Catalogs. New York: R. R. Bowker, 1974.
Rufsvold, Margaret I. *Guides to Educational Media: Films, Filmstrips, Multimedia Kits, Programmed Instruction Materials, Recordings on Discs and Tapes, Transparencies, Videotapes,* fourth edition. Chicago: American Library Association, 1977.
Spear, Mary Eleanor. *Practical Charting Techniques.* New York: McGraw-Hill, 1969.
Stunard, E. Arthur, and Wagner, Betty. *Making and Using Inexpensive Classroom Media.* Palo Alto, California: Education Today, 1976.
Wittich, Walter and Schuller, Charles F. *Instructional Technology: Its Nature and Use,* sixth edition. New York: Harper and Row, 1979.

15

Fair Use of Copyright

Overview

In the process of using library materials, the need to copy information often arises. The availability of inexpensive modern technology makes the copying of information a simple procedure. In fact, the procedure is so simple that libraries and library users are beginning to copy more and more information. The legality of doing so is another matter. Practically all the informational material in the library is protected by copyright; and although some of it can be legally copied, there are limits prescribed by federal law as to how much of the work can be duplicated and how many copies can be made without infringing on the rights of the copyright owner. Just about every library has equipment for duplicating various types of materials, and much of this equipment is directly accessible to the patron. Consequently, the librarian must have practical knowledge of federal copyright law and its effect on the library.

The intent of this chapter is to introduce the reader to recent legislation and other developments pertaining to copyright law. The laws will be presented objectively but no effort will be made to interpret them. In developing policies and procedures for duplicating copyrighted material, the librarian should seek competent legal advice from a copyright lawyer, who can expertly interpret the law.

Purpose of Copyright

Although references to literary property rights can be found in Roman law, modern copyright statutes are believed to have originated in

Renaissance Europe following the invention of the printing press. The prevailing governing powers, in an attempt to protect authors and inventors, gave them exclusive rights over their creative works. Basically, the patent, or what was later more appropriately called a copyright, identified the owner of the work who was to be protected, declared that the work could not be printed or sold without the identified owner's permission, and specified a penalty for anyone who violated a copyright. This description of a copyright remained basically unchanged for many years; the only significant modification in European copyright laws was the addition of some kind of reference to copyright duration.

Copyright laws in the United States antedate the Constitution; the Massachusetts Bay Colony passed copyright laws as early as 1672. The first United States copyright law was enacted in 1790. Since then, general revisions of the copyright law were made in 1831, 1870, 1909, and 1976. The most recent revision, the Copyright Act of 1976, became effective on January 1, 1978. Whereas the previous law, the Copyright Act of 1909, focused almost entirely on the rights of copyright owners, the new law includes provisions allowing the user certain limited rights to reproduce copyrighted material.

Another significant revision is the change in duration of copyright. The 1909 act allowed a 28-year copyright duration that was renewable for an additional 28 years, after which time the material became part of the public domain and was no longer protected by copyright. The new law protects a copyright for the life of the author and an additional 50 years after his or her death. In the case of anonymous works, pseudonymous works, and works made for hire, the copyright is protected for 75 years from the year of first publication or 100 years from the year of creation, whichever expires first.

One intent of copyright is to protect the owner of an originally authored work from unauthorized use of his or her material. Specifically, the material is protected with regard to how it can be used, modified, duplicated, or copied without express permission of the owner. Section 102 of *The Copyright Revision Act of 1976* identifies the following as categories of authored work covered by copyright: (*a*) literary works; (*b*) musical works; (*c*) dramatic works, including any accompanying music; (*d*) pantomime and choreographic works; (*e*) pictorial, graphic, and sculptured works; (*f*) motion pictures and other audiovisual works; and (*g*) sound recordings.[1]

The owner of a copyrighted work, as stated in section 106, is the only one with exclusive rights to the work with regard to how it is repro-

[1] United States *Code*, Title 17, *Copyrights*, section 102.

duced, distributed, and used and presented in public, and under what conditions derivative works may be prepared from it. This protection of copyright is defined in section 106 as follows:

§106. **Exclusive rights in copyrighted works**
  Subject to sections 107 through 118, the owner of copyright under this title has the exclusive rights to do and to authorize any of the following:
  (1) to reproduce the copyrighted work in copies or phonorecords;
  (2) to prepare derivative works based upon the copyrighted work;
  (3) to distribute copies or phonorecords of the copyrighted work to the public by sale or other transfer of ownership, or by rental, lease, or lending;
  (4) in the case of literary, musical, dramatic, and choreographic works, pantomimes, and motion pictures and other audiovisual works, to perform the copyrighted work publicly; and
  (5) in the case of literary, musical, dramatic, and choreographic works, pantomimes, and pictorial, graphic, or sculptural works, including the individual images of a motion picture or other audiovisual work, to display the copyrighted work publicly (United States *Code,* Title 17, section 106).

Although it is beneficial to know how the copyright law protects the copyright owner, the librarian also needs to know what rights have been granted to the user of the material. Special exemptions permitting a limited amount of copying and other use of copyrighted materials are given to schools, libraries, archives, and, in some cases, people who are blind and/or deaf. These and other exemptions are specified in sections 107–112 of *The Copyright Act*.

Fair Use

The underlying rationale of fair use is to allow users of copyrighted material to copy or make expanded use of a copyrighted work without the permission of the copyright owner, as long as such use is within the confines of the law. The problem for the librarian is to understand the limits of fair use. Section 107 of *The Copyright Act* states that fair use is a use

of a copyrighted work, including such use by reproduction . . . for purposes such as criticism, comment, news reporting, teaching (including multiple copies for classroom use), scholarship or research [United States *Code,* Title 17, *Copyrights,* section 107].

Section 107 expressly provides the following criteria for determining whether or not the use made of a work in any particular case is a fair use:

(1) the purpose and character of the use, including whether such use is of a commercial nature or is for nonprofit educational purposes;

(2) the nature of the copyrighted work;

(3) the amount and substantiality of the portion used in relation to the copyrighted work as a whole; and

(4) the effect of the use upon the potential market for or value of the copyrighted work [United States *Code,* Title 17, *Copyrights,* section 107].

The problem confronting the librarian is to apply the above criteria in all situations where copyrighted material is being duplicated or distributed.

With regard to the first criterion, the Senate report interpreting section 107 favors spontaneity of use; for example, the report would allow more latitude to an individual teacher than to an institution. Thus, according to the Senate interpretation, a teacher acting as an individual could make one or more copies of a copyrighted work for temporary use in the classroom.[2] According to the House report on section 107, "spontaneity" occurs when

the inspiration and decision to use the work and the amount of its use for maximum teaching effectiveness are so close in time that it would be unreasonable to expect a timely reply to a request for permission [United States House of Representatives, *Report No. 94-1476,* section 107].

The House Report does not define a "timely reply," but the Association of American Publishers indicates that one should allow 4 weeks to receive a response to a request.[3]

With regard to the second (nature of the copyrighted work) and third (amount and substantiality of the work to be copied) criteria, the following minimum standards of fair use have been discussed as tentative guidelines and do not have the force of law, but might be referred to by courts in an attempt to interpret section 107 of *The Copyright Act:*

Agreement on guidelines
for classroom copying in not-for-profit
educational institutions with respect to books and periodicals

The purpose of the following guidelines is to state the minimum standards of educational fair use under Section 107 of H.R. 2223. The parties agree that the conditions determining the extent of permissible copying for educational purposes may change in the future; that certain types of copying permitted under these guidelines may not

[2] United States Senate, *Report No. 94-473,* section 107.

[3] Association of American Publishers, *Copyright Permissions: A Guide for Non-Commercial Use,* Washington, D.C.: The Association, 1975.

be permissible in the future; and conversely that in the future other types of copying not permitted under these guidelines may be permissible under revised guidelines.

Moreover, the following statement of guidelines is not intended to limit the types of copying permitted under the standards of fair use under judicial decision and which are stated in Section 107 of the Copyright Revision Bill. There may be instances in which copying which does not fall within the guidelines stated below may nonetheless be permitted under the criteria of fair use.

Guidelines

   I. *Single Copying for Teachers*

A single copy may be made of any of the following by or for a teacher at his or her individual request for his or her scholarly research or use in teaching or preparation to teach a class:

A. A chapter from a book;

B. An article from a periodical or newspaper;

C. A short story, short essay or short poem, whether or not from a collective work;

D. A chart, graph, diagram, drawing, cartoon or picture from a book, periodical, or newspaper;

  II. *Multiple Copies for Classroom Use*

Multiple copies (not to exceed in any event more than one copy per pupil in a course) may be made by or for the teacher giving the course for classroom use or discussion; *provided that:*

A. The copying meets the tests of brevity and spontaneity as defined below; *and,*

B. Meets the cumulative effect test as defined *below; and,*

C. Each copy includes a notice of copyright.

Definitions

Brevity

   (*i*) Poetry: (a) A complete poem if less than 250 words and if printed on not more than two pages, or (b) from a longer poem, an excerpt of not more than 250 words.

  (*ii*) Prose: (a) Either a complete article, story or essay of less than 2,500 words, or (b) an excerpt from any prose work of not more than 1,000 words or 10% of the work, whichever is less, but in any event a minimum of 500 words.

Each of the numerical limits stated in "*i*" and "*ii*" above may be expanded to permit the completion of an unfinished line of a poem or of an unfinished prose paragraph.]

 (*iii*) Illustration: One chart, graph, diagram, drawing, cartoon or picture per book or per periodical issue.

 (*iv*) "Special" works: Certain works in poetry, prose or in "poetic prose" which often combine language with illustrations and which are intended sometimes for children and at other times for a more general audience fall short of 2,500 words in their entirety. Paragraph "*ii*" above notwithstanding such "special works" may not be reproduced in their entirety; however, an excerpt comprising not more than two of the published pages of such special work and containing not more than 10% of the words found in the text thereof, may be reproduced.

Spontaneity

  (*i*) The copying is at the instance and inspiration of the individual teacher, and

  (*ii*) The inspiration and decision to use the work and the moment of its use for maximum teaching effectiveness are so close in time that it would be unreasonable to expect a timely reply to a request for permission.

Cumulative Effect

  (*i*) The copying of the material is for only one course in the school in which the copies are made.

  (*ii*) Not more than one short poem, article, story, essay or two excerpts may be copied from the same author, nor more than three from the same collective work or periodical volume during one class term.

  (*iii*) There shall not be more than nine instances of such multiple copying for one course during one class term.

The limitations stated in *"ii"* and *"iii"* above shall not apply to current news periodicals and newspapers and current news sections of other periodicals.]

III. *Prohibitions as to I and II Above*

Notwithstanding any of the above, the following shall be prohibited:

  (A) Copying shall not be used to create or to replace or substitute for anthologies, compilations or collective works. Such replacement or substitution may occur whether copies of various works or excerpts therefrom are accumulated or reproduced and used separately.

  (B) There shall be no copying of or from works intended to be "consumable" in the course of study or of teaching. These include workbooks, exercises, standardized tests and test booklets and answer sheets and like consumable material.

  (C) Copying shall not:

  (a) substitute for the purchase of books, publishers' reprints on periodicals;

  (b) be directed by higher authority;

  (c) be repeated with respect to the same item by the same teacher from term to term.

  (D) No charge shall be made to the student beyond the actual cost of the photocopying.

Agreed March 19, 1976.

Ad Hoc Committee on Copyright Law Revision:

By Sheldon Elliott Steinbach.

Author–Publisher Group:

Authors League of America:

By Irwin Karp, *Counsel.*

Association of American Publishers, Inc.:

By Alexander C. Hoffman,
Chairman, Copyright Committee.

(United States House of Representatives, *Report No. 94-1476, section 107.*

The last criterion listed in section 107 (effect of the use on the potential market) is the one of greatest concern to the copyright owner. Any copying that could tend to reduce the volume of sales of a particular copyrighted work is a potential infringement of copyright.

Performance Materials

Section 110 of *The Copyright Act* provides that certain performances and displays of copyrighted material are not infringements of copyright. *Performance materials,* as encountered by librarians, are those materials primarily intended for use before an audience, and include, among other things, printed lectures, sermons, and sheet music. Perhaps of even greater significance to the librarian are the nonprint media performance materials, for example, audio recordings, slides, filmstrips, motion picture films, and videocassettes. Obviously, the intent of the librarian when he or she purchases a motion picture film is that it will be used by individuals as well as groups. The risk of infringement is reduced when performance materials are used in what *The Copyright Act* calls "face-to-face teaching," that is, use in a classroom setting or transmission in the same building or general area as the classroom. In other cases, performance of a dramatic work will probably require the permission of the copyright owner.

Often, the librarian may feel the need to copy performance material for the purpose of having a spare copy in case the original becomes damaged or worn. Unless express written permission from the holder of the copyright is obtained, any duplication of such material is probably an infringement of copyright.

A problem still exists with regard to copying broadcast materials. Educators feel that some televised information is of educational value, and that users should be free to make copies of educational programs. Obviously, the television networks take a somewhat different view. The issue of off-the-air recording is still being hotly debated, and *The Copyright Act* does not offer any definite resolution of the dispute. The Public Broadcasting System (PBS) takes the position that it will allow schools to copy most (not all) of their programs, on the condition that they be erased after 7 days. Certain television news programs are presently being copied by the Library of Congress, and rights to use such programs can often be obtained through them. The librarian should note that material created and produced solely by the government is not under the protection of copyright; however, the librarian should be certain, prior to copying such material, that it was indeed created and produced solely by the government, and not by a private or quasi-governmental entity acting on the government's behalf.

The technology for copying and transmitting information materials is relatively inexpensive and easy to use. This creates something of a temptation to use material in a way not intended by the copyright proprietor. The purpose of copying or transmitting may be well intended and not for personal gain; however, it may hurt the owner financially. It is always best to know the legal limitations, which may or may not be spelled out in the distributor's catalog or bill of sale. If no specific statement respecting the permissible scope of use can be found, it is strongly advised that written permission from the proprietor be obtained. It is amazing how understanding most proprietors are; if they feel that your request is within reason, most of them will be more than willing to grant your request. In special instances, the proprietor may stipulate that permission will be granted only after receipt of a fee or that it is necessary to purchase a license extending or expanding use rights for the material. Obviously, an additional fee is preferable to the possibility of a lawsuit involving a claim of illegal use.

Photocopying

In most libraries, the print collection contains the largest percentage of material. It is also perhaps the material that is easiest to reproduce by and for the patron. To operate the current generation of print copiers requires no special skill, and the copies reproduced are usually of excellent quality. As with the copying of all material, some latitude is given to the library under *The Copyright Act*. According to section 108(a), one copy or phonorecord of a work may be reproduced by a library if the three following conditions are met:

(1) The reproduction or distribution is made without any purpose of direct or indirect commercial advantage;[4]
(2) the collections of the library or archives are . . . open to the public . . .
(3) the reproduction or distribution of the work includes a notice of copyright [United States *Code,* Title 17, *Copyrights,* section 108(a)].

These conditions apply to the reproduction and distribution of one copy to be included in the library holdings; it does not apply to patrons who make copies using a copy machine on the library premises. The latter situation is discussed in section 108(f), which absolves a library or archive as well as the employees of either from liability for the unsupervised use of reproducing equipment located on the institution's premises, "so long as such equipment displays a notice that the making of a

---

[4] In itself, this requirement is fairly objective, and, at face value, requires little or no interpretation. Clearly, it means that the library can reproduce one copy of a copyrighted work, as long as no profit is involved. But minor nuances can cloud the interpretation (for example, is the manufacturer or lessor of the copy machine realizing a profit by having the copy machine in the library?)

copy may be subject to the copyright law," but which also warns that nothing in section 108 "excuses a person who uses such reproducing equipment . . . from liability for copyright infringement for any such act . . . if it exceeds fair use as provided by Section 107 [United States *Code,* Title 17, *Copyrights,* section 108(f)].

The law stipulates that a notice of copyright restrictions, such as the following, be prominently displayed at the location where copying requests are made.

NOTICE

Warning Concerning Copyright Restrictions

The copyright law of the United States (Title 17, United States Code) governs the making of photocopies or other reproductions of copyrighted material.

Under certain conditions specified in the law, libraries and archives are authorized to furnish a photocopy or other reproduction. One of these specified conditions is that the photocopy or reproduction is not to be "used for any purpose other than private study, scholarship, or research." If a user makes a request for, or later uses, a photocopy or reproduction for purposes in excess of "fair use," that user may be liable for copyright infringement.

This institution reserves the right to refuse to accept a copying order, if in its judgement, fulfillment of the order would involve violation of copyright law.[5]

The notice must be clearly visible and easy to read. In situations where order forms are used to request copy services, the notice must appear on the form. In no case does section 108 permit a library to make more than one copy of a given work, even if more than one patron requests a copy of the same work. According to section 108(g)(1),

the rights of reproduction . . . do not extend to cases where the library or archives, or its employee . . . is aware or has substantial reason to believe that it is engaging in related or concerted reproduction or distribution of multiple copies or phonorecords of the same material, whether made on one occasion or over a period of time [United States *Code,* Title 17, *Copyrights,* section 108(g)(1)].

In situations where the patron can make unsupervised copies of material, a notice, such as the following, must be posted on or near the copy machine, where the patron cannot fail to read it.

NOTICE

The copyright law of the United States (Title 17 U.S. *Code*) governs the making of photocopies or other reproductions of copyrighted material. The person using this equipment is liable for any infringement.[6]

[5] "Warning of Copyright for Use by Libraries and Archives." *Federal Register,* November 16, 1977, pp. 59254–59255.

[6] "Three Words Added to Copyright Notice." *American Libraries* 9 (January 1978):22.

But, as Section 108(g)(1) suggests, merely posting such a notice will not protect a library employee who is aware that illegal reproduction is occurring.

Section 108(g)(2) reads as follows:

> The rights of reproduction . . . do not extend to cases where the library or archives, or its employee . . . engages in the systematic reproduction or distribution of single or multiple copies or phonorecords of material . . . Provided, that nothing in this clause prevents a library or archives from participating in interlibrary arrangements that do not have, as their purpose or effect, that the library or archives receiving such copies or phonorecords for distribution does so in such aggregate quantities as to substitute for a subscription to or purchase of such work [United States *Code*, Title 17, *Copyrights*, section 108(g)(2)].

This requirement basically states that the library cannot copy material or enter into interlibrary arrangements when such copying is in lieu of purchasing the copyrighted material. In such cases, copying the material deprives the owner of the copyrighted material of his or her just remuneration. There is considerable concern regarding this requirement as to what can be copied for purposes of interlibrary loan. The librarian should seek legal advice on this matter and keep him or herself apprised of new developments and interpretations of the law as well as precedents that libraries in general may follow. Generally, in an interlibrary loan, it is permissible for libraries to loan or exchange materials. However, it might be a violation of copyright for a library to copy materials and, in essence, retain the original and loan out a copy. Essentially, if an interlibrary loan results in using or having available the materials in both libraries simultaneously, (which eliminates the need of purchasing a second copy), it is a violation of The Copyright Act. In cases where material is sold expressly for use at a particular library (e.g., showing films to a specifically identified audience), under no circumstances may that material be loaned to another library loan. Libraries entering into interlibrary agreements should carefully consider their exchange guidelines to insure that they are not in violation of copyright.

According to section 108(h),

> the rights of reproduction and distribution . . . do not apply to a musical work, a pictorial, graphic, or sculptural work, or motion picture, or other audiovisual work other than an audiovisual work dealing with news, except that no such limitation shall apply with respect to rights granted by subsections (b) and (c), or with respect to pictorial or graphic works published as illustrations, diagrams, or similar adjuncts to works of which copies are reproduced or distributed in accordance with subsections (d) and (e) [United States *Code*, Title 17, *Copyrights*, section 108(h)].

Under this requirement, the library cannot copy musical compositions, sheet music, pictorial, graphic, or sculptural work, or any kind of audiovisual work, except news and works defined in subsections 108(b) and (c). Subsection (b) allows the reproduction of one copy of an unpublished work, "solely for purposes of preservation and security or for deposit for research use in another library . . . [on the condition that the material being] reproduced is currently in the collections of the library or archives [United States *Code,* Title 17, *Copyrights,* section 108(b)]. Subsection (c) allows reproduction of one copy to be

> duplicated in facsimile form solely for the purpose of replacement of a copy or phonorecord that is damaged, deteriorating, lost, or stolen, if the library or archives has, after a reasonable effort, determined that an unused replacement cannot be obtained at a fair price United States *Code,* Title 17, *Copyrights,* section 108(c)].

This can be extended to include out-of-print works, but it is a good idea to determine conclusively that they are indeed out of print, because they might be available in microform.

Special Rights

On occasion, the library might need copying and distribution privileges that go beyond the scope of what is permissible under the copyright law. In such situations, the library will need to obtain written permission from the holder of the copyright. Some libraries routinely make copies of materials that receive excessive use or are susceptible to damage; thus, the copy that is used by the patron, and the original is preserved. Sometimes material has to be copied in order to conform to a particular format of equipment used in the library. The latter reason for copying is not sanctioned by *The Copyright Act,* and therefore special permission from the copyright owner must be obtained. If the librarian is aware ahead of time that a copy will have to be made for this reason, it is best to obtain special permission when submitting the purchase order and to insist that such permission be part of the sales agreement. It is also very important that the agreement or permission be in writing, and the materials should not be accepted without it.

Display or performance materials may require a special license, especially if the information is transmitted via radio or television or if any kind of admission fee is required to view or hear it. The cost of this type of license is usually prorated on a published scale, and is determined by either the size of the library or the audience involved. Usually, the copyright owner charges a blanket fee, which is subject to periodic review.

Another type of permission is the one-time permission in which the library requests a special privilege to copy or use material that is beyond the legal scope of the copyright law. The library should not subscribe to the position that a "one time only" copy or use will not really hurt anyone, and can therefore be overlooked. The librarian must make a sincere effort to obtain permission to copy and/or use such material. Many companies are willing to cooperate with libraries on such requests and even try to reply fairly promptly. If permission is denied, the library has no recourse beyond the provisions of the copyright law. An unacknowledged request should not be interpreted as a permission; the only rights the library has are those defined in the sections of the copyright law or those expressly conferred on the library in writing by the owner of the copyrighted material.

The librarian should have an ethical and moral attitude toward using copyrighted materials, as well as a journeyman's knowledge of the copyright law. Information materials today are becoming so easy to copy, and the ability to use, display, and transmit these copies is so tempting that copyright infringements could become the rule rather than the exception. In summary, it is well and good to copy and use material within the limitations of sections 107–112 of *The Copyright Act*, as a means of providing services to library patrons; but there should also be a concern to protect the copyright owner's legal rights.

Selected Bibliography

"ALS and ARL Address: Copyright Clearance under the Fair Use Doctrine and Other Provisions of the New Copyright Law." *American Libraries*, 8(December, 1977):624–625.

Copyright and Educational Media: A Guide to Fair Use and Permission Procedures. Washington, D.C.: Association for Educational Communications and Technology, 1977.

Copyright Revision Act of 1976, House of Representatives Report No. 94-1476, 94th Congress. Washington, D.C.: Superintendent of Documents, 1976.

Flacks, Lewis I. "Living in the Gap of Ambiguity: An Attorney's Advice to Librarians on the Copyright Law." *American Libraries*, 8(May 1977):252–257.

Highlights of the New Copyright Law. Sacramento: Creative Book Co., 1978.

Johnston, Donald. *A Copyright Handbook*. New York: R. R. Bowker, 1978.

Librarian's Copyright Kit. Chicago: American Library Association, 1977.

Librarian's Guide to the New Copyright Law. Chicago: American Library Association, 1977.

Miller, Jerome K. *Applying the New Copyright Law. A Guide for Educators and Librarians*. Chicago: American Library Association, 1979.

New Copyright Law: Questions Teachers and Librarians Ask. Chicago: American Library Association, 1977.

Seltzer, Leon E. *Exemptions and Fair Use in Copyright: The Exclusive Rights Tensions in the 1976 Copyright Act*. Cambridge, Massachusetts: Harvard University Press, 1978.

Tseng, Henry P. "The Ethical Aspects of Photocopying as They Pertain to the Library, the User, and the Owner of the Copyright." *Law Library Journal,* 72(Winter 1979):86–90.

White, Herbert S., ed. *The Copyright Dilemma.* Chicago: American Library Association, 1978.

16

Intellectual Freedom

Overview

One of the more perplexing concerns of the librarian when selecting information materials is the matter of intellectual freedom. The desire of the conscientious librarian who is dedicated to the principle of free inquiry is to build and maintain a library collection that caters to the patron's wants and needs but is in no way restricted to what he or she (the librarian) subjectively thinks is best or what any segment of the community feels is best for the community at large. At times information material that is congruent with the philosophy and selection policy of the library may be controversial, and the librarian must have the courage to stand by his or her decision as well as the conviction to defend a selection from any person(s) who might demand that it be removed from the collection.

Selection versus Censorship

It is essential that the librarian subscribe to the position that it is the right of the individual to choose freely whatever information he or she desires. Unfortunately, there are people who sincerely believe they are acting in the best interest of the community when they request that material be removed from the library collection. In essence, these people are restricting the freedom of choice of others by imposing their own tastes or standards of what is acceptable information material on the

community at large. The position of the selector is in direct opposition
to that of the censor; that is the selector justifies the acquisition of information material, whereas the censor must formulate reasons for rejecting it. The selector's views are generally positive, whereas the censor's
are usually negative. It is somewhat ironic that the most severe censorship problem arises not when someone from outside the library wants
something removed, but when the librarian assumes the dual role of
selector and censor. When the censor is outside the library, the lines of
opposition are clearly established, the censor and his or her position are
clearly defined, and the library has recourse to the necessary policy and
procedures for resolving the issue. On the other hand, when the librarian functions as a censor, his or her reasons are not as open to scrutiny.
The decision for censoring becomes somewhat obscure and must be
defended only on rare occasions. Therefore, the librarian must be
genuinely objective and base any decision to censor information on
library policy, not personal reasons. All too often, when the librarian
censors material, it is because of concern that defending a particular
piece of information could cause repercussions that might threaten his
or her job security or possibly lead to character assassination.

Generally library acquisitions are most likely to be censored when
they violate someone's accepted norms, for example explicit descriptions of love and sex, perceived biased treatment of minorities, presentation of opinions espoused by unpopular ideologies, authors whose
purported political views or private lives are controversial, or the use of
what is considered to be indecent language. Usually, it can be ascertained that the person(s) who request the withdrawal of material from
the library are either hostile to free inquiry and open discussion, tend to
be dogmatic and closed minded, or are misinformed and are responding
out of ignorance, unsubstantiated rumor, or neurotic emotion. The censor always believes he or she is acting in the best interests of the community, but fails to understand that intellectual freedom is to be preferred over protected ignorance.

In an effort to protect the community, the censor seeks out the possibly
objectionable features of a work that could be damaging to the weak
mind, not realizing that such actions could lead to thought control. In so
doing, the censor usually does not reject an entire work, but rather only
parts that are deemed objectionable. Rather than assessing the value of
an entire work, the censor analyzes parts of it out of context. The results
of such censorship are often biased, damaging, and lacking in defensi-
ble justification. A popular catch phrase of the emotional censor is "the
concern for prurient interests," which is usually applied to material
considered to be pornographic. In this instance, the censor feels that
there are certain people who are lascivious in their thinking and that

material deemed to be pornographic could have a harmful effect not only on such individuals but on the community at large as well. Such a position is untenable, however, because there is no conclusive proof that any information, pornographic or otherwise, has an adverse effect on prurient interests.

In contrast to the censor, the selector looks at the information material as a whole, and identifies strengths that can overcome objections to any of the parts. Rather than focusing on a somewhat amorphous area that might appeal to prurient interests, the selector considers how the work will affect the rational, intelligent adult. The ultimate concern of the librarian is to protect intellectual freedom and the individual's right to information. Indeed, it should be the individual's privilege to determine whether a particular body of information is suitable or objectionable to his or her unique wants and needs. The general qualities that the librarian should look for in judging information material are good taste, structural or literary excellence, and socially redeemable value.

Response to Censorship

It is inevitable that the librarian will be confronted with requests for the removal of material that is perceived to be objectionable or harmful. The librarian needs to be prepared for such contingencies, and to have the necessary response ready. It is important for the librarian to remain calm; such a request should not be considered as an attack on the library that can only be resolved by entering into full battle with the enemy. Bear in mind that the person(s) requesting the censorship of material is acting in what he or she believes is good faith and a desire to protect the community from objectionable or harmful information.

Any work acquired by the library must first of all be in absolute compliance with the library's philosophy and selection policy. Having satisfied this criterion, the issue can perhaps be resolved without further action. As a matter of record, the library's philosophy and selection policy should be an open statement that is available to the public, especially to those directly involved with the censorship controversy. The librarian should only address him or herself to the issue by being certain that any response is supported by library philosophy and selection policy.

If the censorship problem cannot be resolved by indicating that the selection was made within the precepts of the library's philosophy and selection policy, it becomes necessary to refer the matter to an intellectual freedom or censorship committee for resolution. Ideally, this committee should be a standing committee that is ready to swing into action on request. The committee members should include people who represent the various segments of the community served by the library. Committee members must behave objectively, and their interest should be limited to how the particular problem of censorship affects the community; in no way should they have a personal stake in the matter.

If the material under consideration must be adjudicated by a committee, the complainant should be asked to formalize the complaint in writing. This could be expedited by the library having a prepared form that the complainant could use as a guide in making a request for

Request for Reconsideration of Library Materials

In order to properly respond to your request for reconsideration of library materials, the library would appreciate your providing the following information: (If additional documentation is being submitted, please attach it to this form.)

1. Individual(s) submitting request
   Name:
   Address:
   Telephone:
2. Do you represent a particular community group or organization in this matter?
   ☐Yes
   ☐No
   If yes, please identify group or organization:

3. Please give a complete bibliographic citation of the particular material you are requesting be reconsidered:
   Author or Producer:
   Title:
   Publisher or Distributor:
   Date of Publication:
   Location of Publisher (city and state):
4. Identify media type (e.g., book, film, audio recording):
5. Why do you believe this work should be withdrawn from the library's collection?

6. Are there any specific parts of the work you find objectionable?
   ☐Yes
   ☐No
   If yes, please describe the objectionable parts.

Figure 16.1 Request for reconsideration of library materials.

censorship (see Figure 16.1). The form should clearly identify the requester and should specify whether the individual(s) represents a particular community group. The work in question has to be cited, preferably with a complete bibliographic citation. The complainant should make a statement indicating why, in general, the work should be censored and what, if any, specific parts of the work are objectionable. The complainant should give what he or she feels are his or her qualifications for censoring the work, his or her familiarity with this particular genre of work, and his or her knowledge of the specific work in question. The complainant must state precisely what adverse effect the work will have and must specify the segment(s) of the community he or she believes will be affected. The complainant should also be asked if he or she can provide the names of experts on this issue who would corroborate his or her position. The complainant should determine whether the entire work should be removed from the library or whether it would suffice, if possible, to remove only those parts that are objectionable. Finally in an

7. Why do you believe this work will have an adverse effect on the people who might use it?

8. Please describe the particular type of individual or group on whom you feel this work will have an adverse effect?

9. Should the entire work be withdrawn, or could it possibly be edited to make it unobjectionable?
   ☐Yes
   ☐No

10. Can you suggest any alternative works that can be considered as replacements for the material you are requesting be withdrawn?

11. What do you consider to be your qualifications for judging this work (e.g., knowledge of or experience with this type of material, this particular work, and/or the probable effects the work might have on the user)?

12. List the names and positions of anyone who can provide expert testimony that will support your request to have the material withdrawn from the library:

Signature(s) ————————————

Figure 16.1 (*Continued*)

effort to preserve some semblance of intellectual freedom, the complainant should be asked if there are any alternative works that can be considered by the library as replacements for the work being considered for censorship.

When the formal complaint is received by the library, the librarian must inform the intellectual freedom committee, give the members copies of the complaint, and ask them to stand by for further developments. The librarian should contact the complainant to set up a meeting during which the complaint can be formally discussed and the complainant can be informed of the procedures for handling censorship requests. If possible, an attempt should be made to resolve the problem at this level, in order to avoid the need for a formal committee hearing. It is recommended that minutes be kept of all meetings and that at least two members of the library staff be in attendance at all scheduled meetings. The complainant should be given a thorough explanation of the library's philosophy and selection policy as it pertains to the issue under discussion. If it is the library's position that the material requested for censorship should not be removed from the library collection, this position must be supported by documented fact, not simply based on the librarian's own feeling or supposition. If the matter must be pursued further, the librarian should be familiar with some of the United States Supreme Court decisions regarding the First Amendment of the Constitution as it applies to censorship. In doing so, the librarian has not only the support of the library's philosophy and selection policy, but also the legal leverage of the law of the land. It is well to note here that the librarian is not expected to be trained in the law; and, therefore, should not be expected to perform as a lawyer. Law is a complex field that is in a continual state of flux. The librarian should seek professional advice before taking action that might have legal repercussions.

An important concern with regard to censorship is deciding how to respond to the occurrence of obscenity in prospective library materials. Obscenity is not mentioned in the Constitution, the Bill of Rights, or the First Amendment. It is the task of the Supreme Court to define obscenity; but to this date, the issue has yet to be satisfactorily resolved. In 1957, the Warren Court took a liberal turn on the obscenity issue in *Roth* v. *United States.* The court's majority decision stated

> All ideas having even the slightest redeeming social importance—unorthodox ideas, controversial ideas, even ideas hateful to the prevailing climate of opinion—have full protection of the First Amendment guarantees unless excludable because they encroach upon the limited area of more important areas.[1]

[1] Stanek, Lou Willet. *Censorship: A Guide for Teachers, Librarians, and Others Concerned with Intellectual Freedom.* New York: Dell Publishing, 1976, p. 5.

This decision began a liberal trend, and, although not all obscenity cases were dismissed, the prevailing attitude was that materials had to be proven to have no redeeming social value in order to be censored as obscene.

In 1973, the Supreme Court adopted a more conservative stance by setting forth a new set of rules based on decisions handed down in five obscenity cases. The new guidelines on obscenity enable individual states to ban books, magazines, plays, and motion pictures offensive to local standards, even if they might be acceptable elsewhere. It is interesting to note that this decision was passed on a five-to-four vote of the justices. Justice William O. Douglas said in his dissenting opinion,

> What we do today is rather ominous as respects librarians. The antiobscenity net now signed by the Court is so finely meshed that taken literally it could result in raids on libraries. . . . Libraries, I had always assumed, were sacrosanct, representing every part of the spectrum. If what is offensive to the most influential person or group in the community can be purged from a library, the library system would be destroyed.[2]

The Supreme Court, in its latest decision, does allow censorship at the local level; however, there is a genuine concern to protect the library from a purge of its materials by persons who may strongly influence public opinion. The library's best defense against such an attack is to have a clearly formulated selection policy that has the endorsement of representative elements of the community and a respected, well-informed committee that is ready to resolve any censorship issue.

Granted, there is always concern that information may get into the hands of people who cannot properly handle it. Such people obviously need guidance, but denying them the information is, in a sense, denying them their rights under the Constitution. A partial solution is to select materials that have received recognition in the literature (e.g., booklists, reviews, recommendations) as a means of acquiring material that is likely to have been competently reviewed, judged, and recommended. Of course, it must be realized that of all the books published, less than one-third receive anything in the way of a review or examination. If a controversial piece of information material is acquired, the librarian had better be familiar with it, and be certain that its acquisition complies with the library selection policy.

This makes the selection process appear to be a clear-cut task of buying the best and not providing funds to acquire anything less. However, it is not a clear-cut case of black or white; there is obviously a gray area in material selection that can be susceptible to challenge in terms of its

---

[2] Stanek, Lou Willet. *Censorship: A Guide for Teachers, Librarians, and Others Concerned with Intellectual Freedom.* New York: Dell Publishing, 1976, p. 6.

value or harm to the community. A knowledgeable librarian who is familiar with the material, knows why and for whom it was selected, and is aware of the authority that is delegated to him or her as a librarian can proceed to function as a supportive force in the cause of intellectual freedom and free inquiry. The librarian must have the support of the administration by whom he or she is employed and be able to act without the fear of retaliation or dismissal.

Following the precepts of intellectual freedom which require that all information material is available to all patrons, the librarian must make material accessible on request. This means that even a child cannot be denied material. The librarian knows that some material that is beneficial to an adult is definitely inappropriate for the young mind. However, to deny a child material that is available to an adult is, in fact, discrimination, and, in essence, an infringement of the child's rights under the law. Obviously, the librarian should make every effort to have the child exposed only to information that will improve the mind. If the child does request material that the librarian considers to be possibly detrimental, he or she should counsel the child, but should not refuse the request. If a situation does arise in which a child requests material that may not be beneficial, or if a member of the community demands that certain information not be made available; it is best to subscribe to the position advocated by the American Library Association. The ALA subscribes to the position that it is the parent—and only the parent—who may restrict his or her children from having access to library materials and services. (This position was adopted by the ALA Council June 30, 1972). Thus, it is the parent who decides that the child should not have access to certain materials and who should so advise the child.

The ALA's Position on Intellectual Freedom

It is recommended that every librarian involved with material selection or susceptible to the challenge of material censorship to be familiar with the efforts of the ALA to support the cause of intellectual freedom. The ALA maintains an office for the purpose of promoting and defending intellectual freedom,[3] and librarians can contact this office for information when censorship problems arise.

The ALA does not advocate a specific definition of intellectual free-

[3] Office for Intellectual Freedom, 50 East Huron Street, Chicago, Illinois 60611, (312) 944-6780.

dom, but rather has promoted a variety of principles the purpose of which is to provide an environment favorable to intellectual freedom. As early as 1939, the ALA, confronted with pressures to censor John Steinbeck's *Grapes of Wrath*, adopted the forerunner of what is now called the Library Bill of Rights. The original document focused on unbiased book selection, but it has since been amended, revised, and interpreted to promote intellectual freedom and to oppose all forms of censorship. In addition to the Library Bill of Rights, the ALA has issued several documents that deal with the issue of intellectual freedom and censorship. These documents are included in the Office of Intellectual Freedom's *Intellectual Freedom Manual* (Chicago: American Library Association, 1974). This manual is organized into six parts, the titles of which are "Library Bill of Rights," "Freedom to Read," "Intellectual Freedom," "Before the Censor Comes," "Intellectual Freedom and the Law," and "Assistance from the ALA." Specifically the manual contains the following documents:

1. Intellectual Freedom Statement (June 25, 1967)
2. Library Bill of Rights (June 25, 1967)
3. School Library Bill of Rights for School Library Media Programs (1969)
4. Statement on Labeling (June 25, 1971)
5. Free Access to Libraries for Minors (June 30, 1972)
6. Policy on Confidentiality of Library Records (July 4, 1975)
7. Resolution on Challenged Materials (June 25, 1971)
8. Sexism, Racism and Other-isms in Library Materials (February 2, 1973)
9. Restricted Access to Library Materials (February 2, 1973)
10. Reevaluating Library Collections (February 2, 1973)
11. Expurgation of Library Materials (February 2, 1973)
12. Resolution on Governmental Intimidation (February 2, 1973)
13. How Libraries Can Resist Censorship (January 28, 1972)
14. Freedom to Read Statement (January 28, 1972)

For the convenience of the reader, the following documents are reproduced here: Library Bill of Rights (Figure 16.2); School Library Bill of Rights for School Library Media Center Programs (Figure 16.3); Freedom To View (Figure 16.4); and Statement on Labeling (Figure 16.5). Careful study of these documents will give the reader a perspective on the importance of intellectual freedom, the work that has been done in an effort to protect it, and the support the librarian can expect from the ALA.

𝕷𝖎𝖇𝖗𝖆𝖗𝖞 𝕭𝖎𝖑𝖑 𝖔𝖋 𝕽𝖎𝖌𝖍𝖙𝖘

The American Library Association affirms that all libraries are forums for information and ideas, and that the following basic policies should guide their services.

   1. Books and other library resources should be provided for the interest, information, and enlightenment of all people of the community the library serves. Materials should not be excluded because of the origin, background, or views of those contributing to their creation.

   2. Libraries should provide materials and information presenting all points of view on current and historical issues. Materials should not be proscribed or removed because of partisan or doctrinal disapproval.

   3. Libraries should challenge censorship in the fulfillment of their responsibility to provide information and enlightenment.

   4. Libraries should cooperate with all persons and groups concerned with resisting abridgment of free expression and free access to ideas.

   5. A person's right to use a library should not be denied or abridged because of origin, age, background, or views.

   6. Libraries which make exhibit spaces and meeting rooms available to the public they serve should make such facilities available on an equitable basis, regardless of the beliefs or affiliations of individuals or groups requesting their use.

Adopted June 18, 1948.
Amended February 2, 1961, June 27, 1967, and January 23, 1980,
by the ALA Council.

Figure 16.2 Library Bill of Rights, reproduced with permission from the American Library Association.

SCHOOL LIBRARY
BILL OF RIGHTS
for School Library
Media Center Programs

*Approved by American Association of School Librarians Board of Directors,
Atlantic City, 1969*

The American Association of School Librarians reaffirms its belief in the
Library Bill of Rights of the American Library Association. Media Personnel are concerned with generating understanding of American freedoms
through the development of informed and responsible citizens. To this
end the American Association of School Librarians asserts that the
responsibility of the school library media center is:

To provide a comprehensive collection of instructional materials
selected in compliance with basic written selection principles, and
to provide maximum accessibility to these materials.

To provide materials that will support the curriculum, taking into
consideration the individual's needs, and the varied interests,
abilities, socio-economic backgrounds, and maturity levels of the
students served.

To provide materials for teachers and students that will encourage
growth in knowledge, and that will develop literary, cultural and
aesthetic appreciation, and ethical standards.

To provide materials which reflect the ideas and beliefs of religious,
social, political, historical, and ethnic groups and their contribution to the American and world heritage and culture, thereby
enabling students to develop an intellectual integrity in forming
judgments.

To provide a written statement, approved by the local Boards of
Education, of the procedures for meeting the challenge of censorship of materials in school library media centers.

To provide qualified professional personnel to serve teachers and
students.

Figure 16.3 School Library Bill of Rights for School Library Media Center Programs,
reproduced with permission from the American Library Association.

FREEDOM TO VIEW

The FREEDOM TO VIEW, along with the freedom to speak, to hear, and to read, is protected by the First Amendment to the Constitution of the United States. In a free society, there is no place for censorship of any medium of expression. Therefore, we affirm these principles:

1. It is in the public interest to provide the broadest possible access to films and other audiovisual materials because they have proven to be among the most effective means for the communication of ideas. Liberty of circulation is essential to insure the constitutional guarantee of freedom of expression.

2. It is in the public interest to provide for our audiences, films and other audiovisual materials which represent a diversity of views and expression. Selection of a work does not constitute or imply agreement with or approval of the content.

3. It is our professional responsibility to resist the constraint of labeling or pre-judging a film on the basis of the moral, religious, or political beliefs of the producer or filmmaker or on the basis of controversial content.

4. It is our professional responsibility to contest vigorously, by all lawful means, every encroachment upon the public's freedom to view.

This statement was originally drafted by the Educational Film Library Association's Freedom to View Committee, and was adopted by the EFLA Board of Directors in February, 1979. Libraries and educational institutions are encouraged to adopt this statement and display it in their catalogs or libraries. The text of the statement may be reprinted freely; permission is granted to all educational institutions to use it.

EDUCATIONAL FILM LIBRARY ASSOCIATION, 43 W. 61 St., New York, NY 10023

Figure 16.4 Freedom to View, reproduced with permission from the Educational Film Library Association.

STATEMENT ON LABELING

An Interpretation of the LIBRARY BILL OF RIGHTS

Because labeling violates the spirit of the LIBRARY BILL OF RIGHTS, the American Library Association opposes the technique of labeling as a means of predisposing readers against library materials for the following reasons:

1. Labeling[1] is an attempt to prejudice the reader, and as such it is a censor's tool.

2. Although some find it easy and even proper, according to their ethics, to establish criteria for judging publications as objectionable, injustice and ignorance rather than justice and enlightenment result from such practices, and the American Library Association must oppose the establishment of such criteria.

3. Libraries do not advocate the ideas found in their collections. The presence of a magazine or book in a library does not indicate an endorsement of its contents by the library.

4. No one person should take the responsibility of labeling publications. No sizable group of persons would be likely to agree either on the types of material which should be labeled or the sources of information which should be regarded with suspicion. As a practical consideration, a librarian who labels a book or magazine might be sued for libel.

5. If materials are labeled to pacify one group, there is no excuse for refusing to label any item in the library's collection. Because authoritarians tend to suppress ideas and attempt to coerce individuals to conform to a specific ideology, the American Library Association opposes such efforts which aim at closing any path to knowledge.

Adopted July 13, 1951.
Amended June 25, 1971, by the ALA Council.

[1]"Labeling," as it is referred to in the STATEMENT ON LABELING, is the practice of describing or designating certain library materials, by affixing a prejudicial label to them or segregating them by a prejudicial system, so as to pre-dispose readers against the materials.

Figure 16.5 Statement on Labeling, reproduced with permission from the American Library Association.

Responding to a Request To Censor

Invariably, the occasion will arise in which someone will request that library material be withdrawn from circulation. The librarian should neither panic nor, conversely, react belligerently. As stated several times thus far in this chapter, if the library has a written philosophy and policy for material selection, and if the librarian has used these as guides in selecting materials, he or she should have a solid foundation on which to justify any material being circulated by the library.

The first action to take is to direct the request for withdrawal to the person who originally selected the material because this is the person who is most knowledgeable about the material in question. If the material is indeed somewhat controversial, the selector will probably have given extra thought as to its appropriateness before it was acquired. There is a good possibility that the issue can be solved at this point by providing the complainant with an intelligent reason as to why the item was acquired.

If the problem cannot be resolved in an informal discussion, and the complainant's intention in insisting that the material be withdrawn is sincere, he or she should be asked to submit a complaint on the prescribed form (see Figure 16.1). The complainant should be informed that the reconsideration form will be presented to the library administrator, who will decide what action, if any, should be taken, and that the complainant will be notified of the decision. The administrator, in consultation with the selector, will need to decide on a course of action, the alternatives being (*a*) to withdraw the material in its entirety, (*b*) to remove only the objectionable parts of the material if feasible, (*c*) to deny the request, and (*d*) to submit the request to the library's Committee on Intellectual Freedom for adjudication. With regard to alternatives *a* and *b*, the selector is not infallible; there is always the possibility, given new information or a different perspective, that some form of censorship may indeed be advisable. If the decision is to follow alternatives *a*, *b*, or *c*; and it is agreeable to all concerned, the matter can be considered to be closed. If the decision is to follow alternative *d*, copies of the complaint and a request for a meeting will have to be given to the Committee on Intellectual Freedom. It is advisable that the library keep a low profile on this matter, avoid any unnecessary publicity, and not discuss publicly any views that the library may have on the complaint.

In preparation for the hearing, the committee should be given a written statement that includes an explanation of why the controversial material was acquired and a detailed rebuttal to the formal complaint.

The committee will also be expected to examine the work in question. Consequently, all concerned with the library's position will be thoroughly familiar with the issue, the work in question, and the specific objection to it. If the selector firmly believes that the complaint is unwarranted, that he or she acted within the confines of the library's selection policy, and that the decision to select the controversial material was in agreement with the American Library Association's position on intellectual freedom; the selector should be given the complete and unequivocal support of the library administration. Far too often, the selecter has a tendency to acquiesce out of fear of losing his or her job, security, receiving a reprimand, or some other form of castigation. This sort of situation cannot be allowed to occur. The very essence of the library's selection process is at stake in such a situation; for if the selector is not given the support he or she deserves, all future selection may well be based not on the tenets of free inquiry, but rather on job security, survival, and a policy of following the path of least resistance.

When the committee does convene, the complainant should be allowed to present his or her case first. The committee should see that at least the following information is provided during the complainant's presentation: (*a*) a specific identification of the work in question, (*b*) an intelligent statement as to why the work either in whole or in part is objectionable, (*c*) firm verification of the complainant's familiarity with the work, (*d*) alternatives to a total withdrawal of the work if feasible, (*e*) a specific identification of the persons or groups in the community on whom the work will have an adverse effect, as well as of those on whom the work will have no adverse effect, and (*f*) a specific account of others in the community who share the views of the complainant. (This information is also solicited by the library before the hearing via the request for reconsideration form [Figure 16.1]). Throughout the hearing, the complainant should be accorded every courtesy, and should be treated as a concerned citizen, not as a person whose aim is to attack and destroy the library.

The selector, in presenting the library's position on the controversial work, should give a clear indication as to why it was selected and should emphasize the fact that the decision to select was based not on personal opinion, but rather on what was perceived as the wants and needs of the library patron within the confines of the library's philosophy and selection policy. The ALA's position on intellectual freedom should be stated at some time during the selector's presentation, and it is also helpful to mention, if possible, other similar libraries that circulate the work in question.

After both sides have presented their briefs, they should be given an opportunity to make a rebuttal. The committee should then adjourn the hearing and meet to decide the issue.

It is hoped that the decision of the committee will be final and resolve the issue. However, if either the complainant or the selector considers the decision unfavorable and wants to pursue the issue further, the library should seek the assistance of the ALA, and possibly consider retaining legal counsel. The library should also try to obtain the support of other libraries that are using the controversial material, the endorsement of anyone in the community who has used the work and found it unobjectionable, and/or people who will advocate that the work be kept in the library on constitutional principle.

The resolution of a censorship issue seldom goes to these lengths. But, on occasion, it does happen, usually with alarming consequences. The publicity that the issue receives tends to alert the community to the matter, and usually results in the formation of two vociferous and perhaps radical factions—those who want even more controversial materials to be acquired by the library, and those who want to "burn" all materials that are even remotely controversial. It is unfortunate if the issue deteriorates to this point. When it does, the library is no longer just defending the selection of a specific work; rather it is the entire issue of intellectual freedom that is at stake. The library must muster all its forces to defend the proposition that the library must remain an institution in which intellectual inquiry can be freely pursued without any internal or external intimidation. In the final analysis, it must be realized that the preservation of intellectual freedom and censorship are mutually exclusive; the censor seeks reasons why certain material should not be available, whereas the selector who is conscientious about the preservation of intellectual freedom seeks reasons why certain materials should be acquired.

Selected Bibliography

Anderson, Arthur James. *Problems in Intellectual Freedom and Censorship.* New York: R. R. Bowker, 1974.

Berninghausen, David K. *The Flight From Reason: Essays On Intellectual Freedom in the Academy, the Press and the Library.* Chicago: American Library Association, 1975.

Busha, Charles H. *Freedom Versus Suppression and Censorship: With a Study of the Attitudes of Midwestern Public Librarians and a Bibliography of Censorship.* Littleton, Colorado: Libraries Unlimited, 1972.

Busha, Charles H., ed. *An Intellectual Freedom Primer.* Littleton, Colorado: Libraries Unlimited, 1977.

Cox, Charles Benjamin. *The Censorship Game and How to Play It: With an Appendix of NCSS Statements on Academic Freedom, Controversial Issues and Civil Rights.* Arlington, Virginia: National Council for the Social Studies, 1977.

Daily, Jay Elwood. *The Anatomy of Censorship.* New York: M. Dekker Publishing, 1973.

De Grazia, Edward. *Censorship Landmarks.* New York: R. R. Bowker, 1969.

Dhavan, Rajeev, and Davies, Christie, eds. *Censorship and Obscenity.* Totowa, New Jersey: Rowman and Littlefield, 1978.

Freedom to Read Foundation News. Chicago: Freedom To Read Foundation, 1971–.

Geller, Evelyn. "The Librarian as Censor." *Library Journal,* 101(June 1, 1976):1255–1258.

Haight, Anne Lyon. *Banned Books 387 B.C. to 1978 A.D.,* fourth edition, New York: R. R. Bowker, 1978.

Liston, Robert A. *The Right to Know: Censorship in America.* New York: F. Watts, 1973.

McShean, Gordon. *Running A Message Parlor: A Librarian's Medium-Rare Memoir About Censorship.* Palo Alto: Ramparts Press, 1977.

Merritt, Leroy Charles. *Book Selection and Intellectual Freedom.* New York, H. W. Wilson, 1970.

Newsletter on Intellectual Freedom. Chicago: American Library Association, 1952–.

Pope, Michael. *Sex and the Undecided Librarian: A Study of Librarians' Opinions on Sexually Oriented Literature.* Metuchen, New Jersey: Scarecrow Press, 1974.

Shields, Gerald Robert. "Intellectual Freedom: Justification for Librarianship." *Library Journal,* 102(September 15, 1977):1823–1825.

Index